PRINCE

PRINCE

A Pop Life

Dave Hill

Harmony Books/New York

Published by Harmony Books, a division of Crown Publishers, Inc., 225 Park Avenue South, New York, New York 10003
Originally published in Great Britain by Faber and Faber Limited

HARMONY and colophon are trademarks of Crown Publishers, Inc.

Manufactured in the UK

Library of Congress Cataloguing-in-Publication Data

ISBN 0–517–57282–6

10 9 8 7 6 5 4 3 2 1

First American Edition

Frontispiece: Michael Putland/Retna

For all the good people on the North Side.

For Laura Grace, nearly four, queen of her daddy's disco floor.

For Nicki, from the bloke who lives upstairs.

Contents

Acknowledgements

My greatest thanks are due to all those whose memories and observations appear in quotation marks; also to those who gave of their time, but preferred to remain anonymous.

Gratitude is owed equally to the following Twin Cities residents for their interest, and their provisions of food for thought: Professor Reginald Buckner of the University of Minnesota, Clarence Davis, Mamoud El Kati of Macallester College, Al McFarlane, James 'JB' Bryant, Sir Terry Casey, Gary Hines of Sounds of Blackness, Soli Hughes, Jon Bream, Alan Freed, William Rafferty at the Minneapolis *Star & Tribune*, Billy Robin McFarland, Steve Weise and a good half-dozen people of radio station KMOJ. Regards too to the Best Western University Inn and the charming personnel of Embers Restaurant – not too much coffee, Colleen.

In London, I was generously accommodated by the press officers of WEA. One of them, Ian Blackaby, even wasted valuable leisure time reading the text, as did Lloyd Bradley, Ann Cullis of Gloucestershire School of Art and Technology, and the redoubtable Eileen Murton of the unofficial Prince magazine, *Controversy*, an invaluable source of factual material. Succour and comfort were provided by someone who helped me find out exactly what silence looks like. The resourceful G. K. of Dartair Travel deserves a mention, as does Sue Matthias of *The Observer Magazine*, whose commission got me to Stockholm. Sara Fisher, late of the June Hall Literary Agency, and her successor, Shân Morley-Jones, both did the business on my behalf. Tom Sutcliffe, Arts Editor at *The Independent*, tolerated too many weeks of sabbatical and general distractedness from his rock critic. Nicki and Laura Thorogood tolerated the non-stop domestic distractedness of *The Independent*'s rock critic, who promises to take a weekend off one of these years.

In New York, Robyn Riggs did more than could reasonably be expected, and Greg Tate of *Village Voice* helped firm up some of my many nebulous thoughts. The Metropolitan Library had photocopiers that worked, which earns a gold star in itself.

In Detroit, Mr Charles Johnson put me up, fed me and showed me around in the most hospitable spirit imaginable.

In Miami, Deborah Wilker of the *Miami Post* provided me with cuttings and background information.

In Los Angeles, Marina Rota at Warner Brothers responded to calls without proffering the standard Hollywood flannel. Hardly anyone else on the entire seaboard was any help at all. Even a 'no' would have saved my phone bill.

Finally, a special award for patience, thoroughness, insight and commitment beyond the call of duty to my editor at Faber and Faber, Chris Barstow, whose good idea this was in the first place.

Preface

The reason I wrote this book is that someone from Faber and Faber asked me to. I had reviewed one of Prince's 1986 *Parade* shows in London for the *Observer*, and apparently it marked me out as the man for the job.

Initially, I wasn't as confident as the publisher. I had always reckoned Prince to be talented and clever. A few of his records had impressed me greatly, and I figured him to be saying something worth hearing about the world in his own, very singular way. But I had misgivings too: his reputation for tyranny and his rather debatable stance on important stuff like race, sex and class. Basically, I wasn't sure my enthusiasm for the subject was up to scratch.

But further thought suggested attractive possibilities. One was the chance to do a spot of *real* journalistic investigation. The secrecy surrounding the subject demanded some quite serious legwork if the book was to yield more hard information than previous Prince biographies. I didn't, however, think it should be a biography in the straighforward sense of documenting the events and minutiae of one person's life, with exhaustivity the sole criteria. Work would certainly commence on the assumption that Prince himself would never cooperate with the project in any case – and, of course, so it proved. That didn't bother me, though. If anything, it was a relief. The book-stalls in records shops are packed with sanitized 'authorized' life-stories which insult the readers' loyalty, never mind their intelligence. (They are packed with sanitized *un*authorized ones too – they all have coded messages saying 'don't sue me' in the Preface). Rather, it improved the prospect of writing about the artist in a way that allowed me to put a few ideas and theories to the test during both the research and the writing. And these revolved around the very issues where I found my attitude to Prince most ambivalent – that important stuff about race, sex and class.

Then there was the matter of showbiz. As a bearer of society's favourite fabrications about itself, the entertainment industry takes a lot of beating, which is why millions of people – myself among them – are so fascinated by it. Prince has been a showbiz giant who 'made it from nothing', disseminating a particularly potent blend of American Dreams along the way. This qualified him perfectly for examination in the light of my own nakedly communistic conviction that all entertainment, no matter how glitzy and artificial it may appear, is the product of a culture. And that culture is *always* made by people who will never be stars, many of them regarded by others more powerful as being barely worth consideration as human beings at all. It is a popular joke theory among rock critics that Prince himself is not really a human being, but an alien creature with a gift for assuming the myriad characteristics of the native life-form – a joke which can conceal a certain disinterest in social context as one vital factor in determining in the way creativity expresses itself. It was in an attempt to explore this social context that I spent a total of four weeks in Minneapolis and St Paul, learning a little about the history of black people and black musicians in the area, as well as about Prince himself – who, of course, happens to be one of them.

For a white English writer to study a phenomenon with its roots among black Americans ideally requires a considerable degree of humility and a fair amount of self-examination. I hope I have succeeded in injecting enough of those qualities into this book. It might be possible, should I wish it, to find out one day what it feels like to be an American. I will never know what it feels like to be black in any country, let alone one of the many where whites have a way of seizing and keeping power and resources for themselves.

That is one good reason for reproducing the fruits of my many conversations between quotation marks, thereby enabling the story to be told as experienced or witnessed by those involved. Obviously, a lot of the material is very subjective – there is no such thing as absolute objectivity anyway – and should be absorbed with that knowledge in mind. Any remarks that were clearly false, or inspired by malice alone, have not been reproduced, and although some examples of bitter experience are recounted, I trust this results in vested interests being worn on sleeves. I believe it is journalistically ethical to reproduce one side of a legitimate story if those who could provide the other are given the chance to do so. A few people declined that chance; at least, I presume their failure to respond to messages sent by letter, fax and telephone amounts to a 'no'. Of course, showbiz people are busy, and what they do is important. Their problem, sometimes, is that they don't think anyone else in the world could possibly be busy and doing something important too. That said, it should be recorded – with specific regard to the Prince organization – that the interview with Mrs Bernadette Anderson was, I am told, sanctioned by either Mr Steve Fargnoli, Prince or both, by way of Robyn Riggs at the Howard Bloom Organization, and I am certainly grateful for that.

While we're on the subject of stars and the journalists who spend too much time pursuing them, my feelings are mixed. The obsession with 'personalities' is a depressing indictment of the times we live in, and the way that obsession is catered to by a dismal array of newspapers and magazines even more so. At the same time, publicity is a two-way process. Those who pander to sensationalism cannot complain too much when the whole stupid, sordid business backfires. (This book is not an example of that; there are no revelations about people's personal lives and indiscretions not already known, although there could have been.) But it is also true that when someone becomes a megastar, they join the ranks of an élite; and I have this quaint, old-fashioned idea that the privileged have a duty to make themselves accountable to the rest of us.

The word 'genius' is often used in relation to Prince, and very frequently by those who believe they have reason to dislike him most. And for the record, I think that if there *is* such a thing as a 'genius' visibly at work in the world of popular music, Prince is probably that person. However, it is a word I tend to steer clear of, partly because it's a cliché, mainly because I do not think I know what it means. What I *am* sure about is that 'genius' should be made to do the hoovering, go to the supermarket and conform to common courtesy for the sake of everyone, most of all him- or herself. I think Prince takes his famed reluctance to explain himself through interviews with the press a bit over the top. On the other hand, on a selfish human level, I can understand it. After spending a good part of my time trying to figure out what it is that makes him tick, I have to conclude that if I was him, I probably wouldn't want to talk to me either.

Dave Hill
London, May 1988

1

Cities

Gary Gershoff/Retna

Not everybody in town thinks of Prince, His Royal Badness, as the solvent of racial rivalries, the assuager of sexual neuroses, the champion of the universal outsider, or the man who made Minneapolis the black music hot-spot of the world. Some people really don't approve of him at all.

'What I used to say about Prince, a kind of joke that I did in the black community, was that Prince was the top white act out there right now!' It is not exactly a malicious remark. It just carries the pungency appropriate to what Morris Wilson, saxophonist, activist and archivist, considers to be hard, hidden truths. 'People don't like me saying that because Prince is like their own little piece of the rock, you might say. And when you knock somebody's crutch like that, it's like knocking their religion, you know? And I think those things do a lot more harm than good.'

Back in 1979, before anyone except a handful of local kids and musos from the tiny black districts of Minneapolis and St Paul knew or cared that Prince Nelson from the dowdy north side had a record in the charts, Morris Wilson and his comrades in the Minnesota Minorities Musicians Association were mounting demonstrations in downtown territory, demanding that the owners of clubs and bars put on live entertainment instead of non-stop disco nights. It was hard, and getting harder, for the black musicians of the Twin Cities to find regular work. 'They say there's no racism . . . in *this* town?' Wilson snorts in disbelief.

And yet in the space of just ten years, Minneapolis and St Paul have become synonymous with innovation and success in black popular styles frequently distinguished by their assimilation of white ones. The Nelson kid made it big doing precisely that, and he was only the first. But the question for the compulsively outspoken Wilson is, 'So what?' Prince,

2

to his mind, broke out of the city, broke out of his culture, and never gave anything back – except, he insists, certain incentives for those who follow him to go right off the rails, where reactionary America likes to believe they belong.

'I think a little bit of Prince goes a long, long way,' Wilson expounds, with passion, 'particularly with the kind of messages that are contained there in his material, which is totally absorbed by the young black population. OK, these large increases in unwanted pregnancies and irresponsible sexual behaviour are symptomatic of the society we live in,' he concedes, 'but certainly the rock music and stuff adds to it.'

In the past, Morris Wilson has enjoyed his moments of glory. He's been a sideman and session player with blues and soul luminaries like Muddy Waters and the Temptations, Ike and Tina Turner and B. B. King. He even rubbed shoulders with the doyen of an angry new jazz, the late John Coltrane. Today, he is the man who rocks the boat on behalf of what there is of a local club scene. When Wilson walks into the Artist's Quarter bar, a focus of live jazz in Minneapolis, everybody knows his name.

The reputation of Prince Nelson, though, has spread a little further. Wilson, now in his forties, has seen him rise up from nowhere to international glory, revered as part catalyst, part instigator of a phenomenon now neatly parcelled up as the 'Minneapolis Sound'. Everyone you ask has a different definition of what precisely this 'Minneapolis Sound' is. To Morris Wilson it is the sound of rich Afro-America making good at the expense of its sisters and brothers, with no thought for the consequences.

'Little kids who are eight, nine years old, come into my house, rehearsing with their fathers, and they know all the words to "Erotic City", but they don't know how to write their own name! They know all the words, you know, F – U – C – K, "making love till cherry's gone", all that stuff. Back in that seventies era, there was a whole lot of irresponsible sex lyrics coming out of the black community particularly. But,' he qualifies, 'in the black community you almost can't get a contract unless you're writing that kind of trash. They kind of wanna keep you in that bag. That's the stereotype that you have and they want to keep you there. Prince and all of them, they fall right into line with that.' The harshness of Morris Wilson's judgements may put him in the minority in more ways than one. But his assessment of the music industry's enduring racial assumptions is sound. Whether you consider him a hero or a villain, there can be no doubt that the shadow of cultural stereotype has hovered above Prince Nelson every minute of his career.

The celebrity exponents of the 'Minneapolis Sound' count the black American music that took shape at the back end of the sixties and evolved through the seventies as crucial to what they have achieved themselves. When Sly Stone and James Brown, and then George Clinton's P-Funk project and Earth, Wind and Fire were remaking the music of black America in line with changing times, men like Jimmy Jam, Terry Lewis, Jesse Johnson and Prince were going through their formative creative years. But for expansive, funky new musics to come out of Detroit, Chicago, the cultural hothouses of the South or the ghettos of the urban West Coast was one thing; for them to flourish in the federal state of Minnesota was, and is, something else.

There are huge fat, dusty books which tell the history – at least, *a* history – of Minnesota. Chapters are devoted to the racial and cultural breakdown of the state's inhabitants, and while there is ample mention of Scandinavians and Central Europeans, it takes a keen eye to catch any reference to African Americans at all. In 1850 the census revealed just thirty-nine 'Negro' residents in the state. By 1930 there were 9,445. The majority lived in St Paul and Minneapolis, working in domestic and personal service. About 8 per cent were postal clerks and carriers, 10 per cent were employed in manufacturing and the mechanical trades, and a handful had made it into the professions.

Even by the Second World War, blacks remained statistically insignificant. They were there, though, and if you knew where to look, you could find them making a noise. James Samuel 'Cornbread' Harris II was one of them. He first found out he could command an audience at the piano when he went through his repertoire of two songs – Glenn Miller's 'In The Mood' and Tommy Dorsey's 'Boogie Woogie' – in the recreation room where he was doing his national service. A bunch of his comrades stopped playing pool and asked him to do it again. Once demobbed, Cornbread took up music full time. 'All the little pubs would have a two- or three-piece outfit back then. I thought, "let's give it a try".'

Mr Harris learned to play in many different styles. Apart from blues and jazz, he could do polkas and love ballads, mambas, salsas and calypsos. He is proud of his versatility, but it was an asset he could not have done without. His most affluent audience would probably be white, and they knew what they wanted. On these occasions, most of his fellow players would probably be white too. 'The black music scene was so smothered all the time this was going on. The only way a black musician got to play was for black functions, or as the one black musician in the band, you know? And in some of the areas here, when you got off the stand, you had to go straight in the back room. A lot of people here figure that was only a Southern thing, but it goes on up here too. But there again, do you wanna play music or don't you?'

The proportion of black Minnesotans has not dramatically increased since the forties, even if the status of a few of them has. The whole of the Twin Cities area supports around two million people. Barely sixty thousand are blacks. It is a tiny proportion compared to most other American conurbations, just about 3 per cent. Over on the north side, in the matrix of streets which run, exhaustively and alphabetically, across the Olson Memorial Highway and Plymouth Avenue West, you find the main concentration of black families, about the nearest thing Minneapolis has to a 'Chocolate City' as immortalized in '75 by Clinton's Parliament. It was round here that Cornbread and many of his peers enjoyed their music most. 'This was fun-time. All the musicians in town would come here for jam sessions after their gigs, and play till the sun came up. You'd get into some jazz and clean your pipes out, you know. Some of the best music you ever heard was played round the Olson Highway, before they tore it all down and put in the [public housing] projects.'

One generation later, growing up in the black America that came into being with the Black Panther Party and Martin Luther King, the adolescent Prince explored and fuelled his fascination with music as just one obsessional kid among many who spent long hours in bedrooms, basements and Plymouth's now defunct Way Community Center, singing and jamming and composing and imitating, trying to get their act down. A big slice of the future was being made in the state that produced figure-head Democrats like Hubert Humphrey and Eugene McCarthy. Liberal, accommodating, isolated Minnesota: it was the last place in America that anyone would have come to look.

Craig Rice is one of the people who benefited from what happened in the wake of Prince. With the successful development of Alexander O'Neal's career to his credit during '86 and '87, and with Mark Brown ('Brownmark', to use his solo stage-name) and Mazarati in his care, Rice became the first black manager to really establish himself in the Twin Cities as more and more local businessmen turned their gaze towards a very different, very big-time music scene: attorneys, marketing men, entrepreneurs.

Rice is tall, laid-back, faintly scholastic, and blessed with the type of dark-brown speaking voice of which TV ad-men dream: 'Somebody came up here once, and said, "God, I don't know how you can stay black in this town." ' The conversation took place in an innocuous office-cum-apartment on Pleasant Avenue South. Two minutes from the centre of Minneapolis, and hardly a sound from the street outside. 'You see, it's such a small community. In here you have to fight to be black so hard that it makes you stronger. 'Cause it's so easy in this town to be white, to become just part of the mass. It's just because you're so outnumbered. It would be easy to forget. But you know, you can never *be* white. So if you try to, you're gonna fail. And when you fail, you lose. And when you lose you have nothing.'

For many of the kids who hung out on the north side fifteen years

5

ago, all the evidence must have screamed that nothing was precisely what they were going to end up with if they dreamed too hard of a glamorous musical career. Minneapolis was, and still is, known in industry jargon as a 'vanilla market'. To the world outside, there *was* no black music scene within the city and its twin, end of story. And to the world *inside*, there wasn't much of one either, by that time less than ever. True, there had been a handful of illustrious jazz-players who had made reputations for themselves and earned money outside of town, the best know being pianist Bobby Lyle. But to have pinpointed Minneapolis as a coming force in the black music universe would have been dismissed as lunacy even as recently as 1978, when the first Prince LP, *For You*, was released by Warner Brothers in a flurry of fine talk about 'the new Stevie Wonder'.

There was this sense of isolation. The teenage hopefuls knew the local jazz scene – several of their dads were part of it – and they loved the records by America's florid new funk utopians, even though they often didn't hear them till weeks after New York, Philadelphia or Oakland. But, you know . . . Minneapolis. Never mind that Lipps Inc's worldwide hit record sung by St Paul girl Cynthia Johnson went by the name of 'Funkytown' – she must surely have been singing about some other place. In the Twin Cities, there was no longer an established network of venues where black music could be played by black citizens; no top-quality recording studios; and most of all, barely a single radio station catering to the tastes of the black audience. Nothing, really, but a whole lot of tolerance. And even that, as the word itself implies, had its limits. 'See,' says Morris Wilson, 'the white club-owners were saying, "You're playing the kind of music our customers don't like to hear. They want a little white rock and middle-of-the-road music." But all the white bands were trying to play black cover tunes, so that was not really a valid argument.'

Wilson won the chance to book bands in on the first floor of the only downtown joint patronized by blacks. Resonantly named the Foxtrap, it is remembered as a slick disco bar where smooth dudes with big cars parked outside tried to impress ladies with dangerous fingernails. Morris Wilson brought in jazz combos, and later one of several incarnations of the most famous band from the Way Center orbit. The group went by the name of Flyte Tyme, a handle inspired by the Charlie Parker recording 'Bird in Flight', and then included Cynthia Johnson (just prior to her sudden fame), a noted high-school athlete called Terry Lewis on bass, drummer Jellybean Johnson and a white keyboard player called Monte Moir. Moir recalls one night when the manager suggested he might be advised not to head down to the main floor: 'he said, "there's a guy walking round with a gun down there" '. Flyte Tyme would later be supplemented on keyboards by one of the men who spun the discs on the floor above, Jimmy 'Jam' Harris III – Cornbread Harris's son.

There were further small successes: Felty's Club, the Chicago Bar, where Alexander O'Neal and Wilson's favourite female singing protégée Sue Ann Carwell found work, and one or two others. It was promising, but never meant to last. Wilson cites the white arm of the law. 'What happened was there was such an influx of blacks coming from the north side and St Paul, and the white kids were starting to get frightened, you know? The police department downtown were the ones who really put a lot of pressure on the club-owners, 'cause they don't like to see this congregation of blacks in one place, especially mixing with the white females.'

The live music situation for black musicians has since got quietly worse. Craig Rice remembers being able to at least make a living, albeit a limited one. It was in the late sixties, when he was in his middle teens, that he began plying his trade as a pianist. 'There was a lot of dives, but there was good places too: Dirty Gertie's, the Blue Note, the Cosey Inn, the Peacock Gallery and King Solomon's Mine.' But the Prince phenomenon, when it came, was not a live thing. And while the nucleus of his generation is now making it's way without having had to uproot from Minneapolis, the action is not in clubs, but studios, and most of the artists in them are from out of town. Rice has observed the transformation: 'Today you've got the Riverview and a few others, but that's really about it for black music. What's happened since Prince is that the scene has really changed. There's not really the venues for people to start out in any more.'

Rice gave up being a musician and went to the University of California film school, only getting back into the pop industry when he landed a job as an assistant director on *Purple Rain*. Prince took a shine to him and appointed him tour manager for his subsequent national itinerary. Rice had previously been involved in Pink Floyd's concert trek for *The Wall*, but it was only in a supporting role, and that was the sum of his experience. 'You see,' says Rice, 'he opened the door. The reason I quit playing was there was no way out. You know, I used to play at the Cosey every night and twice on Sunday. Jesus, you know? So, Prince came along and opened the door just wide enough for people to say, "Hey, I can get out too." '

The upshot is a curious dichotomy, a tale with two sides as much as it is one of two towns hugging opposite banks at the cold end of the Mississippi River. On the one hand, Prince has been the provider of opportunity. As stars have been born (the majority at his instigation) and recording facilities opened up, there has been a steady influx of out-of-towners from east and west – even English performers like the Human League, Steve Dante and Junior Giscombe – to sniff out that Minneapolis magic, whatever it's meant to be. But at the same time, because no A & R executive with an eye to keeping their job would ever spend the company's budget hanging around in this mid-west middle of nowhere, the key for Prince and those who've followed was to break out – and that meant business connections on the seaboards and a ready-made product hatched in a soundproof room, not a hot reputation for selling tickets in a town no business type with clout gave a second thought to. Twin Cities showbiz had basically meant two names before: Bob Dylan, from nearby Hibbing, who got out before anyone noticed he'd been there; and the *Mary Tyler Moore Show* – and even that was shot in Hollywood.

The Minneapolis Sound is the unlikely offspring of the shared, unfavourable circumstances of a tiny community, new sound technology, and one little guy's big break. And like all tight local scenes, the history of in-fights and antagonisms is matched only by the sense of loyalty many of those involved continue to express for each other – and the paradoxical loyalty to the Twin Cities which all of them have, at some time, been so anxious to escape.

'We're all really his children,' says Craig Rice, not afraid to show a little sentiment. 'Whether some people will admit it or not, we all come from him, even me. I learned a lot from him and that whole organization. I think there is a certain amount of bile and jealousy came out of it, but that's competitive, that's good, that's what's healthy about this town. It's like a bunch of street gangs. It has that attitude about it. Everybody cares about everybody else, but they all got their own little gang, their little camp together.'

At the time, Rice had just about completed the release of Mark Brown's protégés, Mazarati, from a contract with Prince's Paisley Park label, which yielded a self-titled début album in 1985. He had been unhappy with the company's lack of support. The group was out of pocket, out of work and some of its members had given up and left. But that didn't mean Craig Rice spoke any less highly of Paisley Park's boss. 'He's like everybody, he's got two sides to him. He can be a great guy, prophetic at some points, a genius in his own right. He can be . . . you know . . . a jerk. Just like anybody. But I love him. He's like my brother. I don't care what anybody says that's bad about him. I'll always be there. I don't care what he needs or where he's at, 'cause Prince was there when I needed him. He gave me something that no one else could have, 'cause he believed in me. And that is true for everybody – for Mark, Monte, even Terry and Jimmy. He believed in them too.'

In recent years, the big downtown night out for black-music lovers in Minneapolis has been Thursday's funk disco at the now famous First Avenue and 7th Street Entry – the rock club immortalized in the *Purple Rain* movie that in 1984 would confirm Prince's standing as a major world entertainment star, America's latest black-white 'crossover' icon. The funk night has evolved into an institution. Shuffling through the throng of dancers and drinkers, it is unusual not to catch sight of at least one home-grown luminary: the good-humoured Jerome Benton, fielding the attentions of female multitudes, or maybe Prince himself, often without bodyguards, accompanied by a nurseling or two. It is, apparently, just about OK to say 'hi'. The whole thing is very warm and symbolic – the stars mingling with the mere mortals, in subtle confirmation of their commitment to staying home. Videos run on three giant screens, a team of DJs keep the heat turned right up, and a pack of the get-down exhibitionists you find in any urban dance-setting anywhere in the world disport the night away on the stage – the same stage that plays host the other six nights of the week to the altogether different white hardcore and avant-garde rock scene.

The funk night is a joy, in its way, but it tells only one side of the story of black Minneapolis after Prince. Take a ride a little out of the centre, along the Mississippi's west bank, and there sits the picturesque fulfilment of Mr Jimmy Fuller's career as music-lover and businessman. The Riverview Supper Club looks out over a patio with tables and sunshades, then down the Mississippi itself, affording an almost perfect view of the Minneapolis skyline. It's a clean, modern city, the home of Honeywell Computers, and a major centre of the American advertising industry. Hi-tech and leisure enterprises have flourished in what is the unlikely setting of a settlement founded by the hardiest of pioneer farmers and built up into a major mill town. From the front aspect of the Riverview, the miles and miles of flat suburban streets with their wooden slats and porches – a far cry from the tenement dwellings which dominate most of residential urban America – drop out of sight, and Minneapolis presents itself as a compact vision of pale concrete, tinted glass and glistening steel. A handful of gleaming towers are clustered like a futurist fantasy come true. It is, perhaps, the way the city likes to see itself.

In the early part of the evening, Mr Fuller's clientele wear suits, and scan the business pages of the *Star & Tribune* as they sip their drinks at the bar. Usually everyone present is black, except Mr Fuller's long-time managerial assistant, a fair-haired lady called Nancy Clark. Mr Fuller himself looks just like what he is: a mature gentleman of genuine jazzman's sartorial taste and charisma. He smokes a cigar, talks in a stoneground whisper, and at one point leans confidingly forward, brandishing an index finger crooked across the middle one, and says: 'Me and Count Basie – we were like this.'

Before midnight the tiny dance-floor has filled up with a younger crowd – late twenties and thirties, casual but smart – running through their steps to a blend of happening dance-floor records and established

9

favourites from the local studios: Alexander O'Neal's 'Fake'; 'The Finest', another production by Jam and Lewis, this time for the SOS Band; 'Erotic City', by you know who. But the early part of the evening features live sounds, two forty-minute sets from a Riverview house band, the Billy Holloman Trio.

Holloman, bass-man Sonny Thompson and singer-percussionist William Doughty – 'Hollywood' as he prefers to be known – are three talented players who earn their bread and butter turning out cover versions for Mr Fuller a couple of times a week. Holloman, a tall, superficially impassive man, handles keyboards and most of the vocals. But it is Thompson who comes into his own when the trio deliver their versions of three songs by the local enigma made good. They do 'Pop Life', '1999' and, most impressively, 'Do Me Baby', which shows Thompson to be the perhaps unlikely possessor of an excellent falsetto voice. It is a first-rate imitation, but his links to the originator of those numbers run deeper than that. As another member of Prince's north-side generation, Thompson knows that not every young aspirant from those deceptively silent streets went on to be a star.

'It's one-sided, it's closed up. The mafia runs it!' he guffaws, when asked about the local situation. And though he doesn't mean it quite as literally as that, Thompson seems to have suffered his share of bad luck over the years. In spite of enjoying widespread respect for his skills, the promise of a fruitful partnership with his more celebrated contemporaries has yet to be completely fulfilled. A year-long tenure in Jesse Johnson's band concluded unhappily in a financial dispute which became embarrassingly public when Thompson and his fellow members got in front of a TV crew shooting a Johnson feature to chorus pointedly the refrain from Berry Gordy's 'Money': 'That's what I want'.

Then there was the time Prince himself approached Thompson, just after his best friend André Anderson had made an unhappy departure from the *Dirty Mind* incarnation of his touring band. 'He just called me up and said "I'm going to hire you",' recalls Thompson wearily. 'He had me go to the Y [YMCA], lose forty pounds, you know? Trim up, slim up. I was just working my heart out, practising fifteen, sixteen hours a day. Didn't even tell me when he decided to hire somebody else! The band that Mark Brown played for called me up, 'cause they needed a bass player. I said, "No, I'm getting ready to try to go with Prince", They said, "Haven't you heard? They took Mark." '

This is particularly galling for Thompson, who claims to have played his part in enabling Prince to get to where he is now. 'I was a strong influence on him, even though he won't admit it to this day! Vocally, and the way I play and, you know, arrangements.' There was always plenty of crossover between the three main north-side bands, Flyte Tyme, The Family – with whom Thompson played bass – and Grand

10

Central, the teenage group whose core comprised Prince, Morris Day and André Anderson (who later renamed himself André Cymone). People would sit in on each other's gigs, practise and compose in twos and threes. Thompson talks of long, late hours with Prince at his house: 'We were both into song-writing at that time. We used to sit up and just jam all night. Turn a tape recorder on, see what happened.'

Thompson describes those days when in music industry terms the Twin Cities were just a small, lily-white dot on the marketing landscape. 'It was fun, because we all had our hopes and aspirations of really being big. And it's funny how so many have had their shot at making it.' He recalls well the feeling of being stuck in the middle of nowhere. 'It gets so cold here in winter, and there's not really that much to do except sit down and just practise, go around to somebody's house. And for sure, you *are* cut off here, even now. You got New York and Chicago to the east, and LA and Kansas City to the west, and a lot of music just passes straight over. There was a lot of hot stuff that didn't even hit here.'

No radio station, virtually no venues, and what self-supporting culture there was existed in a partial vacuum. Go back twenty years, and the only way new black music found its audience in these parts was in the form of records ordered up from the South. As a minority too tiny to be perceived as a problem, the condition of Twin Cities blacks in the post-war years has been much akin to that curious, dependent limbo which duplicitous and well-meaning liberals alike sometimes choose to dignify as 'integrated'. Not everyone would think it unduly cynical to conclude that blacks were the more comfortably accepted because of the ease with which they could be ignored.

This, though, is not to deny that Twin Cities people, white and black, are as accommodating as their reputation paints them. It is not for nothing that Minnesota is known as a liberal state. It is a centre for drug rehabilitation programmes, and something of a magnet for lesbians and gays. In the 1984 Presidential Election it was alone in voting for the Democratic candidate, Walter Mondale, in preference to Ronald Reagan. And with regard to *The Negro In Minnesota* (1961), as historian Earl Spangler named his book on the subject, 'It is significant that blacks were granted full suffrage by state action, actually by vote of the people, two months before the Fifteenth Amendment [which forbade the disenfranchisement of blacks] was ratified.'

The same tribulations have weighed upon the black Americans of Minneapolis and St Paul as everywhere else. The same self-organized campaigns have been necessary in pursuit of justice in housing and employment, and of access to power and resources. In the late 1960s there were riots in Minneapolis, on the north side, just like everywhere else. Prince's sister Tyka has recalled in interview that she and her brother were among the first children to be 'bussed'. But maybe the liberal atmosphere has meant that the deeper contradictions of American life have not become visible with the same regularity, or kept simmering with the same vehemence, as in other, angrier cities. That may be yet to come.

And so, as you window-shop around the downtown pedestrian skyways or motorvate painlessly through the broad central streets, explore the vast flatness of the residential districts or cruise the University of Minnesota's inner city campus, it is not hard to understand why more than one Twin Cities resident has described their home as 'a big small town'.

'I think it's a town where people are satisfied,' Jimmy Jam once said. 'In LA, everyone you meet who is a waitress, isn't really a waitress; *really* they're an actress. I guess you have to be in the industry, or you're nobody. Up here, it ain't like that. The waitresses *are* waitresses. The bank teller *is* a bank teller. And they like it. You know what I'm saying?'

But Jam goes on to stress how intensely the ambition of young black musicians of his generation bubbled beneath the unruffled surface of Twin Cities life. 'There were all these white bands, playing white clubs and making a lot of money. Then there was three or four black bands playing in little black clubs and not getting paid. So it was very competitive. That's why the calibre of black music coming out of here is so good.' Jam, like Craig Rice, also employed the metaphor of Prince as father, and himself and his contemporaries as the offspring of one unlikely maverick and his grand scheme: 'Everything he did from the beginning was all a plan. We watched it happen. It was really cool.'

People from the Twin Cities will tell you, in almost the same breath, that it is a great place to be comfortable in and the most soporific urban vacuum on Earth; a haven of harmony and tranquillity that can make contented people complacent, and seduce have-nots and outsiders into forgetting just who they are. It can also make those same individuals long to escape into the limelight. In many ways, the story of Prince is just a tale of Twin Cities writ large.

2

White

Ben Desoto/Retna

Twenty miles west of Minneapolis, along Highway 5, close by a suburban settlement called Chanhassen, sits the Paisley Park studio complex. Set right there on the roadside, gleaming white with turquoise window frames, it is a testament to Prince Nelson's state of independence. He has invested a big chunk of his personal fortune in this building: about ten million dollar's worth, according to Richard 'Hawkeye' Henriksen, a softly spoken white man who looks after things round there.

Getting to look over Paisley Park was billed as an impossible dream, but ended up a piece of cake. The high-profile security surrounding Prince and all he invests in is central to his legend. But once a number and a name had been acquired, all you had to do was explain your interest, and be polite. With a carefully modulated pride, Mr Henriksen led the way through the reception area with its antiseptic aroma of freshly laid carpet, past the café-bar, through 48-track Studio A, into an all-purpose rehearsal space and a vast concrete cavern of aircraft-hangar proportions, where an entire stage-show can be set up, run through and dismantled again inside a few hours. Hawkeye had already been with Prince several years, and had a lot of input into the design and specifications of Paisley Park. Perhaps the complex is a bit like some gargantuan Airfix kit he always wanted to assemble as a boy. Whatever, Hawkeye is someone else with a reason to be grateful to the little guy.

Paisley Park aims to provide every facility any type of act might need: recording, touring, international or – as the construction of an additional, small 24-track studio indicates – local. There is even a basketball hoop for light relief. 'He's really quick,' remarked Hawkeye, nodding at it before heading off towards Studio B, where, at that time, the proprietor himself recorded. 'It doesn't matter that he's not very tall.'

Contemporaries of Prince Nelson would not be surprised by that description. As a teenager, he used to burn up youthful energy on the football field of the now demolished Lincoln Elementary School near where he used to live. Walter 'Q Bear' Banks a DJ with Minneapolis's only black-music radio station, KMOJ, used to be out there too. 'We used to play football and stuff, every Saturday morning, running up and down. His nickname was Skipper. And if you *called* him Skipper, he'd be ready to choke you.' Prince was always diminutive compared to his fellows, but he could look after himself. On the field of play, those who didn't know better would think they could push him around. In the event, so the stories go, no one could lay a finger on him. 'Skipper' was just too fast. Deceptive.

Minneapolis is atypical in many ways, but there, as in many other American cities, sport rivalled music as the main preoccupation among the sons and daughters of the post-war influx of black families from the South. Some promising athletes have ended up making international reputations in the field of music because they lacked the good fortune, or perhaps that extra-special something, to have made them on the field of play. Flyte Tyme Productions founder Terry Lewis set records at North High School in the sprint events. Contemporaries say he might have been the fastest in the state, but that an injury put an end to any such ambition. His younger half-brother, Jerome Benton, went to Iowa State University as a promising footballer until a coach broke it to him that he didn't quite have what it takes.

As for Prince, well, at 5 feet 3 inches (give or take a rumour), guile and pace can only compensate to a certain standard on the basketball court. And as he passed through his teens, music soon asserted itself as his dominant interest. At the now defunct Bryant Junior High School and the Central High, also since closed, Prince enjoyed the tutelage of Mr Jim Hamilton for music. Hamilton had come to the area in 1965 after a spell as a piano-player in Ray Charles's band. In 1968 he picked up the threads of his teaching career, helped, he thinks, by the local school board's desire to recruit more black teachers in the wake of the social disruptions of the period. (The worst instances in Minneapolis occurred when north-side rioters burned down businesses in a four-block spread in the vicinity of Plymouth Avenue).

Central High had a strong music curriculum, and a policy of setting stringent standards in order to attract pupils from outside the immediate catchment area. Prince was an enthusiastic music student, but not an *especially* outstanding one. 'At that age', says Hamilton, 'no one could predict that anyone would become a superstar. But he doesn't really stick in my mind as a super student.' Prince, however, came into his own in one of Hamilton's extra-curricular courses: The Business of Music. 'When I was on the road with Ray, I used to encounter a lot of the business aspects of music. So many of the so-called stars didn't know

15

much about contracts and negotiations. A few times I really thought Ray Charles got ripped off.' Hamilton figured that an insight into the business basics would be invaluable not only to his own most talented and aspiring charges, but also to youngsters from other Minneapolis schools.

The Business of Music class took place twice a week. Among its other participants were William Doughty, André Anderson, Mark Brown and Terry Lewis, who, Hamilton recalls, 'was always wearing a suit and tie, and carrying a briefcase. I was very impressed with Mr Businessman. He was a super kid.' Prince really shone too. 'He was in it for all three years that he was there [at Central].' The class covered contracts and copyright, how to make and shop a demo tape around, the union situation, and more: 'It was letting them become aware that you can't just stroll into this world and be a star.' But Prince already had a strategy for the pop game to come. 'He was kind of a jokester in a way. We did have a few words about some of the lyrics he was coming up with. His quotation was the fact that "Hey, I'm trying to be as controversial as possible. I have to get people to buy the records." ' But most striking of all were his drive and ambition. 'One of his greatest qualities was the work ethic. If he wanted to accomplish something, he would really work at it. If there was something he was going to practise, he would sit there for an hour or two hours, and he would not stop until it had been accomplished. I considered that his greatest asset.'

From this fertile combination of talent, wit and conviction has sprung perhaps the most consistently attractive body of saleable contemporary music of the last ten years. Prince's commercial success has been sufficient for him to construct a creative and business haven, and christen it after the spiritual one of the song from which it takes it name. Paisley Park has the potential to be an absolute hive of activity, but doors and passages have been arranged so that Studio B, where Prince originally recorded, and now Studio A, to which he subsequently transferred, can be completely closed off from the rest of the complex, leaving the star in perfect isolation.

Inside the studio, the 48-track mixing board uprooted from its original setting in his home was the one on which he had produced the albums *Parade* and *Sign 'O' The Times*. An attempt had been made to personalize the control room in keeping with its user's image: a soft peach-coloured drape half concealed a black plastic sofa facing into the sound room; paisley scarves were pinned, almost apologetically, around the walls. The wardrobe department had been doing its job. Inside Paisley Park, Prince can do what he wants, whenever he wants to do it – adding to a vault of over three hundred completed songs, drilling his bands, jamming all day and and deep into the night if required. Paisley Park truly is a monument to a man who had to win, and sustain that victory on his own terms.

16

It goes without saying that the facilities with which an already budding enigma first struggled to express his teenage talents were infinitely more modest. Prince's first serious band was named Grand Central – remembered by some as Grand Central Station – and for much of its life its core comprised Prince on guitar and vocals, André Anderson on bass, and Morris Day on drums – 'a funny-looking kid with an huge Afro and freckles', as one contemporary remembers him. All of them were around fifteen years of age, raw, romantic, perhaps too young yet to consider how difficult it might be for them to break the mould which history had made for black Minnesotan musicians. William 'Hollywood' Doughty, of the Billy Holloman Trio, remembers this youthful aggregation's early public appearances. 'My uncle used to have a barbecue joint up on Broadway, and they used to come up there and play. They had a kind of semi-rock thing: R & B and Grand Funk.'

Contrary to the immediate connotation of the name, this last band (originally named Grand Funk Railroad) was not, in fact, a funk outfit. Rather, it was a brute-force heavy rock band, very popular with American adolescents in the first half of the seventies. The five years from '71 were big ones for Grand Funk, and more generally for the loud, flash, pyrotechnical rock bands that dominated the mainstream of American male teenage taste. And, as the voracious Def Jam label would prove more than a decade later, some of those young American males were black.

There were several reasons why the black youth of the Twin Cities might be especially open to the influence of white-orientated rock. In the first place, the absence of black music on the radio had an effect it is important not to underestimate. During the sixties, and particularly when Berry Gordy's then Detroit-based Motown label was at the top of its form, radio stations across America had reflected as faithfully as they ever would the trans-racial and trans-cultural assimilations which all rock 'n' roll music sprang from. Motown, and other wellsprings of contemporary black pop, virtually insisted on this. If the Beatles and their fellow countrymen provided the backbeat of the British Invasion, then Motown, by its own bold description, was indeed 'The Sound Of Young America'. No Top 40 station, however white, could pretend success like that away.

But as the seventies unfolded, and pop/rock established itself as a permanent commodity form with a broadening market demography, radio stations began to submit more and more completely to the whip-hand of advertisers. Specific audiences were identified and catered to, in line with the dictates of commercials. And that 'specialization' effectively meant the resegregation of radio along racial lines that were no less rigid for justifying their informal apartheid with free-enterprise logic. The implications of this for blacks in the Twin Cities were obvious. They were a tiny, low-income minority. No market meant no advertising; no advertising meant no black radio, and very little – if any – black presence on white radio; and so the people who controlled the airwaves of Minneapolis and St Paul virtually declared that blacks did not exist.

There were spasmodic attempts to correct the imbalance. For a time, station KUXL broadcast from sunrise to sunset to the slightly more affluent black community on the south side of Minneapolis. But in general, black people obtained access to black music – other than what they created themselves – only through records, and from the very occasional visiting star. William Doughty goes so far as to say that 'we didn't even listen to radio stations. Just listened to records.' Even so, the names he reels off express Grand Central's catholicity of taste: 'James Brown, Wilson Pickett . . . The Beatles.'

In the years to come, Minneapolis's black pop moguls would be noted for a succession of hits which forced their way across the colour-line and into the pop charts, or fused black and white styles together in sharp, sometimes outlandish ways. Not that the liaison of (white) rock and R & B/soul/funk was a Minneapolis invention, of course. The musical collage which Grand Central and their rivals were picking up on was something that had blossomed in direct expression of the Civil Rights struggles and radical sub-cultures of the previous decade. Two of the true mould-breakers in this respect were artists regularly named as prime influences by those who came out of the Minneapolis scene: Jimi Hendrix and Sly Stone. In the second half of the sixties, these two special talents suggested creative possibilities for black musicians that would have seemed impossible – certainly by all standard commercial criteria – only a couple of years prior to their emergence.

In 1966, Jimi Hendrix, after learning his trade with a succession of US R & B bands, resettled himself in England and took the celebrated London underground scene by storm. His electric guitar playing, astonishing to this day, revolutionized approaches to the instrument, and soon his refusal to be bound by traditional song-structures – the blues, pop or R & B – found sympathy among the West-Coast Love Crowd. Hendrix had even come to Minneapolis and played.

Sly Stone, meanwhile, burst out of the very heart of flower-power, San Francisco, to express with vivid coherence the ideal of a true family of humankind. His multi-racial, male and female band brought a new dimension to the blossoming counter-culture of Haight Ashbury, directly addressing the issue that no one else could quite look in the eye – that hippies, however wild and free, were a very white tribe indeed. Sly and the Family Stone seized the moment triumphantly. 'A cultural politician of the first order,' wrote Greil Marcus, 'Sly was less interested in crossing racial and musical lines, than in tearing them up.'

The brilliant advances of Hendrix and Stone echoed throughout the world of black music in the years that followed the Summer of Love. Acts like Earth, Wind and Fire, the Isley Brothers, the Temptations under the guidance of Norman Whitfield, and George Clinton's Parliament-Funkadelic adventurers all learned, absorbed, developed or commercialized what those two achieved, and they did it during a period in which the territory of more conventional black pop was becoming annexed by the overground surge of the much derided (and much misunderstood) Disco. Theirs was the new, hot black music of the time. But it was partly rooted in the assumption that black musicians had a perfect right to listen in to the white side of town play far-out guitar solos and project like rock messiahs.

Daring though it was, what these artists did would have made good sense in mild-mannered Minneapolis and St Paul, where black encountered white in the double-edged context of relative racial tolerance and black cultural invisibility. 'Integration' happened logically, in its own backhanded way. Never mind the desire, there had always been a positive *need* for black musicians to mix their historical constituency with that of whites. Cornbread Harris used to get gigs in smart hotels by being ready to cut his cloth to suit the clientele – a compromise not everyone was ready to make. 'Some of these Negroes have never played those places. I used to tell them that I just played the music the people wanted to hear. I said "if you are gonna go into the Minnetonka area, where all these rich people live, who own half the city, you know they are only gonna buy what they wanna hear. You're doing a service. If your service is cleaning rugs, and that's all you can do, fine. But don't expect them not to ask you to wash the walls. Now, if you can wash the walls *and* do the carpet, you're gonna get more work." '

It was standard, and in itself perfectly healthy, that even the few black venues – meaning venues where blacks might be the majority on stage – attracted mixed-race audiences. Meanwhile, on record, white bands that had based their act on black styles were popular among blacks because, as Craig Rice explains it, 'that's what you were exposed to on a daily basis. Even groups like the James Gang was hot here. I mean, you couldn't have a black party without the James Gang! Most black people here know about Def Leppard and Led Zeppelin too.' Rice remembers the kind of set he used to play at the Cosey Inn, one of Jimmy Fuller's venues. 'It was basically black music, everything from Harold Melvin and the Blue Notes to Wilson Pickett and Motown, and then you'd throw in something by a white artist. If it wasn't the Beatles, then maybe the Rolling Stones.'

It was against this backdrop that Grand Central, all a few years younger than Rice, put their adolescent energies into action, and it was as a band aspiring to many styles that William Doughty first perceived them. He went to the same school as André Anderson, North High, and was

19

already a practised singer and dancer by the time he joined Grand Central. Like Anderson and Prince, his father had been a jazz musician working locally. Doughty, then, became a logical addition to a band which at one time also included one of Prince's cousins, Charles Smith, on drums. Morris Day's advent on the scene precipitated his departure. Anderson's sister Linda joined in on keyboards, and Grand Central soon became the dominant enthusiasm of their lives. 'Back then everybody was wild,' Doughty recalls. 'Just teenagers having fun. We was all too ambitious, as a matter of fact. We devoted everything to it. That's all we did. Half the time we didn't even stay in school. Half the day in school, half the day in the basement.'

Grand Central rehearsed upstairs at Day's house, or in the basement that doubled as Prince's bedroom at the home of André's mother, Bernadette Anderson. Playing a blend of contemporary covers and a few numbers of their own, they performed fairly regularly at school functions and the like, plus the very occasional club gig, including the Cosey Inn. Nancy Clark from the Riverview remembers these appearances well. 'They were all there with their chaperones, doing the early set. It was basically a little jazz thing they did there. Their moms had to come in with them to make sure they finished at nine o'clock.' Meanwhile, based around the same bunch of blocks on the north side, Grand Central's main competitors would be working just as hard to perfect their riffs, grooves and moves. There was no lack of competition. 'We had a little rivalry going on,' remembers Sonny Thompson, greatly amused by the recollection. 'We all lived in a little three- or four-block radius. And every so often, we'd all run into each other at the Way Community Center. It was a different time. Eveybody would throw dances, and there would be battles of the bands. Sometimes it would be all three of us playing! It was pretty funny.'

Thompson recounts his own enthusiasm for the new funk formulations of the time. 'It was the new sound, not the same as everything else. That was when the style of thumping on the bass first came out, what Larry Graham had been doing for Sly. Me and André was the first to really get it down. Then Terry [Lewis] eventually came up with it too. We played a lot of Sly, some James Brown, Jimi Hendrix. Also Herbie Hancock, 'cause our keyboard player was really into him. A little Tower of Power; they were really hot back then.'

The Flyte Tyme band, meanwhile, were a story in their own right. The received wisdom has been that this was just one more teenage band, two of whose members, Jam and Lewis, revived the name for their production company several years later. But far from being just a short-lived venture which formed the nucleus of Prince's first protégés – The Time – Flyte Tyme had a life-span of close on ten years; they were a little miracle of young, black self-organization. Further, Time member

20

Jimmy Jam did not actually hook up with Flyte Tyme until late on in its existence. Nor did Monte Moir. Terry Lewis, though, was one of its mainstays, along with drummer Jellybean Johnson (also later of The Time), and a horn section which included one James Anderson, a fellow called Big Bob, and David 'Batman' Eiland, whose family basement provided the group with its rehearsal space. In Minneapolis everyone has a basement.

Cynthia Johnson was one of Flyte Tyme's longest-serving members. Born and raised in St Paul, she started singing with her siblings at home, encouraged by her mother. At sixteen she became a member of her church choir, and soon after was approached to join Flyte Tyme when the group's then guitar-player, Joey Kerium (later of Alexander O'Neal's road band), whom she had known at elementary school, heard her singing at a funeral. 'I went to one of the band practices, and I brought my saxophone. I think that's what really did it, 'cause I could play and there was a four-piece brass section there then. Gee, there must have been ten of us altogether.'

Throughout the seventies, Flyte Tyme cultivated a flair and versatility that made them the north-side band remembered with most widespread admiration. Jimmy Fuller first employed them around 1974 at a short-lived and notorious venue on 14th Street and Hennepin Avenue called the Filling Station Bar. 'Flyte Tyme was always one of the more professional groups around,' says Nancy Clark. 'The guys worked hard, they got along well, and it wasn't a band that changed members constantly.' It was also a self-managed group which worked on as regular a basis as Twin Cities options allowed. And though they too cut their cloth to fit the crowd, Flyte Tyme were less inclined to stray into rock country. 'We pretty much stuck to the R & B material,' says Cynthia Johnson. 'We did Chaka Khan, Stevie Wonder, James Brown. But there was never a time when we did not include some of our own songs.'

Ms Johnson found the Flyte Tyme atmosphere positively familial. She was the only female member, but that never caused any problems for her. 'I mean, these guys were just so *clean*. I was the bad seed at the time, 'cause I was trying to smoke cigarettes and be cool. I was fortunate, 'cause it could have been a group of guys who were totally the opposite, and I could have been sucked into a really bad scene. But Terry and Jellybean and Batman . . . they were my brothers.'

While most of its personnel were still in High School, Flyte Tyme made themselves busy in and around town. They played at fraternities, weddings and Hallowe'en parties. They got gigs at the obscure Nacirema club (that's 'American' spelt backwards) and a 'little cracker box' called the VFW (Veterans of Foreign Wars). There were a few of what Cynthia Johnson calls 'real gigs' too. 'We got paid. We did a lot of Thunderbird Motel gigs, on the [entertainment] strip on Highway 494, which was one

21

of the best jobs we ever got, 'cause it was a nice classy hotel. We got pretty good money, but normally we didn't end up with anything, 'cause it all went back into buying equipment.'

Whenever they had the finance, the group would make use of the Twin Cities' limited studio facilities. They had ideas and ambitions. Johnson would type out covering letters to accompany the cassettes they sent to anyone who might be ready to listen, though they never got the response they wanted. But such was the energy of the Flyte Tyme operation that they actually organized tours out of town, using their own 'raggedy old bus' to play shows in Chicago and even Memphis, set up by Johnson and Lewis themselves. Yet for all their initiatives, even Flyte Tyme found that the road always led back home and to 'the same two or three little holes in the wall that didn't pay even 35 dollars a night. So it was mostly just the love of the music that kept us going.'

In the end, what Cynthia Johnson got out of eight years with the band was 'a lovely new saxophone' and a great deal of fun. She remained with Flyte Tyme until around 1980, when she was twenty-four years old. Not too long before Prince moved in to recruit the Flyte Tymers for The Time. Steven Greenberg, a local songwriter/producer with financial means, tracked her down to record one of his own compositions, a synthesized bubblegum-funk thing called 'Rocket'. It became a hit, and was followed up by the famous 'Funkytown' – a number one in over twenty different countries.

But her success as the Lipps Inc singer had its price. After three albums and too many arguments, Johnson left, withdrawing from the music industry altogether until 1987. Her return to the scene has seen her pick up the threads of many old Twin Cities friendships, working on the Chico DeBarge album Mark Brown helped to write and produce, and doing back-ups on the most bizarre Flyte Tyme Productions project yet, the Pia Zadora LP. 'There's a real close-knitness among musicians here. Most of us that made some kind of mark between '79 and '82 grew up together, sometimes as competitors, but also as friends. So it wasn't like in some big cities where there's that kind of bitterness. None of that existed.'

Q-Bear Banks, looking on from the sidelines at that time, underlines those sentiments. 'A lot of people think that Flyte Tyme and Prince were against each other. But it's not like that. They were the greatest of friends. After they performed and they did rehearsals and sometimes studio time, they would all sit back and lounge about and talk and laugh. Some of 'em did smoke and drink. Not all of them were good. But they all hung out together, went to movies. There'd be like twenty of 'em, twenty guys. And people would be wondering, "what is this, a gang?" '

Prince is remembered by some of his mischievous humour, but mainly for his reticence. The picture that emerges is that where Flyte Tyme were outgoing and active, and The Family an accomplished covers band, Grand Central were a looser line-up whose dominant individuals had yet to fully exert themselves – a confusion of egos looking for a direction of their own. Some north-siders say that Prince was always around but they never really got to know him very well. 'To see him dance across the stage today is a revelation,' remembers Cynthia Johnson. 'It really is like seeing a star being born. It must have just been inside there waiting for the moment to break out.'

What finally emerged was a unique musical animal, his potential formed in the context of the particular social climate of the Twin Cities, the route to its fulfilment anticipated by his prowess in Jim Hamilton's Business of Music class. From Minneapolis and St Paul, Prince would have absorbed the idea that black and white noise *could* be moulded together and be created by collaborations between black and white human beings. Maybe, too, he grasped the notion that for a black musician to maximize his audience, it was positively *necessary* for such hybrids to occur. There is no doubt that he caught on very soon to the idea of pop as a game, something that involved hard practicalities together with a willingness to go out on a limb. His determined but more gregarious contemporaries in Flyte Tyme plowed a more conventional furrow, sticking to the R & B lineage, and finding the achievement of widespread local acknowledgement like squeezing blood out of a stone. But there was a bigger picture forming in the quiet boy's mind.

For Prince, from moderate Minnesota, Sly Stone and Jimi Hendrix were not really political, they were *sensational*. Not only was their finest work inspired, but it suggested a potential for escape into a universal music that combined idealism with a premeditated emulation of the shock tactics employed by all the greats of rock 'n' roll. In the San Francisco of 1968, it would have been a vision that put him at the centre of the ferment of the time. In mellow Minneapolis, it was a brilliant fantasy, a vision that set him apart. Not surprisingly, his fulfilment of it had to be achieved pretty much alone.

3

Deals

Darlene Pfeifer/*Minneapolis Star Tribune*

Prince Nelson has a cousin called Shauntel Manderville. Her mother and Prince's mother are twins. In 1972 she married a black New Yorker by the name of Linster Willie – or 'Pepé', as he had been known since infanthood. Pepé Willie's uncle, Clarence Collins, was a member of the R & B group Little Anthony and the Imperials, and through this family connection, Willie got involved in the music business from the bottom. Starting off as the Imperials' valet and errand boy, he moved on to singing and songwriting, and before long had picked up a thorough grounding in the subtle and manifold ways in which the wide-eyed beginner can be stitched up a treat. The fifteen-year-old Prince Nelson used to ring him up for advice, and, says Willie, 'he was family, so I was happy to help out if I could'.

Soon, Pepé Willie and his new wife packed their bags and left the dim lights of Brooklyn to settle in the relatively pristine peacefulness of the ultimate mid-western town. Willie insists he always maintained that Minneapolis was going to be the next urban centre to spawn a great musical explosion. And when he first saw them performing – at a ski-party thrown by his then father-in-law – he agreed with LaVonne Daugherty, Morris Day's mother, to put his experience at the service of the very young, very promising, but, he says, exceedingly erratic Grand Central band.

Pepé Willie remembers: 'They would be rehearsing round at André's house, or in Morris's attic. It was fun. There was a lot of laughter. They were great musicians, but, like, Morris had a seven-piece drum set, and only played three of them.' Grand Central's material was, apparently, also a little lacking in construction. 'I would help them out be getting André, Morris and the others to put down their instruments and just sing, while Prince played guitar. Because, you know, one guy would be singing, "well, thank you", and another would be singing, "well, spank you"!'

Getting them to write down and memorize the words was one thing. Another was that Grand Central had a tendency to jam. 'They would start a song, sing a verse, and then all of a sudden they'd be off somewhere else for fifteen, twenty minutes! Hey guys, wait a minute! When they'd finished, I would say, "look, that was great. But I forgot the name of the song. And if I did, I'm pretty sure the public would have too." But Prince was always good. You can't take nothing away from him. He was always very helpful to the other members. When they were practising one of his songs he would sometimes go over to the keyboards and say to Linda, "No, I don't want you to play that." He'd put the guitar down, go over to the keyboards, play it, and she would just copy it back. He was telling her what to play.'

The group and Mrs Daugherty both aspired to greater things, and with this in mind, Pepé Willie recalls arranging for a friend called Dale Menton (who once had a recording deal with MCA) to take a look at Grand Central one night at a studio he part-owned called Cookhouse (now known as Nicollet Studios) on Nicollet Avenue. The band set up, and went through part of their own repertoire, which included compositions by André Anderson called '39th Street Party' ('a really nice song', says Pepé Willie) and 'You Remind Me Of Me'. By this point, Willie says, he had been working with the band for around six months, and their original material sounded pretty good. But then Menton suggested they play a couple of cover tunes, maybe something by Earth, Wind and Fire. It was soon apparent that they had mastered delivery of other people's hits better than the stuff they had created themselves.

'They went back to the drawing-board. But I knew at the time that Prince was a major talent,' Willie insists. More than a year later, some time in 1977, Prince was back at Cookhouse again, not with Grand Central but as a session man, helping Pepé Willie to demo some of his own songs. The sessions were, Willie says, paid at the proper rate in accordance with Musicians Union rules. And Prince was a pretty cost-effective guy to hire. 'In the studio, he was all I thought I needed, 'cause he could play everything.' Willie remembers an incident which showed Prince to have acquired a studio affinity that would turn out to be a crucial factor in his future career. After doing some work on a Pepé Willie track, Prince rang up worrying that he had made a mistake on a guitar part. 'I didn't hear it,' recalls Willie, 'but *he* heard it. He said "I want to go back and clean it up." And I said "OK", 'cause I knew that he could do it. He was the only one I could leave in the studio on his own.'

It was on the strength of these Cookhouse demos that Pepé Willie went on to secure a recording deal with Polydor in New York. The A &

R man who got them in was Hank Cosby, formerly a writer-producer with Motown, and best known as the co-composer and producer of Stevie Wonder's 'My Cherie Amour'. By this time Pepé Willie had a pair of regular singers, Marcy Ingvoldstad and Kristie Lazenberry, and soon after put together a short-lived multi-racial band comprised of local musicians Pierre Lewis, André Lewis, Wendell Thomas and his brother Dale Alexander on drums, a character who would crop up ten years later in the touring incarnation of Prince's jazz protégés, Madhouse. 'We fired him, 'cause he was late for rehearsals all the time, and we put an ad in the paper.' It was answered by a drummer from a Jewish Minneapolis family, Bobby Rivkin. Rechristened 'Bobby Z', he would later go on to greater fame in Prince's first road band. Lacking a name to put on the label of their planned début single release, Pepé Willie and company decided to call themselves after the main routeway out of the Twin Cities in the direction of the Big Apple – 94 East.

But by this time, Prince had already assembled the groundwork components of his future glories. The blend of imagination, expertise and perfectionism that later afforded him so much control over his output had begun to reveal itself, as had his ability to harness the creativity of those around him. But the most intense of the creative relationships that helped set Prince on the road out of the backwoods of Minnesota, and on the way to the remarkable alternative universe inside his head, involved a white expatriate Englishman called Chris Moon.

With a curious half-and-half accent veering from slightly nasal middle-class English to acquired American flash, Chris Moon gives due warning that he is among the more singular individuals to have had an input into the life and times of Prince. It is an image he appears to enjoy. Born in a caravan in Southampton, UK, Moon and family moved to suburban Surrey when his father made a dramatic career move: he gave up being a street-artist to work instead in public relations for the British Air Corporation. Geographically, it was the least spectacular in a series of changes which resumed during the teenage Christopher's adolescence with a move to Aloha Airlines in Hawaii, followed three years later by another move, when his father took up a new post as vice-president of advertising with North West Orient, Minneapolis's very own air travel firm.

It was in the depths of the freezing Minnesota winter that Moon entered the American education system, sporting 'English trousers, Hawaiian shirt, a deep tan and a British accent. I was immediately misunderstood, a social outcast from the beginning . . . which I quite enjoyed.' On leaving school, Moon embarked on a loose ten-year plan. He wanted to get into music, but 'I didn't have much music talent. So

I decided it would be fun to own a recording studio. Besides, I thought it would get me some girls.'

Supporting himself by working for a cassette-duplication company, he learned from the engineer how to edit and duplicate tape. At nineteen, his boss left and Moon was promoted to replace him. He asked for a raise, and didn't get it: 'so I left'. Instead, he took advantage of the last of the free international flights his father's position entitled him to. Teac had just introduced their four-track recording machines. Moon scraped together his every last cent, flew to Hong Kong and bought one for about one thousand dollars. He was in business.

For the next two to three years, Moon, his upper lip appropriately stiff, set about establishing his name from nothing. First off, he arranged his sparse equipment in the basement of the house he was renting on 25th St and Portland Avenue: 'It looked like an English dungeon down there.' With carpet on the walls and plastic microphones hanging from the ceiling, Moon began recording people for free. Anyone who came along, never mind the style: country, polkas, rock, or, his favourite, R & B. His English accent then got him work doing ads on the radio for upcoming Twin Cities rock shows, among them the Rolling Stones, and soon he was talking visiting acts into letting him record their performances for broadcast on the main progressive rock station, KQRS.

After five or six changes of location, Moon moved his studio once more, this time to a former hairdressing salon by Lake Nokomis on the southern fringes of Minneapolis, close to the international airport. By this time, he was charging thirty or forty dollars a time for use of his facilities, which were now considerably improved. In a town with only half-a-dozen studios to its name, his credibility was on the up and up. The new location certainly had its assets – 1,500 square feet of space, including living quarters – but also its drawbacks. While Moon, his mother and father were refurbishing the premises downstairs, they started hearing footsteps up above. Inspections yielded nothing. Then a neighbour gave them the news: the previous occupant, a photographer, had been found one day by his father, hanging from the ceiling, naked, surrounded by pornography. 'It seemed we had a bit of a ghost upstairs,' grins Moon.

It was to this latest setting for Moon Sound that Prince showed up one summer's day in '76 with LaVonne Daugherty and the rest of the teenage band, who, aware that Larry Graham had formed a group called Graham Central Station, had now renamed themselves Champagne. 'They were fairly timid and shy,' remembers Moon, who let them have the studio at a discount. 'I think there were three or four sessions. They'd come in, do the rhythm track one day, then the vocals, and then the mix and so on.'

By now, Moon had another regular job, this time in the recording studio of the biggest advertising agency in the Twin Cities, Campbell-Mithun Inc. He was hired on April Fool's day, and celebrated his august new position by treating himself to 'a giant Afro hairdo'. The hours were eight a.m. till one p.m. 'I would turn up at about ten and finish about two or three.' The first part of Moon's day would involve putting together jingles for, among others, national clients like Ford and the locally based Honeywell. Before long, the second part of his day would be spent almost exclusively in the vicinity of another giant Afro hairdo, the one belonging to Prince.

A secret lyricist and poet, Moon had aspirations as a songwriter. What he needed was a musician. During the Champagne sessions, his attention was drawn to Prince. 'I thought, "he's fairly quiet and mild-mannered. There's a guy with not much ego. Why not work with him?" ' Moon is hugely amused by his misjudgement of the superstar in waiting. Not that things didn't work out well for a considerable while. 'I cornered him in the studio, and said, "I'd like to talk to you about something, why don't you come back later on?" ' Prince did, and a bargain was struck. 'I said, "Here's the deal in a nutshell. I'm looking to produce some original material with somebody. It's very uncomplicated. I'll provide the studio and the lyrics, record you, and if you want, teach you how to produce yourself. We'll put some material together, and if anything comes of it, we'll split it 50/50. How does that sound to you?" '

Prince responded in the way Prince tended to respond to new people entering his world. He said nothing – but he managed to dredge up a nod. 'Then,' continues Moon, 'I reached into my pocket and handed him a set of keys to the studio, which I'm sure blew his mind – a sixteen-year-old black kid from the north side of Minneapolis. It kind of set him back. I said, "Let's shake on it." ' And so they did. It was the start of a curious friendship. For close to a year, Prince Nelson and Chris Moon devoted long hours to composing and recording their material. Prince quickly made it clear that he could not only handle the singing and the guitar, but the piano, bass and drums as well. 'He had a driving force to play as many instruments as he could. Although not highly touted or expressed, it was definitely there, because at my [earlier] suggestion that we bring in other people, I remember his reaction as being one of a little disappointment.'

They made an improbable couple: Moon, a bohemian white Brit in his early twenties; Prince, a pint-sized black American still in his middle teens. 'I took Prince down to Campbell-Mithun one time to do some work for them. They've still got a tape down there with some original Prince stuff that they don't even know about. I remember when I was walking with him through the halls. Everyone was looking at me – "here comes the white guy with the Afro with the black guy with the Afro!" – and thinking, "Oh, my God." '

There was no social contact between the two of them, and probably just as well. Prince was already firm in his disapproval of traditional rock 'n' roll ways. 'I remember it was a Friday night, still recording, and I was pouring myself a rum and Coke or something,' says Moon, 'and Prince said, "You're not gonna drink that, are you?" He didn't like the idea of drinking or drugs or anything like that. He had fairly strong opinions about it, and was quite willing to express them.' If religion lay at the root of this – and Prince had been a church-goer – he didn't say so. 'There was never any discussion of religion. I'd say "Why", and he'd say, "Well, you don't need to change yourself. You're OK the way you are." I think it was just basically a personal belief that he had.'

Pepé Willie had also experienced the clean streak in Prince. 'We used to have a beer or two, or some wine at rehearsal, during a break or something, and he'd come back upstairs, when we was in the attic at LaVonne's house, and Prince used to laugh at us, because we were somewhat . . . tipsy. He would just look at us, and point at us, and say "Look at yo' eyes! Yo' eyes is red!" And we'd look at him and say, "Man, this dude!" We used to look at him like he was just the squarest guy in the world.'

Moon and Nelson worked round and round the clock, evenings and weekends. Prince had been booted out of Champagne for pursuing this solo interest, but if it hurt him, he didn't let it interfere with his work rate. 'We both had a musical hunger that we were trying to satiate,' says Moon, though, with his morning job to keep up, he needed the occasional break. These were the times Prince refined his studiocraft on his own. 'When I would go away at the weekend, Prince would stay in the studio. He'd sleep on the sofa, right under where this guy had hung himself. I never told him the story, 'cause I didn't think he needed the aggravation.' If Prince ever woke up, rigid with fear in the night, he kept it to himself. It was a different story for another of Chris Moon's friends. 'He looked very pale in the morning. He told me, "I woke up in the middle of the night and saw two legs swinging in front of me." And he didn't know the story either.'

One midweek night, Moon went out on a bender. The next morning he staggered into work late, locked the doors from the inside, and 'lay there in a major recovery mode'. He put his mind to the Prince situation. Things were going OK, but 'I decided what we needed was a marketing direction. There had to be some vein of continuity.' Moon came up with a now celebrated catchphrase: 'I thought, "Naughty Sexual Innuendo". I set about writing a song which I envisaged as being the spearhead of this marketing direction.' The result was an item entitled 'Soft And Wet'. 'I think the original opening line was, "Angora fur/The Aegean Sea/It's a soft, wet love/That you have for me" . . . You know. A real

31

masterpiece.' Moon showed it to Prince. 'He read it through, and said, "Yeah, I like this!" '

Prince was already working hard on his steps and spins, and snappy ways of signing his autograph. Moon, though, claims that it was his idea to have his partner drop the surname Nelson, and just use 'Prince' for showbiz purposes. Whatever, with 'Soft And Wet' they 'kicked off the demos properly'. With their new entrepreneurial stratagem in mind, Prince and Moon eventually completed fourteen songs. Three of them would finally end up on Prince's first LP. Then, one day, Prince put a proposition to Moon: 'He came to me and said, "I want you to be my manager." '

The events by which Chris Moon persuaded Prince he was not the man to be negotiating contracts and hussling him onto airplanes are clouded by a fog of rumour and memories faded by the passing of time. What *is* clear is that Prince decided to go out to New York, stay with an older half-sister on his father's side called Sharon, and see if he could rustle up some kind of interest in the results of the Moon Sound sessions.

The tapes generated inquiries from at least one source. There is the well-trodden tale of Sharon Nelson introducing Prince to a French woman called Danielle Mauroy, who supposedly wanted him to record a blousy, string-laden rendition of a ballad from the tapes he carried with him called 'Baby'. Also, Pepé Willie, in New York at the time on 94 East business, recalls receiving a phone call: 'He called me up about a contract some label offered him out there. He said, "Man, they don't want my singing, they just want my playing", or something. I said, "Don't sign it", but he went ahead and did it anyway.' Pepé's recollection is that this contract – whoever it was with – turned out to be meaningless anyway, due to Prince's tender years. A clearer anecdote from this period again involves the resourceful Chris Moon. 'He called me up and says,"Oh, man. I called up all these record companies and they won't have anything to do with me. I can't even get in to see them." He says, "I need your help. I want you to get me an appointment with one." I hung up and thought, "Jesus Christ." '

Moon made a few straightforward phone requests to companies in New York. Predictably, he met with no success. Sensing the need for drastic measures, he secured the name of the President of one of the major labels, and told his personal secretary that he was representing Stevie Wonder and could he please have a word? 'So this guy's on the phone. I said, "Hello, my name's Chris Moon. I told your secretary I'm representing Stevie Wonder, but, to tell you the truth, I lied. But if you think Stevie Wonder's good, you're gonna love my artist. He plays all the instruments, writes all the songs, and sings. Plus, he can see." '

Astonished, the President was sold. 'He said, "Send him in tomorrow at nine o'clock." ' Nothing came of the meeting, and Moon says he cannot remember which company it was. Atlantic, maybe? Or Arista? Somewhere, there is one horribly ulcerated executive, hoping he never does.

Apart from dealing with Prince's increasingly anxious phone-calls from New York, Moon was trying to sort out the management problem. As usual, when it came to black musicians, there were implicit difficulties in working from Minneapolis and St Paul. 'There was no black music scene in town. There was nothing to hook on to, nothing you could work with.' Cynthia Johnson puts it another way. 'I don't think there was a [black] band in the Twin Cities that had a manager, 'cause there wasn't a manager that believed in the black music scene.' Given this, it is hardly surprising that Prince's solution to the management problem and the realization of his wildest dreams came about not from within his own community, tiny, isolated and predictably under-represented in the professions, but through a chain of connections linking three white men: the first was Chris Moon, the third, Russ Thyret, a vice-president of promotions at Warner Brothers' record division in Los Angeles, and in between the two, a Jewish Minneapolitan entrepreneur with his own advertising agency, Owen Husney.

Moon decided to pay a visit to the office of the best man he knew with entrepreneurial rock 'n' roll experience. One day Owen Husney walked in to find Moon sitting on his couch. 'You won't believe this,' Moon said, coining a deathless cliché, 'but I've got the new Stevie Wonder.'

Chris Moon was perfectly correct. Owen Husney did not believe him. 'Well,' says Husney, 'I'd heard so many stories like that, I really didn't pay any attention. But he continued to sit on my couch, and wouldn't leave.'

Moon had come bearing a tape. 'It was about fifteen minutes long, or something. "Soft And Wet" was part of what was on there, and there was another song called "Aces".' (Moon recalls that 'Baby' was also among those selected from their collaborations. Another from this period, entitled 'Machine', was, reputedly, very rude indeed.) 'It was a combination of different things. I said, "Who's the group? These guys are good." He said, "Sit down." I said, "Why?" He said, "Because it's one kid playing all the instruments and singing all the voices." '

Moon's version of events suggests that Husney was impressed by the versatility and youth, but took a little longer making up his mind about the quality. He says he delivered the tape on a Monday morning, and spent the rest of the week hassling for Husney to express some interest

– which he finally did. Husney obtained Prince's sister's number from Moon, called him in New York, and recalls the ensuing conversation thus: 'I said, "Look, you're young, a lot of people aren't gonna take you seriously. You should be your own producer, but you need somebody protecting you creatively." '

As a potential manager, Husney did have certain attributes. Though working in advertising, he had experience in the world of rock which went back fifteen years, starting when he was in a group himself. He and a bunch of friends – 'we were just a bunch of idiots out of high school' – formed a band called the High Spirits and did 'a lot of material by black artists'. They recorded a song by the bluesman Bobby Bland called 'Turn On Your Love Light', and 'kind of updated it for pop radio'. The promotion of the record was very much a DIY venture for the band, but Husney and his buddies did not lack nerve. 'We physically took the record to radio stations ourselves,' he says; and it seemed to work, because the track went to number one locally, and 'we were in *Billboard* for about two minutes'. 'Turn On Your Love Light' also topped local charts in Kansas City, Florida and California, and its success was, says Husney, sufficient to support the High Spirits on the road for six or seven years.

Once their hit record's fallout had well and truly exhausted itself, Husney went into business, keeping his ears pinned back. 'I started doing the food backstage at national concerts, folding the baloney and salami. I heard a lot of stories about what went on between managers and artists.' Moving into management himself, Husney had looked after a varied range of performers, from acoustic acts to a hard rock band called Rings. He was competing with the manager of Black Sabbath to secure their favour at the time Prince came into his life.

'We were involved in a very heavy battle, then all of a sudden I got that Prince demo tape, and I never even bothered to call the group back.' Certainly Prince seems to have excited him enough for him to think it worthwhile making a serious investment of effort. From Husney's own account, that investment began right there on the telephone to New Jersey. He tells the story well. For a man with a reputation, deserved or otherwise, for keeping well out of the limelight, Husney describes his role with the polished expansiveness of a natural salesman.

'All I can do in my role is enhance the artist's true vision, not change it. In other words, I saw Prince for what he was, and I knew that's what I had to fight for for him. I think that struck a good chord, because he came back, we met a couple of times, he came over to my home, and we just sat there and talked about it. I said, "You need someone to fight for you, because who on earth is gonna let you play all the instruments in your sessions, and who is going to let you be your own producer? You need someone out there that is willing to cut their arms off for you.

And that is what I want to do because I believe you are indeed that talented." '

Moon says his unwillingness to act for Prince himself was 'not well received. We had developed a comfort with each other, and the idea of working with somebody new . . .' It just didn't appeal. 'But I talked to Prince about it quite a bit. I explained to him that I had somebody with experience.' It is not difficult to imagine what would have attracted the teenager in the end, for all his usual caution. Not only did Husney express faith in Prince's ability to accomplish precisely the type of approach to music-making he had been edging towards in the preceding months – that is, increasingly self-directed and self-contained – he also seemed ready to put his heart and some of his money where his mouth was. So Chris Moon receded from the scene. 'I said, "The only thing that you have to do is make sure that my interests are protected, and everything goes down the way it should be." '

It was the end of a working relationship, but not the end of the line. In 1986, ten years after their first encounter in the haunted Moon Sound studio, the Englishman became one of the very few aggrieved former associates of Prince to extract what he considers was owed to him. For a long time, stories had circulated that Moon had copyrighted a bunch of songs resulting from his and Prince's long collaboration, and would one day release them. But in the end, Moon decided not to commit his Prince sessions to vinyl. What he *did* do with them is not something he cares to elucidate on. But the truth of the matter is that he sold the songs to Prince's publishing company Controversy Music after a meeting with Prince's management at which a suitable fee seems to have been agreed. Reparation, Moon might think, for his disgruntlement over writing credits for three songs which appeared on Prince's début album of 1978, *For You*. One was 'Soft And Wet', for which Moon was named co-lyricist, but not co-musical composer. The other two songs in dispute, 'Baby' – a song of which title appeared on the tape Moon had given Owen Husney – and 'My Love Is Forever', were both credited solely to Prince.

This episode is but the most dramatic of an ongoing, long-distance relationship between the two. The first incident, about which Moon is far more open, occurred a couple of years after their original parting: 'Prince sent his dad over to see me. It was funny, 'cause we hadn't spoken for a long time and suddenly I got this call from Prince. He says, "Will you produce my dad?" His dad came in and met with me and we talked. I think I told him that I needed to hear some additional tapes or something, and I never heard from him again.'

Moon says that he and Prince have not met face to face since about 1982. But he reckons that Prince has sent out coded messages. A few minutes into Prince's 1986 film, *Under the Cherry Moon*, we see Prince lying on a bed reading a piece of A4 paper, with a distinctive logo at the top – a capital letter 'C' facing a symbol in the shape of a crescent moon: C Moon. It pops up again during the closing footage, only this time the paper is covered in writing. And remember, the film's hero goes by the name of Christopher – and, so the introduction informs us, all *he* cares about is money.

From his end, Moon has kept up the communication more directly. On the wall of his little home recording studio, there is a large framed picture of Prince with his adolescent Afro, an early publicity shot. Moon is proud of their work together. Since those days, he has exercised his entrepreneurial urge as a property agent, and spent some time in Kenya working on, of all things, a proposed movie sequel to *Born Free*, though he is still involved in music when the fancy takes him. In 1987 he put together an anti-drug single called 'Proud, Straight And Strong', sung by Cynthia Johnson. On the back it says: 'Special Thanks To Skippy Nelson'. There have been other little tweaks. 'What I do, like when I was in Africa or when I was in the Caribbean, I always send him these postcards: "I'm in the middle of the African bush. These natives were dancing to your music. Just thought you'd like to know." ' On one occasion, not long after *Purple Rain*, Moon discovered that Prince was visiting a Minneapolis bookshop, attended by his usual crew of body-guards, 'I was going out with a very tall, blonde, attractive aerobics instuctor at the time,' he recalls. 'I said to her, "Just walk up to Prince, and tell him Chris Moon says 'Hello'." He came running out of the store looking all around for me, saying "Where is he?" I was across the road in a phone booth with dark glasses on, watching.'

In 1985, an album attributed to 94 East, entitled *Minneapolis Genius – The Historic 1977 Recordings*, was released in America. Though basically all instrumental, the title and packaging dropped some pretty heavy hints as to the identity of one of its participants. In the light of a US number one single of the preceding year called 'When Doves Cry', the mauve backdrop with a silhouette of a dove holding a red rose in its beak on the front did not leave too much to the imagination.

Minneapolis Genius features some of the last studio recordings Prince was involved in before Owen Husney and his partner Gary Levinson negotiated his solo contract with Warner Brothers. Released on the Hot Pink label, the only 94 East members involved in the work it contains were Pepé Willie, Kristie Lazenberry and Marcy Ingvoldstad, while the vast bulk of the instrumental and compositional credits are shared by Willie, Prince and André Anderson, known in that context by his stage name André Cymone. The six songs originate from sessions involving Prince and Anderson as session instrumentalists at three different studios:

one was the Cookhouse in Minneapolis; another was also a local facility, the only top-flight recording space at the time, Sound 80; the third was a studio in New York.

The trip to the Big Apple occurred in the first place because of Pepé Willie's connection with Little Anthony and the Imperials. Tony Silvester, leader of the group The Main Ingredient, was going to produce the Imperials, and needed to hire some musicians to make demos of songs he was considering recording with them. Knowing Willie's connection with the Imperials, he called him up to discuss who might be recruited for the job. 'I said, "I have two guys here that can play everything",' Willie recalls; ''cause André could do it all just like Prince can. It's like kids roller-skating, and one says, "Hey, watch this trick", and the other one says, "I can do that too." So whatever Prince could play, André could play. These guys were just phenomenal. Prince would pick up the bass and say, "Hey André! Play this!" and show him, and before he had even finished, André would say, "Yeah, I know what you mean, man." And then he went and played it just like that.'

At this point, 94 East's deal with Polydor had fallen through. A song called 'Fortune Teller' was intended to be their first single release, written for them by Hank Cosby. Prince had contributed to the recording (as had another artist destined for future fame, the soul singer Colonel Abrams – according to Willie, Abrams was a 'freelance singer' who sang the lead vocal on 'Fortune Teller', but he and Prince never actually met), which would have marked his vinyl début. But when Hank Cosby was fired, 94 East lost their 'in' with Polydor, and the project was shelved. Pepé Willie says that Prince was 'kind of angry' about the incident.

Nevertheless, both he and André Anderson agreed to take up Tony Silvester's offer. This time Prince would go to New York in style. 'We got a room at the Hilton,' remembers Willie, with some satisfaction. In the studio (Willie cannot remember its name), Willie, Prince and Anderson demoed some songs of their own. Two of the tracks on *Minneapolis Genius* were recorded at this time: one is the closing track, 'One Man Jam'; the other is a voiceless version of the Pepé Willie composition 'If You Feel Like Dancin' ', which opens side one, crediting Willie on keyboards, André Cymone on bass and Prince on guitars and synthesizers.

But those weren't the only two original compositions committed to tape in New York. Pepé Willie also believes that these sessions saw the first-ever recording of Prince's 'I Feel For You', the song which would eventually appear on his self-titled second album and (in 1984) be covered and taken to number one in Britain and the States by Chaka Khan. Nor was this the only future hit to get an early airing. 'Everybody had their own songs,' says Pepé Willie. Prince had 'I Feel For You', and Anderson had a number called 'Thrill You Or Kill You', which Kristie Lazenberry

37

believes may have been a precursor to a tune recorded in 1987 by Jody Watley, written and co-produced by André Cymone and future Prince engineer, David Z, entitled 'Still A Thrill'.

There was also a ballad, which Pepé remembers André considered to be one of his: 'Do Me Baby'. Willie states plainly that it was André who performed it in the studio in New York. And yet it would be Prince who not only released the song on his 1981 album *Controversy*, but claimed authorship too. 'André called me up on that song, that "Do Me Baby" song. He said, "Hey, you remember I did it New York?" I said, "What, the slow jam?". He said, "Yeah, well, Prince has taken it for his album." ' Prince's alleged act of appropriation did nothing to heal the rift between the former best friends that occurred after the *Dirty Mind* tour, four years after that trip together to New York.

The Minneapolis studio Sound 80, where Bob Dylan recorded *Blood on the Tracks*, was the setting for three more of the *Minneapolis Genius* tracks: side two's opener, 'Just Another Sucker', jointly credited to Willie and Prince, and jointly published by Prince's Controversy Music house and Willie's own PMI – Pepé Music Incorporated; 'Dance To The Music Of The World', by Pepé Willie alone; and 'Lovin' Cup', whose authorship is shared by Willie and his friend from Harlem, Ike Paige (who also splits copyright with Tony Silvester for 'One Man Jam'). The sixth *Minneapolis Genius* cut is 'Games,' another Pepé Willie tune, and the only one on the album to emanate from Cookhouse.

Pepé Willie says he was intending to sing on the songs he wrote himself – those recorded in New York and at Sound 80 being part of his 'brand-new thing' after the collapse of the Polydor deal. (It seems that Prince's record deal came through, and the project had to be abandoned; hence the various contributions credited to one Alvin Moody on 'Games' and 'Just Another Sucker', which were overdubbed later, just prior to the album's release). Loosely, the goods here might be fairly characterized as cool, polished (though not fully fine-tuned) street funk that slips into a nice clean groove and stays there. The lack of vocals, save for the ladies' backups on 'Just Another Sucker' and 'Lovin' Cup', lets us hear one of two of the players showing off a bit. The special interest in 'If You Feel Like Dancin'' is what the guitar player gets up to.

Throughout the seven-minute-and-ten-second duration, Prince solos almost without respite, sending the instrument through the entire repertoire of heavy rock pyrotechnics, from lightly distorted fast-finger fretwork to screaming high notes which hurtle right off the high end of the ecstasy meter. There were two guitar players who he really admired: Carlos Santana – an enduring influence – and Jimi Hendrix. 'He felt', says Pepé, 'that any guitar player should be able to play Hendrix's [version of] "Star Spangled Banner". That was mandatory, like playing your scales.' 'Just Another Sucker''s rhythm lick is a good one, with a nice crisp shuffle on the backbeat: occasionally the guitarist deigns to come back to the beat and flirt with it before heading off for the stratosphere again.

Not surprisingly, Prince's name pops up under each of *Minneapolis Genius*'s half-dozen titles. His presence is, after all, the albums's selling-point. His guitar work appears on all but 'One Man Jam' (the Silvester/Paige number), where he provides synthesizers, percussion and clavinet on a disco-orientated, electronics-dominated number whose melody strongly recalls the Philadelphia International hit 'Where Are All My Friends' by Harold Melvin and the Blue Notes. On 'Just Another Sucker', 'Dance To The Music Of The World', and 'Lovin' Cup' he is credited for guitars, keyboards, drums and synthesizers, and on the latter, an easy-paced ballad featuring plenty of Anderson's popping bass guitar, he exhibits both a more restrained rhythm-guitar style and a mastery of a quite complex drum part.

But if *Minneapolis Genius* could later claim to be documentary evidence of one teenage musician's unusual versatility and skill, and if the Moon Sound sessions had showed this same individual could bring them all together under his own direction in the studio, on paper that still didn't add up to 'the new Stevie Wonder'. It was going to take a more than musical expertise for one quiet adolescent from the north side to light up the Minnesota skies.

Owen Husney, meanwhile, was hot on the trail: 'I put together some financing, and we raised some money. He was living with André, in his basement, so we got him an apartment and we bought some instruments for him and got him into a 24-track studio.' The address of the apartment, as contained in Pepé Willie's notebook of the time, was 2012 Aldridge South, where, according to a famous anecdote (in Jon Bream's biography *Prince: Inside The Purple Reign*), he made a lot of mess and had a Chaka Khan record nailed to the wall. The 24-track studio was Sound 80, where Husney paired Prince with the engineer who would work with him throughout the next ten years, David Rivkin.

Like his brother Bobby, David Rivkin also went on to assume the professional surname 'Z', derived from a Yiddish pet-name their grand-father used to call them: 'Butzie'. David Rivkin had been in a band with Owen Husney, while Bobby had worked as a session drummer at Chris Moon's studio – he would probably have been the one to contribute to the tracks Prince recorded there, had the teenager not been so determined to do it all himself.

Sound 80 and Rivkin were hired so that a fresh demo could be made for Husney to hawk in LA. He had a dream, one he believes has come true: 'I'm convinced that it takes two things to cause an explosion,' he says, embarking on a theory he has expounded more than once. 'One is a major artist. The second is a business entity. That's what puts a town on the map. The young black artists in Detroit would have been forced to go to New York or Los Angeles if there had not been a Berry Gordy. What our company did specifically back in the mid-seventies was we formed the business entity here. When Prince came to me it was because I was the person in town who had the vision.'

There are some comparisons to be made between the growth of the Minneapolis Sound and the phenomenon of Motown Records two decades earlier. But in that statement, Husney has pushed them about as far as they could possibly go. Detroit in the late fifties was certainly a city where blacks were still seeking to establish themselves, though for them the battle was to become something other than production-line fodder for Henry Ford. Because of the blue-collar wage opportunities that existed, Detroit's black population was large. Consequently it was possible for a separate and more self-supporting black musical culture to exist. The magnificence of the superficially simple Motown Sound owes everything to the jazz-players of that huge underclass, its superb rhythmic basis laid down by forgotten session men of whom drummer Benny Benjamin and bass-player James Jamerson were only the most talented and prolific. There was nothing comparable in Minneapolis and St Paul, as Chris Moon had already realized. Owen Husney, the burgeoning 'business entity', would have to be Prince's emissary to Tinsel Town.

'We attacked it all first class, 'cause if we went in as just the average Joes, it wasn't gonna look like a first-class effort.' Husney employed 'a first class attorney', Lee Phillips, who still represents Prince today. With him he took David Rivkin's demo tapes, containing reworked versions of songs from the Moon Sound demo including 'Soft And Wet' and 'Baby', plus, Husney believes, some other, newer Prince material. But he didn't just take the songs; he took the packaging too. 'We spent 1,500 dollars on fifteen press kits,' Husney says. 'The usual press kit has clippings, and stories about your mom, and all the other bands you played in. All I did was have a picture of Prince on the cover. It said, "American Artists Presents Prince", and inside there was just five sheets. And on those sheets there was just one picture, and one quote from Prince above each one.' With the tapes put together on special silver tape reels, Husney had it all worked out right down to his own wardrobe. 'We knew that everyone in Los Angeles was going to be wearing jeans, so we went out there in three-piece suits.

'I had to lie and fib to get into the labels,' he recalls, beaming. 'I called up CBS and I remember them saying, "Well I don't know if I want to make an appointment with you", and I said, "Well, I'm out here to make a presentation to Warner Brothers, would you care to see me too?" So then they said, "Oh yeah, oh yeah!"

'When people heard the tape, they asked the same question I did: "Who's the band?" Then I told them it was one kid, and this is the way it's got to go down. We wanted three albums, because it was gonna take that long for him to develop. We wanted him to be his own producer, and to play all the instruments. And those were the terms we made the deal on.'

CBS, A & M and Warner Brothers became the leading candidates for the signature of this creature from the town Husney likes to think of by its popular title, 'Island of the North'. The first of these liked the artist but stalled on the three-album commitment. But that wasn't all Husney was after. 'We also knew that Prince needed a family type of thing, an organization behind him. It couldn't just be a regular signing. And we demanded a lot of money for him.' A & M, says Husney, came very close to agreeing terms. But Husney's personal connections at Warner Brothers gave them the edge. He describes Russ Thyret as 'a friend and a man of heart. It felt good with him in there fighting for us.' And so it was that Warner Brothers came through, pretty much meeting Husney on the required terms. 'It was six figures,' he says, preferring not to get too specific. 'Well, the whole deal was a multi-million dollar deal, but the initial [sum] was well into six figures.'

The only sticking-point was on the question of self-production. Warners were not ready to relinquish the final authority over the output of what has rightly been described as a historic signing. Prince's contract made him officially the youngest producer in Warner Brothers' history, and it is hardly surprising that such an organization was unwilling to risk the huge commitment of cash and trust without a safety net. So manager and monolith came to an arrangement.

Husney explains it like this: 'One thing that Prince probably doesn't know is that I set up a plan with them. It was to call Prince and tell him that after we were signed, Warner Brothers was gonna offer some free studio time to him in LA. We were gonna fly out there, and he was just gonna fool around and make some demos and stuff. But the *real* plan was that we'd put him in the studio and have him fool around, but have major producers come down! All these were just regular-Joe-looking guys, and Prince didn't know who they were. But while he was in the studio, guys like Lenny Waronker (now president of Warner Bros), Gary Katz, producer of Steely Dan, Teddy Templeman, who did the Doobie Brothers and a number of other major-league names. They were just coming in and out like janitors. He made, like, half a song on his own. And Lenny and Teddy came back and we talked in a corner of the building, and they said "You're right. This guy has a record sense and should be doing his own albums." '

But whatever convictions Waronker and Templeman may have expressed to Husney on this subject, Warners still demanded and exercised the right to impose a young executive producer – Tommy Vicari – over the first Prince album. And certainly to have done anything else would have made their break from standard record company procedure even more complete than it already was. For what is remarkable about the first Prince contract with Warner Brothers is not simply that he was very young and totally unheard of, but most of all that he was black.

With only a very few superstar exceptions, Afro-American artists had never enjoyed the same power to control and explore their creativity as their white counterparts. When Stevie Wonder became a legal adult in 1971, he put his contract up for the highest bidder, only returning to Motown, his original home, when he had secured the leeway to write, produce, and play whatever he wanted on his own LPs. It was an unprecedented situation for a black performer to negotiate his way into, notwithstanding the fact that Motown was the first black-owned record company to make it big in the USA. Over fifteen years later, Wonder's situation was still very much the exception to the rule.

The new Warners signing sent ripples of envy and admiration through American popular music circles. It marked Prince out as an exception even before he had made a record, and his subsequent output would be measured against the expectations raised by his arrival. Without doubt, Stevie Wonder was the market role-model Warners must have hoped he could emulate: a multi-instrumental composer, producer and singer who might prove to have the potential to burst out of the black music charts and eventually 'cross over' into the other, more profitable musical compartments which American leisure capitalism had evolved. He would be self-generating and self-contained. A special case from day one.

4

Fame

Warner Bros.

One year after becoming Warner Brothers' black teenage celebrity elect, Prince found out what fame could be all about. He was making a promotional appearance at a radio station in North Carolina during a pre-Christmas 'food drive' for the local poor. Listening in the car with Pepé Willie *en route* from airport to hotel, he heard the DJ announce that their plane had just landed, and they were on the way to the station, '*right now*'.

Prince had recently become a Name, at least in certain circles. His first album, *For You*, came out in the States in April 1978, with 'Soft And Wet' released as a single at the end of June to make number twelve on the *Billboard* black singles chart. A follow-up, 'Just As Long As We're Together', was new in the shops. In the South, Prince's career had got off to a good start. People knew who he was, and now they knew where he was going to be. They showed up in generous numbers, and by the time Prince and Pepé Willie had rushed to the hotel, freshened up and hurried to their appointment, boredom had sharpened the crowd's anticipation. Inevitably, there were those who found the reality a disappointment in one particular respect. 'We got out, and we were walking through all these people,' remembers Willie, 'and I heard somebody say, "Oh, he's so *short!*" I was so embarrassed. But then I thought, Hey, he *is* short, you know? He had to deal with it sooner or later.'

As a studio prodigy with no serious track-record as a live or TV act, Prince's reputation as a phenomenon preceded his actual physical self. The risk of ridicule was always there. Later, as his command of flirtation improved, he would endeavour to turn his stature to his own advantage through mischievous methods of self-reference. But for now, being a major signing to one of the world's biggest record corporations ensured that the maker of *For You* attracted plenty of publicity when his album

44

came out, and plenty of speculation to go with it. So when he finally did step out before his public, unprotected by the trimmings and peculiar power-relationships of showbiz, his ordinary mortal failings were pitilessly exposed. All that talking dirty, and look at him – a proper short-ass. 'That was his first really big thing,' says Pepé, 'and it scared the total mess out of him. He did not even know what was going on.'

The circus rolled on, introducing Prince to stardom's seductive possibilities even as its downside goaded him. His radio interview complete, he went on to a theatre to do an autograph-signing session with a member of the band Cameo, a major black attraction even then. 'There was a long line to see Prince,' remembers Willie, 'and a short one for the other guy. We had security, but the crowd was getting kind of hectic.' The celebrities were sat up on the stage. The nobodies were supposed to file past in an orderly fashion. 'Then I noticed some guy had snuck up on stage, pretending he was security. Then there was two, then three, then four. I said, "Prince, are you ready to go?", but he said, "No man, I just gotta keep signing . . ." He would never stop signing. He loved those fans.' Willie arranged for their car to pull up backstage. 'I said, "Prince, let's go", and he just grabbed my arm, and we flew to the car and got right out of there, back to the hotel. That's when he said he felt like a piece of meat being carried around. But he was high, really high up there, you know? To bring him back down to earth was a real chore.'

The R & B success of 'Soft And Wet' proved that Prince had arrived, but only in the hearts of what the rock industry would have considered his natural constituency – other blacks. In the beginning, he did not inflict much damage upon the edifice of cultural apartheid. Nor was he much expected to, certainly not by his record company. 'I *was* looking at him as a multi-formatted artist,' explained Russ Thyret, ten years later, 'as both a pop and a black artist. But I actually and truly did not realize the dimensions of his talent.'

Warners envisaged Prince's place as being in a specific pop tradition. The Black Teenager had been 'discovered' in the first months of 1970, when the Jackson 5 dramatically emerged as Motown's perfect mating of bubblegum and soul. It was to this market that Prince was first directed, and to which he first appealed. The truth was written in the charts: 'Soft And Wet', a splendidly immature piece of teen erotica, only crept up to number 92 on the national Hot 100. Black hit, white miss. But 'Just As Long As We're Together', the follow-up, fell short of both targets by a mile.

Listening to the two songs, it is not hard to account for the difference. 'Soft And Wet' is bursting to be sweaty, slick and funky, and just about makes it, despite being in a bit too much of a rush. The hot breath of the typical teenage male. 'Just As Long As We're Together', meanwhile, was a shortened version of that on *For You*, and indicates the stylistic diversity of the album. More freeway jazz than funk, it has a cool West-coast sensibility with nothing like the instant hook, nerve or novelty value of its predecessor. It is not really a 'black' pop song at all; yet neither it or its maker was anything like 'white' enough to qualify for the category of FM rock. Even so, *For You* performed reasonably well for a début. In its immediate post-release period, it sold more than a hundred thousand copies in America (it was not made available in the UK till much later), which suggests encouraging interest from the 'specialist' (read 'black') audience, but not much from anywhere else. Prince was already looking into the crossover void: he could maybe go on being a star in his own limited constituency, but the fulfilment of his artistic ambitions implied the need to go beyond it. If he was going to keep on signing autographs *and* doing things how he liked, it was already clear that he needed to span the great divide – and that, in the end, would take more than good records to achieve.

But however you like to look at it, *For You* was a determined start. Recorded over five months at the Record Plant, Sausalito (near San Francisco), it is one of the clearest musical statements Prince made in the first period of his career, in the sense that he began work on it unencumbered by financial pressures, and free from the complicating ideological baggage which he would ultimately take upon himself. This, by all accounts, was the record he wanted to make, and he made it the way he wanted.

In some ways *For You* is an archetypal teenage epistle. It is earnest, uptight, over-sexed and struggling hard to sound grown-up. The album opens with its title track, more a fanfare than a song in its own right. Celestial in its sweetness, 'For You' is one minute and six seconds of artificially constructed *a capella*, comprising layer upon layer of Prince's cherubic falsetto. As an opening gambit, it amounts to a dual-dimensional definition of intent: first, it graphically underlines the claim that, yes, the album was the work of one single individual, its multi-track construction 'explaining' how it could be done; second, in its lyric Prince makes a metaphorical gift of his talents to the listener. It is, at root, a display of devotion and personal sacrifice – a thoroughly Christian gesture.

There is another sense in which 'For You', in its antiseptic sensitivity, heralds the predominant blend of sensations to follow: a slightly pedantic compromise between studio technology and mannered, adolescent eager-ness to please. But the album is also impressively eclectic, and consistent in its quality. As such, it amounted to a distinct improvement on the norm in black pop, where a couple of hit singles are too often padded out with shoddy filler. Stylistically, the first side proceeds to draw on technological funk, acoustic MOR, a reggae-ish poppiness and jazz. The vocals are almost all delivered in falsetto, and synthesizer strata dominate the sound. The results are at their best when at their most gauche, especially in their sexual self-consciousness. 'Soft And Wet'? Its rudery might give you a jolt, but as a shock tactic it is undermined by its over-anxiety, the lyric surrounded by brash rhythmic challenges which are ultimately lightweight: so what do you think of *that*!? From a suitable adult distance, this lends the track a certain pubescent charm. Prince told one interviewer at the time that the song was about deodorant.

His quest for the clinching suggestive metaphor had already announced itself on the preceding, first full track, 'In Love'. Contriving an engagingly liquid innuendo on the theme of messing about in a river, its author makes the most of this lubricious analogy, employing the key image as an exaggerated punchline to each yearning verse. Indeed, extreme libidinal tension makes its fidgety presence felt throughout most of the first side. Even the slapped acoustic-guitar-dominated ballad 'Crazy You' enjoys a handsome quota of sharp inhalations through teeth clenched in the effort of self-control. No pat dividing-line between lust and romance here.

One important ingredient was the way sexual implication – always endemic in the very physicality of soul – was taken a significant step closer to being explicit than in the majority of teenage music. Such overt eroticism was not, of course, new to black music in the commercial sphere. Adult downhome singers like Tina Turner and Millie Jackson had become famous for their willingness to discuss soiled underwear and oral sex with both live audiences and the record-buying public. Marvin Gaye's *Let's Get It On* album (1973) had defined a mature art of seduction to perfection, proclaiming the potential of physical desire as the ultimate expression of love. But stuff like 'Soft And Wet' spoke directly to *adolescent* erogenous zones in a way that large numbers of radio stations found unacceptable. Consequently, airplay for that first 45 was restricted not only by 'race' but also by 'good taste'.

There was, however, fleeting evidence of a sober side to the new star, or perhaps just a small appreciation of the need to contemplate the possible consequences of spilling all that juice. 'Baby', which opens side two, is a quiet, carefully crafted tale of unplanned pregnancy between young unmarrieds. It is a tiny bit soppy, but quite beautifully sung. It is also the sole realist deviation from the album's predominantly romantic-erotic spirit. The greatest musical diversion, though, occurs on the final track, 'I'm Yours', which plunges into rock territory head-first. All the orgasmic guitar exhibitionism displayed on 94 East's 'If You Feel Like Dancin' ' steps up for an encore, but this time within the sort of song structure you would expect: that is, slamming riff-play of the type popularized by such as Boston, Foreigner and other anodyne white bands of the burgeoning FM radio scene.

But aside from the brief moments of near-explicitness, what struck most vividly about *For You* was the diversity and hand-me-down nature of Prince's musical roots. What is most lacking is a true synthesis of them. In all, it remains an engaging collection of songs, accomplished, and with some memorable quirks, but lacking in the sense of spontaneity, however illusory, which would ultimately characterize Prince's best work. *For You* is a real patchwork, stitched together with a precision at times so neurotic as to make it almost joyless: quite an achievement in a bunch of tunes overwhelmingly concerned with sexual exploration and fantasies of the heart-strings.

In keeping with this, the making of the album was far from a casual business, with the young star exhibiting an almost obsessive blend of perfectionism and self-sufficiency. Owen Husney explains that the original plan was for Tommy Vicari to come up and help make *For You* in Minneapolis, but the available studio facilities were not up to scratch. So, with a view to keeping his promise that he would protect Prince's creativity, Husney made sure the studio that was picked was comfortably out of interfering range of the Warners folks in LA. Then he, his wife, Britt, and Vicari travelled out to Mill Valley in the Sausalito environs, and set up a temporary base.

The guts of the recording seem to have involved just Vicari and Mr Nelson, although the story is clouded by the occasional presence of André Anderson and David Rivkin. Anderson would later complain that he had assisted in the recording of *For You* and should have been listed in the credits, although Owen Husney's memory tends to contradict him: 'I know André gave Prince a lot of support. He flew out there and was living with him, and they would hang out together.' But as for the actual studio work, 'I don't remember André doing a whole bunch'. Rivkin's contribution, following on from the Sound 80 demo, seems to have been more tangible. An experienced musician and songwriter, he had worked with the country singer Gram Parson, among others, and also as a freelance composer. In person he prefers to be rather vague and guarded about his involvement with *For You* and his many subsequent inputs into Prince's work. He makes a few throwaway remarks about 'guitars underwater' – both the Rivkin boys are noted for their engagingly off-the-wall sense of humour – but doesn't get specific. After all, he is one of Prince's few creative collaborators to remain in favour to this day. 'I'm like a SWAT unit,' he says. 'You know, I can do anything. I'll come in and save something in a mix, or I'll help overdub. A lot of times Prince will have me come in and help with the vocals 'cause he just doesn't wanna deal with it. It's different with every project.'

On the inner sleeve of *For You*, Rivkin lines up alongside Husney, Bernadette Anderson, Chris Moon, Prince's parents and God as deserving of 'Special Thanks', though his name is billed jointly with the Minneapolis studio where he produced the demos which Warner Brothers first heard: 'David Rivkin/Sound 80 Studios'. He does not appear in the official outer-sleeve album credits at all. Yet Owen Husney seems confident that Rivkin made some direct engineering contributions to the album. 'Mainly Tommy did the album, but I think he [David] helped out on some areas of vocals, because [he] had a good sense of pitch and could move very quickly.'

If this might be interpreted as casting some doubt over the exact accuracy of the legend 'Produced, Arranged, Composed And Performed By Prince', Tommy Vicari's own comments on the Record Plant sessions (as reproduced in Jon Bream's *Prince: Inside The Purple Reign*) leave little doubt as to Prince's earnest desire to be seen as responsible for as much as he possibly could. After reportedly erasing Vicari's name from the engineering credits on the tape box and substituting his own, he is then said to have asked, 'If I do some mixing on the record, can I get mixing credits?' Vicari replied: 'Look, why don't you press the record and take the picture too?'

Husney recalls the way the balance of their relationship changed: 'I think in the initial [stages] Tommy was very helpful. But Prince is so bright that even at that young age he was able to learn what Tommy was doing. I felt the relationship changing from one where Tommy was the guiding father, to where all of a sudden Prince was taking his knowledge and going beyond it. I remember Tommy complaining to me, "God, how can this guy be doing this? He's so young." I think things may have gotten a little shaky towards the end.'

In the event, Prince *was* attributed with designing the dust cover, while Vicari enjoyed status as Executive Producer and for engineering and remixing the tapes at Sound Labs, Los Angeles. But whatever the precise balance of inputs between Vicari, his engineering assistants, Rivkin, André Anderson, and Prince, the album was pushed to the public consciousness – truthfully enough – as essentially the work of one teenage prodigy. And so the Prince mystique was let loose upon the world.

5

Business

Warner Bros.

At first, it was the black teenage pop glossies that got on the case with the freaky boy enigma who sat po-faced and naked behind a huge acoustic guitar in the inner-sleeve photograph of *For You*. As the first black teenager to command a six-figure sum and almost complete artistic control, Prince, the boy wonder, was the automatic object of attention, curiosity and esteem.

Right On! and *Soul Teen* found Prince easy to accommodate within their pages. His hit song, with its barely subliminal theme of adolescent sex, made him an ideal teeny heart-throb, and his success plunged him for the first time into the publicity whirlwind. It was not an experience he much enjoyed, and those early interviews read like nightmares of evasion for the journalists concerned. As Pepé Willie relates, Prince regarded all potential predators with extreme caution: 'I did a promo thing with Owen in Chicago, in the depths of the ghetto – record shops and stuff like that, taking posters and pictures and copies of the album. We were showing up, and all these kids were waiting outside, and everybody was asking where was Prince at? We had lunch with the radio people there, and when we came back I told Prince, you know, "Why don't you just call up these guys and thank them for playing your record?" ' Willie has an amusing impersonation of Prince when someone has put his nose out of joint. The voice goes all sulky and the words are delivered as if with a stroppy bottom lip stuck out. 'He says, "No, I'm not talking to them", and I said, "Why not, it will help your record", and he said, "Oh, don't you think the record's a hit now?"'!

Willie asserts that Prince had definite ideas about how he wanted to conduct his career even at this stage, what he would and would not do towards presenting himself and his work to the public at large. 'He just didn't want to do interviews, or nothing like that. It was probably because he was too afraid, or he didn't know what to say, or he was ashamed of something or other. I had a big argument with him about that.' But Willie also remarks on the young star's capacity for being an equally pronounced extrovert if the circumstances suited him. 'We'd go out and play basketball, and he'd be the first to go up to the other, bigger guys and say, "Hey, you want a fight?" He wasn't shy at all, you know? But maybe because of all the people who were suddenly all around him, he got kind of humble, or he felt that he should be that way so he didn't seem egotistical. He just pretends to be shy. But it was very sensible of him in a way.'

Owen Husney considers that Prince was a naturally reticent character when confronted with attention from strangers, but at the same time he has a rationale for his growing ability to turn that reticence to his advantage: 'We had discussions, that less is more in this business. If you're truly talented, like Prince is, then you're better off not giving it all away.'

Prince had also made up his mind what kind of people he wanted to be seen with on stage. 'He didn't want to tour with black artists,' recalls Willie, very specifically. 'He wanted to tour with Mick Jagger and Foreigner, the big guys. He didn't want to be on the so-called chitlin circuit, and I can understand it. I always told him that the black artists have a double thing to do. I said, "You can make it to number one on the R & B chart and it don't mean *nothin'*. Now you've gotta go Top 40." '

This desire to confound expectations of what a black performer could and should be in the public and corporate mind extended to the actual composition of Prince's first road band. The line-up that accompanied him on his first, low-key tours and would, bar one member, survive to form the basis of the Revolution, was put together in Minneapolis during the summer of 1978. It was with careful deliberation that Prince selected his five musician employees, seeking a combination based not only on their proclivities as players, but also on their sex and race. André Anderson, as his close collaborator and surrogate brother, was an automatic choice as bass-player, but there was no place for Morris Day. He and Prince were having one of their disagreements at the time, and anyway, 'He wanted a white drummer, you know,' says Pepé Willie. The job went to David Rivkin's brother Bobby, by that time employed as a runner by Owen Husney. One minute he was Prince's chauffeur, the next, he was sat behind the skins. Anderson, Bobby Rivkin and Prince formed the nucleus of the band. Rivkin had considered giving up playing all together, but he sensed something special about Prince.

Together, the three of them jammed and planned. They even spent some time in LA looking to complete the line-up out there. In the end though, an ad placed in *The Reader*, a Twin Cities entertainment paper,

53

sufficed: ' "Warner Brothers artist seeks guitarist and keyboardist", I think it said,' recalls Dez Dickerson, who at that time swung his axe as leader of a local glam-rock band called Romeo. He knew who this anonymous artist must be, because his sister had a copy of *For You.* 'I remember thinking it was OK, though I wouldn't go crazy about it. I just thought, "Well, this is the first train out of town", and I tried to get on it, you know?'

Dickerson's musical pedigree possessed precisely the unconventional characteristics Prince would have been looking for. Born in St Paul of lower-middle-class parents who had moved up from Tennessee, he grew up listening to a mixture of jazz and R & B – Coltrane, Miles Davis, early Aretha Franklin. But at the age of four or five, his favourite record was the B-side of a single by the legendary saxophonist King Curtis. 'It was this real rock 'n' roll thing. I just loved it.'

Dickerson shaped up as that living incongruity, a black rock 'n' roller, someone who used to watch Ricky Nelson's cheesy TV shows, and loved them anyway. Romeo had made a fair success of themselves around north Minnesota and neighbouring North Dakota, playing a circuit of bars and ballrooms that were usually the preserve of polka bands performing for farmers. Dickerson's tastes meant that he mixed almost exclusively with white musicians, with predictable results. 'I ran into some problems even though we were a rock band, because I was black. There were some places that wouldn't book us.' Romeo went through a big velvet and silk phase. Then Dickerson, who liked to change his look like other people change their smalls, began to tune in to the outer fringes of the New Wave. 'I started wearing a tie, Johnny Mathis meets Cheap Trick. My hair was real short, very *GQ.* I sort of brought that image-consciousness into Prince's band.'

The audition took place at the band's rehearsal space in a building called Del's Tyre Mart, located on what is known as the West Bank, near the university, around the junction of Washington Avenue and 35th Street. Dickerson had two hours in which to do his bit, then get to an out-of-town Romeo gig. 'I got there not knowing that they were notorious for being late. I had waited with some other people for an hour and a half. Graciously, they let me go first.'

The entire experience amounted to a crash course in the way Prince worked, and continues to work, both in rehearsal and in business matters. 'We just sort of jammed. I found out later that he liked how I didn't instantly try to solo for fifteen minutes. And that was it. We went outside, we talked for a minute, he asked me some career-minded questions and I gave him some answers. After that he kept calling me, asking me if I could come over to his house and learn some of the tunes, or play with him and André. He never told me that I had the job. I mean, to the day

I left, he never told me. I just figured when I started getting paid, I must have it.'

Among the keyboard-players Prince tried out was Jimmy 'Jam' Harris. Dickerson lobbied for him at the time – 'I liked his playing, and I liked Jimmy' – but to no avail. Instead, Prince opted for a pair of white musicians, one a man and the other a woman. Matt Fink, who, like the Rivkins, came from the St Louis Park suburb, came to Prince's attention by way of Bobby Rivkin, Owen Husney or both. Husney says that Fink mailed him a tape: 'I remember playing it to Prince. Next thing I knew he was on the phone trying to get the guy in the group.' But the fact that Rivkin and Fink knew each other, and had been to the same school probably had something to do with Fink's recruitment.

Doctor Fink, as he was later rechristened, is the only one of the original Prince band to have lasted right through to the *Lovesexy* tour (1988) and beyond. Noted for his rather strange, straight-faced sense of humour and equable nature, he is widely regarded as an outstanding player. His female counterpart, Gayle Chapman, was also from St Louis Park. She was known to Pepé Willie, who had collaborated with her as a writer, and had been first introduced to Prince by his cousin, the ousted Grand Central drummer, Charles Smith. A young woman of strong religious convictions, her tenure turned out to be brief, but while she lasted, her impact was significant.

In the first place, women musicians were still relatively rare in all forms of pop. But for a young *white* woman musician to turn up in a group whose leader, most visible sidemen, and primary musical orientation were all black was not only unusual, it offended against some of the most deeply held conservative taboos in the land. Even growing up in liberal Minnesota, it would be a strange thing indeed if Prince had not had at least some conception of the mischief he might be perceived as instigating. 'The whole thrust of what we were doing was to shock people,' says Dez Dickerson. 'That was what Prince wanted to do more than anything, and at that time I was certainly into it.' The fact that Prince's initial popularity was in the South only maximized the line-up's risk-potential, something Dickerson suspects that Prince, even in his wilful non-conformism, may have underestimated at the time. When the band finally started touring regularly, a good year after its inception, unpleasant realities blundered in.

Dickerson remembers one particular incident at a Holiday Inn in Shreveport, Louisiana: 'André and myself, and I think Prince, went into the lounge with Gayle, and this guy leaned over to her and said, "You aren't in here with these niggers, are you?" It jolted us, because when we were on stage, and in our own environment, it was just our own musical Disneyland.' In redneck philosophy, the sanctity of womanhood is paramount. It is central to racist mythology that the greatest threat to it is posed by that most potent of folk-devil stereotypes, the footloose, rapacious black male – and Prince used to seize Gayle Chapman and French-kiss her right up there on stage.

Chapman's other crucial input was spiritual. While he liked to tease her streak of piety with his rude-boy routine, her religious influence seems to have impinged directly upon some of Prince's immediate, and most drastic, business decisions. The formation of the band had barely been completed when his affairs entered a period of upheaval, much of it precipitated by a falling-out with Owen Husney, who was still running his ad agency. In short, the faith Husney professed to have in his young discovery was not reciprocated. Pepé Willie describes finding himself involved in a kind of shuttle diplomacy between the two, which soon degenerated into shuttle abuse. 'Prince said, "Hey, why am I calling him up on the phone, and he says, 'hello, it's the ad company'? How come he's not in LA or New York doing management work for me?" He told me, "Can you go to Owen and tell him there's an argument?" ' Soon their communication became more blunt. 'Both of these guys are my friend, OK?', says Willie. 'So, I go to Owen and say, "Owen, Prince says, 'Fuck you.' And Owen says, "Well, you tell him, 'Fuck him too!' " So I go back with that, and Prince says, "OK, he's fired!" ' '

'I guess there was a bit of a disagreement of philosophies,' reflects Dez Dickerson. 'Owen, like a lot of managers, was more geared for delegating, or being the overseer. Prince wanted someone who was there to pretty much cater to whatever whim he had.' But this was not just a matter of a burgeoning adolescent ego. It is Dickerson's view that Gayle Chapman actively encouraged Prince in thinking he had, quite literally, a divine right to special attention: 'It didn't help that Gayle was telling him that he had been blessed by God with some special dispensation, and because of that he couldn't go to grocery stores or do the normal things that normal people do. He sort of ate all this up. It was very convenient information, and I think it allowed him to indulge himself in certain ways. I think that maybe Owen could have been more intricately involved in the day-to-day things, but maybe Prince took the other thing to an extreme. I *do* feel that he has a special talent, and that God gave it to him. But that doesn't mean you have to have people fawning over you, like you're an emperor or something.' Or, maybe, like you were God Himself.

The summer of 1978 saw the steady evolution of what Pepé Willie jokingly calls 'the Napoleon Syndrome', the authoritarianism for which Prince is famous. It is a trait which has since left several one-time associates with a bitter taste in their mouths. But whatever the justice in that, his professional circumstances during this time were unlikely to discourage such tendencies in a young man with a giant talent and a point to prove.

The band had moved out of Del's Tyre Mart, which had been broken into, and – suddenly managerless – found themselves, in Dickerson's words, 'sort of cast adrift'. As a temporary measure they resettled in the basement of Pepé Willie's house in a salubrious stretch of Upton Avenue South, near Lake Calhoun. Ostensibly, they were getting themselves in shape for a tour. But for Prince, there were other things to contend with: managers (or the lack of them), publishing deals, fan mail. 'He was under a tremendous amount of pressure,' considers Dickerson. 'There were so many decisions that suddenly people were looking to him to make. Pepé offered to be a sort of interim overseer.'

It soon became obvious that whatever the disorder afflicting his business affairs, Prince was going to be clear about one thing: he was indisputably the leader of the band. 'He wanted everyone to know that he was definitely the boss,' recalls Willie, who sometimes found himself playing a mediating role between the star and his charges, who, he says, rarely felt inclined to confront Prince directly themselves. 'He was right to be in charge, because he was paying all the bills, and he was the one that Warner Brothers was backing. But I didn't really understand what he had over them, or why they feared him. One day I went down there, and I was saying to Prince about the complaints of certain individuals in the band. I turned around and said to Bobby and André, you know, "Isn't that right, guys?", and no one said *nothing*. It totally amazed me. I looked at them and said, "Jesus, does he have a gun on him or something?" '

Prince instigated a rigorous programme of rehearsal. 'He was a harsh task-master at times,' says Dickerson, 'but I understood that, which is why I think we had a different relationship than his with most of the people in the group. I had led my own band before. He would confide in me, and get information from me as to how to go about doing what he was doing. You've got to have organization and some discipline, otherwise it's anarchy. There were times when he was a little extreme. I didn't agree with every decision he made. Certainly he was a workaholic, to say the least. But it was his prerogative. He was paying us.'

The band, though, was not exactly coining it at this stage in the proceedings – probably about a hundred dollars a week for a lot of hours, and very little artistic say in how things would finally go down in a show. When it came to the crunch, Prince decided what everyone would play. But the marathon jam sessions still excited Dickerson creatively. 'It stretched me in many different ways. One thing about Prince is he's always pushing himself. He doesn't get complacent. If anything, he's almost neurotic about it. We were always playing, and trying different styles, and just jamming, you know. We experimented with jazz types of things and rock 'n' roll and R & B. To me that was a new thing. It was a neat period. He had this idea that we might become a kind of black Rolling Stones.'

The six months in which the shared home of Willie and his business partners, Ms Ingvoldstat and Ms Lazenberry, became Prince's base also afforded him something of a practical crash course in the ways of the industry: some hard practice to add to Jim Hamilton's theory. All his fan mail, his cheques and other correspondence were being sent to Upton Avenue. Then there was the copyright situation to sort out.

'I told Prince, "We gotta get this publishing thing all set up," ' remembers Willie, ' "then no one can take it from you." I had him write a letter to BMI [Broadcast Music Incorporated] and told him exactly what to say. He went out and bought the stamp himself, thirteen cents or whatever, and put the letter in the box. The forms came back about a week later. We filled it out, and mailed it back, and that was the start of Ecnirp ['Prince' spelt backwards, later Controversy Music], his first publishing house.' At the same time Willie says there was a Californian attorney supposedly acting on the matter on Prince's behalf. 'We got a letter from [him], opened it up, and there was some more BMI forms and a bill. It said nine hundred dollars!' The band was practising as Pepé Willie opened the mail. He headed straight downstairs. 'I broke up the rehearsal and said, "Prince, look at this. See how they rip you, man? Here is something you already did, and it cost you a stamp." I tore it up right in front of his face. They even tried to charge him twenty cents for the postage.'

On Friday, 5 January 1979, Prince and his new band made their first public appearance before a hundred or so people at the innocuous Capri Theatre at 2027 West Broadway, Minneapolis. Though officially a benefit show for the converted cinema itself, the real purpose was to make ready for a second performance the following night. 6 January would be the date when the VIPs of Warner Brothers, Burbank, rolled up to see if their precocious and high-spending studio newborn was seriously viable in the big, bad world of showtime. There was to be a third, ordinary show on the 7th too, and Willie, Ingvoldstad and Lazenberry of Pepé Music Incorporated claim credit for all the arrangements. 'We did all of it,' remembers Kristie Lazenberry. 'We made the tickets, we sold them, we even did the door. We were the security too!'

Among the Warners bigwigs was Carl Scott, on whom the raw Prince stage show seems to have made a particularly deep impression: 'It was unbelievable. I remember being up in a balcony that was jam-packed with people looking down at this little guy, literally climbing over amplifiers and electronic equipment, going from one place to another to create these sounds. I just couldn't believe I was watching this. There was something absolutely *genius* taking place. It was totally different to anything that I had ever really experienced before. I knew that something in there was magic, but I didn't know what it was.'

Dez Dickerson's memories of this show are equally dominated by visions of disorder. His assessment of its artistry, though, is rather less esoteric. 'Boy, he was at a different show. The weather was bad, we had all sorts of monumental equipment problems. All I remember is Prince spending most of the evening with his back facing the audience, and in between songs, mumbling into the mike with his eyes closed. I remember André and I *far* overdoing it. I had a wireless fitting for my guitar for the first time that night. I was like a horse that had been let out of a stall. I took every opportunity for running into the audience, to the back of the auditorium, and back up on stage. Just stupid things. It must have been very *different* for whoever saw it.'

Not only did they act weird and play weird, they *looked* weird too – although as yet there was no unifying visual concept. Dickerson was still sporting his pin-stripe and tie look; André Anderson showed up with a bandana lashed around his thigh in an echo of Jimi Henrix. Prince, his mighty Afro dwarfing his tiny frame, is remembered for his thigh-high boots or leg-warmers, and flare-sleeved blouse: all told, a bizarre blend of black hippie, big-city spiv and ambisexual Glam provocation – and a glimpse into the future.

Backstage after the show, Carl Scott had a rather awkward introduction to the architect of the evening's strange entertainment: 'Meeting him, he was so different to how he was on stage, where he was very outgoing, and in control of that environment. In person he was very quiet, and laid back and shy almost to a fault. I honestly thought that it had to be me, you know. He was polite, but with very few words. Anyway, we went back to Burbank, and were totally shell-shocked by what we had seen.'

Shell-shocked or not, Dez Dickerson's recollection is that on the strength of the Capri shows, the gentlemen of Warners concluded that Prince was not yet ready to do the tour everyone had been practising for. 'They decided that he would have to cut another record first. At least, my understanding is that they heavily influenced that decision.' Another disappointment was the turn-out. True, there had not been enormous advance publicity, but a rare Prince interview had appeared in the *Star & Tribune*. More than that, the local boy was a historic signing to a massive entertainment corporation, and tickets were on sale downtown, four dollars in advance. In the end, 'we sold just enough to pay for the lighting,' says Pepé Willie; 'I think I came out with about five dollars' profit.'

Prince was still invisible back home, in that definitive vanilla market.

59

Station KUXL was a small-time operation, while the community outlet KMOJ, tucked away among the project housing in a shabby part of Bryant Avenue, broadcast only to a handful of blocks and at the time had only just introduced a smattering of gospel music into its original public service format. So what if Prince had scored a substantial début hit? There was hardly any way that 'Soft And Wet' could actually have been heard in his home town, or its maker heard of. But if the Twin Cities were in some respects a special case, in others they merely represented an exaggeration of the situation that applied across the United States. Prince knew that he wanted to transcend a racially defined market divide. But it was a bigger matter altogether to make it actually happen.

After his falling-out with Owen Husney and American Artists, Prince considered a number of managerial options. Among them was the Jamaican-born Don Taylor, who had taken care of the career of reggae king Bob Marley and been badly wounded by the Kingston gunmen who made an attempt on Marley's life in 1976. Taylor had cut his teeth with Little Anthony and the Imperials, for whom, like Pepé Willie, he had originally worked as a valet. At the time of Prince's inquiry, he was back in the USA and living with Pepé Willie's sister.

Making use of his family connections, Willie instigated a meeting with Taylor in Miami, making sure Prince knew who was supposed to be courting whom – it was Taylor who paid the plane fare. 'I was trying to explain to him [Prince] that this is how it's done,' Willie claims. 'When a manager wants you, and you're kind of popular, you know, *they* fly you wherever you want to go. You don't pay.' Prince reportedly gave Taylor a short trial, but it was not a lasting match. 'I just wasn't the man for the job,' Taylor explained, his remarks appearing in Steven Ivory's 1985 biography *Prince*. 'This guy was just too weird for me. I never knew *where* he was coming from. He'd start recording at one studio, and if something went wrong, he'd want to just scrap the project and book time someplace else.' Pepé Willie is not surprised by this response. 'Yeah, Don never went for none of that weird shit.'

Prince's basic distaste for the niceties of promotional work and his preference for his home town as a working base, appeared to stack the odds higher still against his evolving a mass public profile. Any manager taking him on would need not only to provide the minute-by-minute personal attention he had found lacking in Owen Husney, but also a creative input which could help this introverted *Wunderkind* avoid becoming just another unfulfilled dreamer stuck in the R & B ghetto.

The eventual solution to the problem came at Carl Scott's instigation. Before joining Warner Brothers, Scott had managed the hugely successful American blues and boogie band Little Feat. On his acceptance of the

60

Warners' post, Little Feat's affairs had passed into the care of the Hollywood-based management company of Bob Cavallo and Joe Ruffalo. Friends since their shared boyhood in New York City, Cavallo and Ruffalo had made a favourable impression on Scott, and among the artists they handled were the black 'crossover' successes Weather Report – the premier hip jazz act of the time – Ray Parker Jnr and the massive Earth, Wind and Fire, whose leader, Maurice White, had actually been approached to produce the début Prince album (he declined for lack of time). When Prince asked him for recommendations, Scott called Cavallo–Ruffalo up: 'I told them I had seen the situation in Minneapolis, and I assured them that they should pay attention to this guy, maybe talk to him, and they wouldn't be sorry.'

Cavallo and Ruffalo responded by sending a subordinate named Perry Jones and his cousin Tony – whom everyone irreverently addressed by his middle name, Maylon – up to Minnesota to get the flavour of things, or as Dez Dickerson understood it, 'to secure Prince for them. They laid the groundwork.' The two of them showed up for the first time shortly before the Capri Theatre gigs. They went on to function essentially as tour managers for the dates the band lined up in support of Prince's second, self-titled album. And it was during this period that Steve Fargnoli appeared on the scene: 'He just showed up one day,' Dickerson recalls, 'and he's been there ever since.'

Fargnoli's experience in the music industry had included promotions at college level, working in a New York booking agency, and even singing. But what may well have made him especially attractive to Prince was his experience as road manager for Sly Stone – not, so legend has it, one of the more soothing occupations in rock 'n' roll. At that time Fargnoli was, like Jones, just an employee of Cavallo and Ruffalo, but a rising one. 'He turned up at a rehearsal,' remembers Dickerson. 'Prince sort of explained who he was and what this meant to us. We supposed that we'd better play well and impress the guy.' Not long after, Fargnoli was promoted to become a full partner with Cavallo and Ruffalo, the trio known at their own comic instigation as 'Spaghetti Inc'. He has since gone on to enjoy the intense loyalty and respect of Prince, and seemingly, in the great tradition of rock 'n' roll managers, the almost unanimous dislike of everyone else who ever had to work under him.

Prince was gradually assembling the business apparatus he would need to shift his career into a higher gear. Though he continued to base himself physically in Minneapolis, his management, his accountant and his record company were all out in the West Coast nexus of the American entertainment industry. Rightly or wrongly, inevitably or avoidably, his initial circle of confederates and advisers – Moon, Willie, Husney – was being left behind.

With hindsight, Owen Husney projects a serene and thoroughly rationalized perspective on their split. 'I think I was lucky and unlucky. You know, a lot of managers start off helping with nephews who can sing, or tap-dancing parakeets. But my first experience at really getting into the music business, I was there to discover an international superstar! Even though I had the vision and the fight and the belief in Prince, there was a lot of things that I just didn't know about the business then. I knew I was limited to a certain extent.'

Husney prefers to by-pass whatever acrimony occurred at the time. 'Basically, I rapped it down to Prince. After he made his first album I realized I was short of knowledge in the international areas, in touring and in publishing. I maybe wasn't the best person to look after him. It was a very amicable thing. I just said, "Look, as long as I'm taken care of, I'm not gonna be the asshole manager that's gonna hold on to you and sue you, and do all those kind of things. I'm here because my belief is there for you." I was there to be helpful, because I think the guy's a stone genius, and I didn't want to be the one who got in his way, so I let it go to the next step. I think it was a very mutual thing.' The legal niceties appear to have been settled, as they say, out of court. 'I got taken care of. I have no complaints.'

Husney seems to enjoy an ambivalent status among the black musical community of Minneapolis and St Paul. As he points out himself, altruism aside, it would have made little sense for him to have courted a reputation as a difficult manager – other local talent would have come to regard him warily. And while he and Prince have not been on friendly terms ever since, Husney has signed eleven more acts to major deals, among them black Twin Cities artists Sue Ann Carwell, Jesse Johnson, and a solo André Anderson in his showbiz incarnation as André Cymone. But none of these subsequent liaisons has been free of rancour, and only Johnson's has stood the test of time. Husney sees himself, and not without justification, as the catalyst that sparked the explosion from 'the Island of the North'. Some members of the Anderson family look upon him less favourably. Mrs Bernadette Anderson – André's mother and the woman who raised Prince through his teens – is quite clear where she stands. Let us simply say that relations between Husney and the Anderson family have been far from friendly ever since.

The bust-up with Husney exemplified how the mixed blessings of celebrity were already homing in on Prince. On the one hand, fame and acclaim, on the other, a heightened and volatile potential for losing friends and squabbling over matters of cash and gratitude. 'We were in the house once,' Pepé Willie recalls, 'and Prince had just got a royalty cheque for thirty thousand dollars or something like that. I just said to him, "Well, you know, when you make it to the pop charts, just say my name. That's all you gotta do." But he never did.'

In the event, Pepé Willie joined Cavallo, Ruffalo, Perry Jones, and André Anderson among the small-print appreciations on the *Prince* album, released the following year. 'We still maintain to be friends,' said Willie. 'I call him up before he starts out on each tour and wish him good luck.' But the two of them would enjoy a turbulent relationship through Prince's rise to superstar status, one whose nadir was the eventual release of *Minneapolis Genius*, which Prince regarded as an act of pure, cheap exploitation. There was a heated scene in a hotel room with a bouncer apiece on hand. 'I said, "Listen, I gotta make a living too." '

But Pepé Willie remembers with amusement other transformations which fame imposed upon His Royal Badness. The business pressures of evolving stardom may have helped him to lose friends – but there were droves of contenders lining up to fill the space if ever he felt lonely. 'When Prince wasn't famous, he complained how some girls treated him.' But all that was changing fast. 'I remember once him saying, "Pepé, man, four months ago that girl wouldn't even talk to me. And now she's knocking on my door." '

6

Myth

Chris Walter/Relay

The north side of Minneapolis does not look like a ghetto. At least, it does not conform to the popular idea of what a ghetto is supposed to look like. The streets are long, straight and tree-lined. The scene is dominated not by forbidding concrete tenements, but by neat, detached houses, set a little off the road in their own grounds. It is the poorest part of Minneapolis, mainly black with some Jews, but at first sight it might almost be genteel. By comparison it was, when Bernadette Anderson moved into the area in 1948.

'For years I didn't lock my door,' she remembers, then a fourteen-year-old bride, with a new home in the north side's public housing. 'It was very nice in the projects then. Now I wouldn't dare leave my door unlocked. It's gotten to have a lot more crime, a lot of people have moved in who are just fleeing another city. There's not the family structure there was at that time.'

In the mythology of Prince, Bernadette Anderson makes a cameo appearance as the woman who took him in when his own family structure seemed to be falling apart. The tales surrounding his parents' divorce, his fallings-out with first his stepfather, then his natural father, and his eventual admittance into the Anderson household, assumed a virtual life of their own after *Purple Rain* made Prince the hottest name in showbiz – especially since the plot of the film seemed to bear some resemblance to the tapestry of rumour and half-fact that the star-making media embraced as biographical truth. What lies beneath this continuing shroud of speculation and hearsay is a story of black America remarkable for its everyday heroism.

Bernadette Anderson was born and raised on the south side of Minneapolis, not too many blocks from where Prince's father, the pianist John Nelson, lived with his first wife and family. 'Long before Prince was

66

even thought of I knew his first wife, as much as I could being a kid.'
Soon, there were further connections with the Nelsons, one of them
nurtured by the church; the Nelsons, like many black families, were
practising Seventh Day Adventists, and so was Mrs Anderson's husband,
Fred. But also, there was music. 'My husband had always been a
musician, and he played the upright bass. He and Prince's dad played
together a lot of times. He was in Mr Nelson's band, the Prince Rogers
Trio.'

It was on 7 June 1958 that the first child of John Nelson's second
marriage was born, and christened after the band. After all, it was
because of the Prince Rogers Trio that Mr Nelson had met Prince's
mother, Mattie Shaw, whom he had recruited to sing with the group.
On his birth certificate (as reproduced in Jon Bream's *Prince: Inside The
Purple Reign*) his middle name is listed as just plain Roger, without the
's', but most people have assumed it was meant to have been there,
Bernadette Anderson included. Mattie Shaw and her sister Edna Mae
had come up to Minneapolis from Baton Rouge, Louisiana, in the fifties.
Both migrants would have been of fairly tender years. Mrs Shaw was
still only twenty-four when she gave birth to Prince, while her husband
was past forty. Mr Nelson had a steady job at the Honeywell Computers
complex, one of the bigger local employers. His music, though it was
his abiding passion, did not pay the bills.

Together, Shaw and Nelson had one other child, a daughter called
Tyka, who in 1988 released her own album through Chrysalis, with
production by David Z, but no input from her brother. For his first ten
years, Prince grew up in the family home on 5th Avenue South, among
the mixture of blacks and Scandinavians that predominates there. It was
when his father left and a stepfather, Hayward Baker, arrived that things
began to go seriously wrong. Prince eventually moved out, and after
short, troubled stays with his Aunt Olivia and his estranged father, finally
showed up at the home of his best friend, André Anderson, asking if he
could stay. By then he would still have only been around thirteen years
old.

'It was after the [Grand Central] band had played somewhere the night
before,' says Mrs Anderson; 'and his dad had got mad at him and put
him out. Some girl had followed him home, and she'd stayed there. He
[Prince] said, "I didn't do anything wrong, but I can't explain that to
dad." His dad was very strict. So I said, "Well, you can stay here, but
I got to check with him first." ' John Nelson approved the deal. So
Bernadette Anderson, by then a divorcee, suddenly had another young-
ster to add on to an already considerable brood: Fred Jnr, Sylvia, Eddie,
Patricia, Linda, André . . . and now Prince.

For an itinerant adolescent to just step into a hard-pressed single-
parent family might seem a bizarre, if not plain improper way for people

67

to carry on. But set the situation in context and it seems significantly less strange – if in certain ways no less sad. In black American society it tends to be considered less unconventional to take on responsibility for the children of broken homes, without automatic recourse to agencies of the state, than it does among whites. Practicalitites imposed by hardship have worked against the evolution of neuroses about private property – and that includes children. There are plenty of living products of this resourceful and supportive communality in the world of music. James Brown, for instance, was brought up amid vice and poverty – but also with loving care – by his Aunt Minnie on the fringe of Augusta, Georgia.

So the indomitable Mrs Anderson took her place in a grand tradition of domestic survival. A warmly formidable woman who radiates a potential for enormous energy and drive, she had begun establishing herself as a pillar of the community in the early sixties. 'It was during the [Martin Luther] King era, when people were beginning to stand up and demand their rights. Kids were starting to wear 'fros [Afros] and being proud of being black. I started working for the schools as an aide. I was heavily involved in Parent Teachers Associations and that kind of thing.'

Mrs Anderson had strong views about schools and how they conduct themselves. Fred Junior was once suspended from North High School for not shaving. He was well into his teens and, as Mrs Anderson puts it, 'he had a little fuzz. They felt he was attracting too many of the young women, and they didn't want that. I took an attorney to the school, and said that *I* would decide when my child could shave, and not the principal. It was quite upsetting. But we won, of course.'

But while she was prepared to fight the education system, Mrs Anderson stuck by one iron rule. Never mind its shortcomings, all her children *had* to go to school. 'There was a lot of argument about schools not giving the right curriculum, and at that point, maybe I wasn't too militant. My *kids* said I wasn't too militant! I feel that yes, the schools did not address the black kids' culture, but that at least they were learning, and once they had learned to read, then they could read about their culture. I didn't want them out of school. That was my fight.'

It was in such a domestic environment that Prince finally found his adolescent home. Mrs Anderson's policy towards André and Prince appears to have been simple, practical and, judging by the results, extremely effective: so long as they stayed out of trouble and kept up their education, she would leave them pretty much to conduct their own affairs as young adults. Deviation from this agreement could be firmly punished: 'She did her job as a mom, let's put it that way,' says Pepé Willie, remembering an occasion when Mrs Anderson suspected that Prince had – unusually for him – played truant one day. 'She did not mess around. I stayed there until he stopped crying . . . and then we went to Cookhouse to do some work.' In the event, both boys graduated from their respective High Schools – André from North, Prince from Central – and Prince even made it six months ahead of his scheduled time. 'I never had a problem with Prince,' says Mrs Anderson, glowing. 'He doubled up on his credits, and took them all at once. You could get them by going to school say from eight till two. Well, he went from seven until four. He wanted to get done, because his entire goal was music.'

This picture of earnest industry in a single-parent foster-family of extremely tight financial means contrasts vividly with the received impression of Prince's teenage years that would prevail ten years later. By then, Mrs Anderson, head of the household once voted Family of the Year by the Minneapolis Urban League, appeared in the Prince myth only as the benevolent matriarch who let Prince and her son André get away with everything – 'everything' meaning, of course, Wild Teenage Sex.

The Wild Teenage Sex talk got into its stride during February and March 1984, in the aftermath of Prince's first incursion into the territory of major-league crossover with *1999*, and just as he was gearing up for world domination with *Purple Rain* later that year. André and Prince were feuding at the time, and had been since André left the band in the summer of 1981. With his solo album *Survivin' In The Eighties* just out on CBS, he consented to a kiss-and-tell interview with an ill-fated Los Angeles-based monthly called *Rock Magazine*. It is probably the most regularly reproduced Prince-related interview ever published.

'We had this room with really small beds,' ran André's story. 'We were really separate people and wanted to divide the room to prove it. So I took a piece of tape and put it in the centre of the floor and up the walls. My side was packed with junk: clothes, T-shirts, trumpets, saxophones, guitars, you name it. Prince's side was immaculate. His clothes were always hung up or folded. He even made his bed every day!

'When I first met him, he didn't even cuss,' said André, Mr Streetwise, car thief, lady-killer, hell-raiser compared to little goody two shoes. At first 'Prince's parents did not want me around him. They would ground him just so he would stay away from me.'

In the two *Rock Magazine* pieces (the interview was spread over consecutive issues) the world read of torrid sexual experiments with girls in groups, girls tied up with tape, girls dangling from the ceiling. 'Prince's crazy thing was passing girls around,' screamed André's purple dialogue. 'Maybe twenty, maybe more – not all that many. It didn't really matter who went first. It was "He's my brother, and we do everything together." We didn't like to be bored. It was a challenge for us to get these girls to participate in some lewd activity.'

How much of all this was fact, and how much fabrication, only the alleged protagonists could possibly know. Prince's cousin Charles Smith

69

told *People* magazine that 'everybody was basically scared of girls . . . we talked a lot of mess.' But whatever the sins they actually committed, Mrs Anderson has little doubt as to the existence of intent. 'Naturally they got interested in the ladies, you know, and I'd have to keep a close eye on their activities! Music was cut off at ten o' clock generally, and I used to have to check the basement every now and then, to make sure it was cleaned out completely. I'm sure there was things I didn't notice.' But as for André's *Rock* Magazine interview – 'I don't know about all that stuff! I said to him, "Boy, why'd you do that? Makes me look like I'm too fast!" '

The stuff about the divided bedroom is true enough. 'When Prince moved in they were really tight,' says Mrs Anderson. 'They were just like brothers, almost twins – their birthdays were only twenty days apart. Then it finally came to a point where they argued all the time, so they decided they needed to go their separate ways as far as rooms went. Prince said he wanted to move into the basement. I said, "Prince, if I let you go in there, they'll think I've got this foster kid, and now I'm shoving him in the basement." He just said, "No, no, it's nobody's business. I can fix it up and it'll be sharp." '

While Grand Central rehearsed at Mrs Anderson's, the place was always full of kids. As well as Prince, André and his sister Linda (who was so shy at gigs, she never looked up from the keyboard and buttoned her clothes up tight), there was William Doughty, Charles Smith, Terry Jackson – an only child from the house next door – and later, Morris Day. 'All the time they'd play,' marvels Mrs Anderson. 'Sometimes it'd drive me crazy. I'd be in bed, and everyone's supposed to be sleeping, and all of a sudden I'd hear this guitar in the basement, and he [Prince] was playing Minnie Riperton, and singing it. Sometimes I'd go holler, and other times I'd just let him go ahead. Then above my head was André doing the same thing. Terry and Will, they were a little more girl-crazy. They was goofing off all the time. They liked their music, but they wasn't as dedicated. The smoking and the drinking, Prince and André didn't care anything about. They were very serious.'

Throughout this time, Prince and Mrs Anderson maintained their links with the rest of the Nelson family. It must have been a big jump for the young man – from the stringent respectability of his previous homes on the south side to this controlled but teeming liberality. As well as his mother and father, Mrs Anderson knew his Aunt Olivia. In fact Aunt Olivia lived in the house on the south side next door to where Mrs Anderson was raised. 'She was very strict, very religious. She preached a lot. And of course, she didn't go along with all that noise.' Meanwhile, Mattie Shaw had moved north and lived close by, as she still does. She would call Mrs Anderson from time to time to make sure Prince was going to school. Today she introduces Mrs Anderson to people as 'Prince's other mother.'

John Nelson has moved up to the north side too, living on his own. Testimony to the way he and his famous son have patched up their relationship stands at the back of his house in the shape of a mauve BMW car (he used to drive a white Thunderbird, which he has since given to Prince). When Prince first settled into his new home, Nelson Snr provided him with an allowance. 'At first it was about ten dollars a week,' Mrs Anderson says, 'though I think he raised it a bit later on. There wasn't a lot of money in the house, and I couldn't give him any. He wanted to continue going to Central High in south Minneapolis, where he'd been going. So I said, "Fine, you can go. Keep that money for your lunch and your bus fare. If you can take care of that, you won't have to worry about anything else." So he did, and he'd even save out of it. I never went to welfare to ask for any money, because he didn't want that stigma. So we just said, "We'll work it out." '

Such was the chronology and varied domestic framework of Prince's childhood. It is not the way they were presented to the great capitalist public as his rise to international fame really got underway in 1981, and as it continued for the following four years. Instead, the more the consuming masses latched on to Prince's elaborate matrix of audio-visual spells, the more completely the nuts and bolts of his reality faded into the seductive tapestry of myth. By the time *Purple Rain* had turned him into front-page news, Prince, unreachable behind his wall of silence, was being explained to the world as a variety of things that he patently was not. But this was not just a matter of shoddy reporting. Someone had been tampering with the script.

The first significant distortion is down to Owen Husney. Prince's age at the time *For You* was released was officially claimed to be eighteen. The truth, of course, was that he was just two months short of twenty. 'Yeah, that was definitely my idea,' Husney reveals. It was a fib which the media swallowed whole, and seems, one way or another, to have been absorbed at Warner Brothers too. Certainly Russ Thyret cannot recall knowing anything about the deception.

Then there was the question of race. Prince seems to have inherited the relatively light skin-colour of his natural parents, something which went some way towards helping him avoid being labelled 'black'. Both Mrs Shaw and Mr Nelson reportedly define themselves as black, as do people who know them. Given this, it is an education to observe how a succession of newspaper interviewers built up an image of Prince as some kind of exotic mulatto. 'My dad is black and Italian,' he explained to Dennis Hunt of the *Los Angeles Times* as the *Dirty Mind* tour hit the

71

road in January 1981. The album was Prince's first to stand a real chance with the 'crossover' audience, and opting out of a decisively black identity did him no harm. 'My mum is a mixture of a bunch of things. I don't consider myself part of any race. I'm just a human being, I suppose.' He also declined to reveal his second name, and offered an explanation for inheriting his father's stage handle that was rich in intimations of wounding psychological conflict: 'I think my father was kind of lashing out at my mother when he named me Prince.'

By the time he got into *Rolling Stone* (19 February 1981), his genes had been juggled slightly. 'The son of a half-black father and an Italian mother,' ran the report. On 29 March, the New York *Daily News* had straightened daddy out: 'His mother is Italian. His father, black.' A dramatic picture emerged of underdog making good: 'His music is from the ghetto, with its punctuated street rhythms and simplistic charms.' Prince was, we learned, 'one of nine children struggling to survive, [but] Prince cut away from the hand me down home life to carve out a career of his own at the age of 17'. Pulsating stuff. You have to wonder just what kind of deadpan mischief was going on with some of those interviews. In the Boston *Real Paper* John Nelson was 'half black' again, and Prince was crediting Quaker Oats oatmeal with saving him from malnutrition. Then he was asked to define his greatest ambition. 'Senility,' said Prince; 'I'm close to it now.'

It had not taken Prince long to decide that all interviews were really good for was a nice little wind-up. 'I think there were two things at work there,' reflects Dez Dickerson. 'To a degree there was an attempt to if not erase, then sort of blur the heritage. But I think there was something else at work. Early on in his career he had had some experience of doing press interviews where what he said had got pretty well mangled, misquoted, misrepresented. He took that very, very hard. If you see yourself as a star, you want everybody to take what you say as seriously as you do. So what he said was sacred to him. When people misused what he said, it upset him greatly. So he just decided that he was never going to tell them the truth again. You know: "They don't print what you say anyway, so you might as well make up something that sounds good." '

Prince liked to play manipulation games. They weren't necessarily meant to be cruel; just a bit off the wall. Mrs Anderson remembers going to the band's early gigs, and watching Prince and André exploit their relatively similar appearances to confuse their fans: 'All the kids were running, looking for Prince. He was sitting downstairs in the hotel, saying "No, no, Prince ain't down yet!" André would show up and they'd all run to André, saying "Prince, Prince!" ' 'He's got a great sense of humour,' affirms Dickerson. 'He used to do things just to totally put people off. He would shake hands with someone left-handed, and so force *you* to shake left-handed, just almost as an exercise in control.'

Soon, every aspect of Prince's identity in the world's mind's eye would be bound up with a great morass of rumours and blurred identities, diversions from and refractions of the truth. But the fragments of dubious information that emerged as the reality of his early life are worth close consideration, if only as a yardstick of how far the mythology they comprised would ultimately be stretched. In the quest for biographical 'fact', it is easy to forget that the fictions which always attend celebrity comprise another kind of reality in themselves. At the point of actual consumption – when someone hands their cash over the counter and goes home to get cosy with their precious new disc – the legends which circulate round the maker of that record might be said to be the only 'truth' that really counts: the background (dis)information that can confer extra dimensions of meaning upon what is in the grooves.

The monarch of Paisley Park's inclination has been to revel in his own labyrinth of legend, and hide inside it, no matter who stepped up to add new twists from outside his immediate control. His retreat from the entire sector of the media world that deals with context, explanation and analysis would leave him vulnerable to exterior forces clouding the picture he wanted to project of himself. But the thing about that picture was that it was already pretty cloudy in the first place. So maybe nothing mattered so long as his own enigma was magnetic enough. All attempts to spoil the image he promoted could only draw people's gaze back to that image again and again. And that meant more raw material to conjure with. The important thing was to make that image *matter* – and never let it crack.

On 22 August 1979, 'I Wanna Be Your Lover' was released as the new Prince 45. It was his first record successful enough to evolve a mystique which would make him count for more than just the sum of the product shifted. The song was an instant R & B smash, making number one on the *Billboard* chart during a run totalling twenty-three weeks in the black Top 100. This handsome success carried over into the national Top 40, where the single climbed to number eleven and eventually achieved sales of over one million copies.

It is a marvellous record – and on closer inspection a startling one. More sinuous, more persuasive and altogether more *comfortable* with itself than anything on *For You*, 'Lover' steps straight into its stride with a taut guitar and synthesizer lick that effectively maintains the song's exquisite tension from intro to fade. There is a good bass-line, important to the rhythmic mettle of the track, and the drum pattern is neat, if uncomplicated. But the real sting lies in the treble frequencies rather

73

than the basement, as guitars, keyboards and percussion peel off each other in close formation – a light, fly-footed framework in which Prince's falsetto could lead a melody, tell a story, *and* keep hold of the beat, without ever becoming subordinate to it.

With this combination of strict rhythm and fingertip deftness of touch, 'I Wanna Be Your Lover' unlocked the secret of how to make a pop record funky and a funk record pop. Likewise, its lyric also mixed tough with tender, a subtle mechanism for making an unusual romantic pitch. Prince's confessional message starts off about as *humble* as you can get, giving us an instant snapshot of a guy who's broke, super-sensitive, and probably not very big. The male adolescent self-effacement is finely tuned to suggest an inadequate quota of the traditional masculine so-called virtues. He is without power, without machismo, without cash. He is apologetic too, but he takes a deep breath and lets it all come out. He wants to be your lover. OK. But he wants to be your *mother* . . . and your *sister*? And most of all, in the clinching last line of a memorable chorus, he wants to be the sole guardian of your orgasm. A man who wants a lot.

The candour and completeness of this reversal of standard heroic male wooing techniques is extremely impressive. But although his advances are trailed with heavy hesitation, there is no lack of confidence in his power to deliver, if only it can be on his terms. Prince cannot stand the way his chosen She treats him like a child. But trust me, he insists. His devotion will be that of a female parent, his loyalty, easy in its intimacy, like a girl sibling. And if She can only invest in so strange a relationship, the pay-off will be dramatic – this love will not only be different, but its satisfactions too special for words. And so finally, ego delivers the finishing touches; after *his* love, no one else could measure up. And that, he finally confesses, is what he most wants her to feel.

'Lover' was a winner from the second the needle hit the radio groove, and Warner Brothers seemed to have sussed it. It would be a couple of years before the advent of the promotional video on its subsequent world-dominating scale, but just the same, they financed a clip to support the single. By contemporary standards the 'Lover' video was a primitive affair, a mimed performance with no set or props, just the singer himself dancing and mouthing the words, with phased-in sequences showing him to be playing drums, guitar and keyboards as well as the bass slung low around his waist during the verses – the one-child band angle was still a selling-point. More interesting, though, was Prince's look, which had undergone a major transformation. The bum-fluff moustache still discol-oured his upper lip, but the Afro hairstyle, emblem of Black Pride, had given way to a coiffure, which to some would have signified its absolute antithesis. To straighten the hair, in the radical rhetoric of the late sixties, was to be ashamed of your blackness, a state which white supremacists would be only too keen to encourage. And for the video of 'I Wanna Be Your Lover', Prince's hair was long, wavy and swinging down low. This was no warrior helmet, not for any race – rather, it flaunted its 'femininity' with an insolence that was almost inspired. Such a very pretty boy.

An overt and visual representation of 'I Wanna Be Your Lover''s wounded passion served as the cover for the album that followed the single. Nude from the nipples up, our man gazes with heavy sincerity into the lens. Jurgen Reisch's photo presented a sublime, cherubic vision of wistful uncertainty and innocent promise – if just a little slimy. On the reverse side, Prince sits apparently stark naked astride a winged horse along the lines of the mythological Pegasus. Chris Callis, from New York, was the commissioned photographer, and the horseback shots were his second assignment with Prince. The first had been to do promotional pictures just after the first album. 'He came to the studio by himself for those,' Callis recalls. 'He had an Afro, and we did the picture with his shirt off . . . and he didn't say anything.' Prince, though, was a cooperative subject, and he liked Callis's work. For the 'Pegasus' session, Prince had him flown out to LA. 'By this time he had a larger entourage,' says Callis, probably a reflection of Prince's new management situation. 'There was four or five people. We all rented horses, and I don't think any of us particularly knew what we were doing. They were going to put in some wings later on, dove wings that someone else had photographed. He rode around in his underwear, and I just photographed him. I don't know if we even spoke at all. The only impression I have of him is that he just didn't talk.'

Simply entitled *Prince*, the LP went into America's record shops on 19 October 1979, buoyant on the back of 'Lover' 's bubbling profile, and secured a British release two months into the following year, so avoiding the pre-Christmas rush which might otherwise have swamped an artist quite unknown to most record-buyers across the Atlantic. *Prince* is a succinct, consummately professional album that sought primarily to consolidate the artist's inroads with the black audience while making encouraging gestures towards the whites he needed on his side if his grander ambitions were to be fulfilled. 'I Wanna Be Your Lover', which opens the proceedings, indicated real progress in the dance department (something his surprisingly ungainly hopping and bopping in the video did not). On the LP version it breaks down into an extended instrumental groove which nodded its approval to the disco floor – and probably gives a good idea of what a Prince band rehearsal sounded like.

The excellence of 'Lover' is almost matched by one of the two other floor-fillers among a total of nine tracks. 'Sexy Dancer' was a terse piece of straightforward lusting funk. More interesting is the strutting 'I Feel For You', which suggests a rather less spiritual variation on the outsider's

75

ardour defined in 'I Wanna Be Your Lover'. But although the protagonist is breathily insistent that he really means it, this time it's just your body he's after. The lyric contains one of the more literal declarations of physical attraction to appear on disc. Sheer lust had rarely expressed itself with such a disarming blend of naïvety and nerve.

Prince is not a concept album as such. Nor does it fit together the impulses and priorities of black and white music with the same natural consistency as Prince records to come. It did, however, indicate the versatility of the artist more completely than the début had done, and his execution of the various styles is accomplished with bolder strokes. More than this, though, *Prince* reveals the beginnings of an intriguing and idiosyncratic kind of philosophical carnality.

The track 'Bambi' was the joker in the pack. Never mind the grandstand ecstatics of the closing solo on *For You*'s 'I'm Yours', 'Bambi' was a pure rock guitar statement. Prince grinds the instrument up and down through the chords like a muscle car changing gear. It is far too earnest to be a parody, except that even the most perverse rock neanderthal might think twice about so upfront a confession of desire for – whisper it – a lesbian. Puerility is the key. Sat between a placid, sweetly modulated ballad of devotion ('With You') and an almost country-style piece of insouciant longing ('Still Waiting'), 'Bambi' is wilfully incongruous. And it's *loud*. Yet here we have a little lost soul utterly bemused and scared to death by his heterosexual passion for young and winsome, real-live dyke. In his ignorant wishful thinking, he pleads with her to go the other way. 'Bambi', the person, even gets a mention in the thank-you list, along with God. Extraordinary: a falsetto, heavy-metal cry for help.

What unites much of the eclectic content of *Prince* is the suggestion of a male dynamic of seduction which seemed fresh and new in the territory of black pop – or, for that matter, white, where ambisexuality has a far stronger line of succession. The unbridled expression of sexual urges was not in itself new, especially in the R & B field. Nor were naked displays of impossible tenderness. But the signalling of an erotic personality which could only be assertive upon legitimation of its submissive exterior – *that* was a little different.

Prince is full of songs that plead, quite unashamedly, for acknowledgement and understanding, or make petulant demands for attention. In this sense it is vintage young love material. And yet behind the signifying, his impulse to possess, control, even dominate has a way of revealing itself in the punchlines. The basics of this absorbing routine – romantic or erotic entrapment through intimations of helplessness – works to greater or lesser effect in the scenarios of 'Lover', 'Bambi', the closing weepie 'It's Gonna Be Lonely', 'I Feel For You' and the limpid, almost ethereal 'When We're Dancing Close And Slow', where the waif seducer prepares to clinch the 'feminine' deal he proposed in the classic, opening single. It's quite a performance. Even if you don't quite believe it, you have to believe that *he* probably does.

What Prince does in these songs is not so much challenge conventional sex roles as *invert* them – or simply take on some of the traditionally assumed characteristics of the 'opposite' sex in order to effect entry into the feminine world. Never mind that he wants to be someone's sister, and not like those other men at all. By the time we get to that last dance he wants to, hey, *come inside of you*, girls – and actually says so too. His horny heterosexual motives are never in any doubt. The thing is, how could you resist?

The *Prince* album was, he told the press, a piece of cake to make after the long haul that was *For You*. Several of the songs had been written, rehearsed and demoed well in advance, with at least one ('I Feel For You') pre-dating his Warners contract altogether. With the benefit of his greater experience, Prince and his studio staff were able to put the record together at the Alpha Studios, Burbank, in just six weeks.

The album did well, ultimately selling a million copies worldwide. But 'Why You Wanna Treat Me So Bad?' – like 'Bambi', a rock guitar-orientated cut – was released as a single in January 1980, and bombed. For now, Prince could slam riff all he liked. But in the eyes of the American media (and hence, the American public), he was still a 'black' act, and that was that. What *Prince* did achieve was confirmation of a substantial R & B audience, and the heightened interest of black pop glossies – and some rock critics – in the personality behind the pubescent sexual outlaw posture: something which became more apparent when he took his band out on the road, and in his rare forays on to television.

The most famous of Prince's early TV appearances came when he and the band guested on that staple of US rock 'n' roll television, *American Bandstand*. Dick Clark, the show's gleaming veteran host, conducted a painful one-way conversation with young Mr Nelson before millions of viewers. Clark asked Prince how long he had been a musician. The brat held up four fingers to indicate the number of years.

A story has since circulated that this display of mute insolence was due in part to Prince's infamous shyness, but mostly his annoyance at Clark's first question, which implied his incredulity that a Hicksville like Minneapolis could be the band's home town. In truth, the whole dumb-struck performance was a premeditated stunt. Dez Dickerson: 'Before we went on we were sitting in the green room and he [Prince] hatched this idea not to say anything. He said, "If he asks you anything just shake your head, don't talk." When I came home and saw somebody's tape of it, I thought it just made him look foolish, but other people thought it was brilliant. I thought it made us look like total buffoons. I remember thinking, "Oh, this is so stupid. I feel so dumb!" You know, "We're illiterate, but we play well." But I guess one man's ceiling is another man's floor.' News of this contrived piece of non-cooperation even filtered across to the UK, where the weekly *Black Echoes* magazine reported it with glee. Behaving like that to Dick Clark is a bit like being invited to Buckingham Palace, then hanging your arse out at the queen.

If Prince was showing signs of shaping up as a bit of an outlaw, he was not on his own. During the same period, Rick James, a product of Buffalo, New York, had already emerged as a major and imaginative new talent on the American funk scene, and a possible saviour of the faded reputation of Motown records. His early works had cut a vivid dash across the rather jaded face of black music, all sky-high funk and space-age mock-heroics. But at the start of 1980, it had begun to look as though James's popularity might be on the wane. Prince and his band were booked as second act on a string of 'Slick' Rick's East Coast dates, part of the rationale being that James needed a strong supporting act to maintain his drawing power. An intense rivalry between the two of them springs directly from this tour, one whose causes were partly personal and partly philosophical. It is worth a closer look at how the pair of them compared and contrasted at the time.

On the face of it, the two had a lot in common. Both were fascinated by the potential for incorporating aspects of rock into musical repertoires whose central drives were those of R & B, soul and funk. James appealed to a young black audience, and he already had his entire act – sound, ideology, stage show – worked out. His brash, eclectic funk and spoof Marvel-comic warrior postures made a lot of Prince's studio work at that time look stilted and rather fey. James aspired to the flash of white rock 'n' roll. But his underlying sensibility was a clear celebration of hip black cultural mores and the ways in which they had evolved through contact with both the broader American counter-culture and other, newer black politics from different parts of the world. The name of his group – the Stone City Band - was a punning metaphor for a state of mind in which black idiom (a random example: the Stylistics' 'Stone In Love With You') and his delight in a state of 'stoned' pleasure through dope were parts of the same whole. His hair, meanwhile, was a processed version of the Rastafarian dreadlocks internationalized by Bob Marley and other Jamaican reggae stars.

Out there on the road, though, Prince was leading his band in such a way as to prove that the rock influences on his second album had been no gimmick. And the kinky intimations of some of those songs were made live and visual in performance. 'It was a rough period for Rick,' says Dez Dickerson. 'But in terms of the way we went over it was good, if you can term someone else's misfortune as good. We would go over like gangbusters, because the black audience was just dying for something new.' Not that the increasingly freaky Prince repertoire met with no resistance. 'We came out with a very heavy punk influence. For a lot of black people the word "punk" had connotations of homosexuality, and there's always that macho thing with funk. But for the most part, it was warmly received.'

Backstage, though, the situation left something to be desired. 'I remember Bobby and I went to Rick's room one night, because there had been this escalating tension that we found later had just sprung out of insignificant, fairly stupid things: someone perceived a slight in an elevator when André didn't talk to someone, and they thought André had a bad attitude. We just cleared the air. But Prince at that time was just so shy, and not given to seeking people out. He and Rick really didn't talk too much. And silence has a way of prompting people to provide their own dialogue.'

Meanwhile, critics were beginning to provide an interesting new dialogue too. A small headline gig at New York's Bottom Line prompted a rave notice from the *Soho Daily News* of 20 February 1980: 'Judging by the album you'd never know that Prince is anything but a rock dilettante. In concert, it's clearly his lifeline.' The review remarked with interest the punkish demeanour of Bobby Z and Matt Fink in their wraparound shades and skinny ties. It marvelled at Dez Dickerson and his incredible technicolour hair, and the introduction into the set of a new song, 'Head'. Most of all it noticed Prince: 'Scantily clad in tiger-striped black and white bikini shorts and loose-fitting vest, the set begins with his back to the audience and tiny ass waving from side to side.' It continued: 'The hour and a half set concluded with the hit "I Wanna Be Your Lover" with Prince necking on the platform with his sexy blonde keyboardist [and] a black patron screaming out beside me euphorically, "rock 'n' roll!".'

Here were the first stirrings of the 'crossover' euphoria which Prince and Dez Dickerson craved. But it was a crossover provoked by a carefully nurtured cocktail of shock tactics. For Gayle Chapman, the 'sexy blonde keyboardist', involvement in such a strategy invoked contradictions that were too much for her to take. She became the band's first casualty. 'No one to my knowledge got a really clear handle on exactly what the problem was for Gayle,' says Dickerson. 'I know that she had some conflicts. She loved it, but she didn't love it. She wanted to do it, but at the same time there were some other things tugging at her.' In the end, Chapman's dismissal was precipitated by something relatively trivial, a dispute over a reheasrsal. She wanted to be somewhere else, and Prince wouldn't have it. But the real reasons were, of course, more complex. Maybe it was the adulation that she found hardest to take. 'She freaked out on the road,' says Pepé Willie, her one-time song-writing companion. 'It was just too much for her to handle all that running around: Florida,

North Carolina, South Carolina, Atlanta. She went back to religion. All these people were coming up, saying "I love you, I love you", and she was saying "I don't even *know* you!" '

As for Rick James, well, he made it his business to denounce His Royal Badness at every possible opportunity for several years after. 'Prince is a mentally disturbed young man,' he opined briskly to Britain's *Blues And Soul*. 'He's out to lunch. You can't take his music seriously. He sings songs about oral sex and incest,' as, by that time, he was. James was far from averse to a spot of grandstand erotica, but for him, it seems, Prince was just too much. Maybe the final insult added to James's injury at the hands of the upstart support act concerned a young Canadian model called Denise Matthews, whose main claim to fame was a commercial for Pearl Drops tooth polish. Prince threw a party after the American Music Awards Show, a year or so after the tour, and Slick Rick brought Ms Matthews along. 'The story goes that somehow or other Prince enticed her away from Rick,' shrugs Dickerson; 'and a few days later, there she was on the bus, on the road with us. One day she was Denise, and then she was Vanity, and suddenly she was a star.'

The girl group Vanity 6 would be among the many protégés on whom Prince bestowed his golden touch as his stock began to soar. Rick James remained unimpressed. 'Something else,' he told *Blues And Soul*, 'he doesn't want to be black. My job is to keep reality over this little science fiction creep. And if he doesn't like what I'm saying about him, he can kiss my ass. He's so far out of touch with what's really happening, it makes me angry.'

James would spend too much of the following years in drug-detoxification clinics, and too little making music. Prince would become the biggest pop star on the planet. Whether he had to kiss anybody's ass to get there rather depends on if you think Slick Rick had a point.

7

Manifesto

Rex Features

Prince's third album, *Dirty Mind*, was released on 15 October 1980. On 12 January 1981, top New York PR operative Howard Bloom, commissioned to work on Prince's media profile, sent a progress report to Steve Fargnoli in Los Angeles: 'Here's the material I promised on Prince. The verdict from the press is clear: Prince is a rock and roll artist! In fact, the press is saying clearly that Prince is the first black artist with the potential to become a major white audience superstar since Jimi Hendrix.'

Bloom's conclusions about the album's likely buyers were backed up with a list of quotes from gig reviews from major city newspapers and hip, serious cultural publications like *Village Voice*. 'As the critics keep pointing out, Prince's star potential is explosive,' Bloom enthused. 'And as the critics imply, the task with Prince is to hold his black audience while aggressively pursuing the rock and New Wave audience.'

With *Dirty Mind*, Prince began to move into that domain of dreams and contradictions which is the real stuff of American stardom, a place emblematic of the agonies and ecstasies of its time. It was an album that challenged the prevailing market categorizations, and so urged listeners to place it in a category on its own. *Dirty Mind* is a record with *attitude*: it would either tickle your fancy or turn you right off, and responses of both kinds were inspired within each of the tidy consumer divisions that, in all its impurity, *Dirty Mind* was half-related to. The upshot of these tiny disruptions in the compartments so subtly infiltrated into the minds of records buyers would not be instant idolatry and profit, but the generation of a consumer community – people whose pleasure in a record would be connected to illicit sensations of secrecy and defiance. A community based on such commitment can grow into an army. It just needs a little faith and a helping hand.

'. . . the strategy on Prince's next tour could be critical,' wrote Howard Bloom. 'I'd suggest booking him two dates in each [regional] market: a date as second act on the bill to a major black headliner like Cameo, Parliament, etc *and* a date at the local New Wave dance club. The idea is to go after the black and rock audience simultaneously. Neither date will conflict with the other. The white kids who would go to see Prince at the Ritz would never go to the Felt Forum [a New York funk auditorium] to see Cameo (they're sure they'd get mugged or raped). The black kids who flock to see Cameo wouldn't think of going to the Ritz.'

So the marketing question, or part of what lay behind it, was: how un-black could white people be convinced Prince was? Or maybe, how close to a new variation on a mythic vision of blackness they could better understand? And by that, what might be intended is: how many white people could be persuaded that this Prince character was not involved inextricably in those alien musical languages of dance and gospel-derived exhortation? The stuff lots of them – well, the ones too young to remember the sixties – would think of as all feet and no brains; and no *authenticity*. How could Prince's deviant disco be made to feel both more 'intelligent' and more *dirty*?

That is one way of looking at the way rock-business people were looking at Prince. Maybe it is a cynical one. After all, could it not be argued that the only way for the nonsense of artistic apartheid to be challenged was for performers to be sold in imaginative ways, with long-term market integration in mind? No question, a single man or woman could not move the mountain alone. But all the good things, all the grand, romantic possibilities conjured up by post-war popular music culture, at least suggested that the mountain might be bullshit. The bearers of these messages, if briefly, and at considerable personal cost, evolved into the great inspirational stars: Elvis Presley, James Brown, the Beatles, Sly Stone.

Whatever, when the latest lean, hungry outsider comes along with a strange new message from some self-invented parallel world, at odds with all the diminishing definitions – racial, sexual, social – people like them are supposed to be grateful for, it *has* to be a thrill for any functioning liberal media mind: hey, everything can be *all right*! Howard Bloom did not exaggerate; the white rock press *loved* the wilful non-conformism of *Dirty Mind*. 'A pop record of Rabelaisian achievement', decided *Rolling Stone*. 'This is lewdness cleansed by art, with joy its socially redeeming feature.' After the very New York headline show Howard Bloom had recommended for Prince, Pablo Guzman in *Village Voice* glowed, and at the same time suggested Mr Bloom may have got one detail a little bit wrong: 'It was the night after Lennon [died] and it did seem right to rock all night . . . The crowd . . . was a surprise –

heavily street and black – but the show was not.' The Ritz performance, then, proved that blacks *were* prepared to move into white territory to see something they liked. And that territory did not just mean the venue – it could mean the music too.

With the libertarian idealism *Dirty Mind* rekindled, Prince became a stick with which sane journalists on white publications could beat upon radio segregation. And why not? It deserved it. But while the *New York Times* headline of 2 December 1981 would optimistically ask, 'Is Prince Leading Music To A True Biracism?', it is worth considering what the cost of achieving so utopian a state might be – and who would be paying.

The great black American writer James Baldwin once surmised: 'At bottom, to be colored means that one has been caught in some utterly unbelievable cosmic joke, a joke so hideous and in such bad taste that it defeats all categories and definitions. One's only hope of supporting, to say nothing of surviving, this joke is to flaunt in the teeth of it one's own particular and invincible style. It is at this turning, this level, that the word color, ravaged by experience and heavy with the weight of peculiar spoils, returns to its first meaning, which is not *negro*, the Spanish word for black, but vivid, many-hued, e.g. the rainbow, and warm and quick and vital, e.g., life.' He continued: 'How hard it is though, to speak of negro life in these terms, Negroes being so bitterly maligned and so brutally penalized for those very qualities of color which have helped them to endure.'

Baldwin's words were written in a different context and a different time, but his analyses are worth carrying in the head as we listen to some of Prince's finest, most impassioned moments. *Dirty Mind* was nothing if not the flaunting of a particular style, and in the face of suffocating expectations. It is not simply that it could not be ruder, but that it could not be more *personalized* in its rudeness. It could not be more dismissive of the rock-business assumption that black musicians were only viable when they dealt in traditional black music forms. It could not be more at odds with the full-blown, divisive Puritanism of the American power-structure, just at that moment undergoing a fierce, white-hot revival, with Ronald Reagan its presidential standard-bearer.

This was a *rock 'n' roll* record which had a song about how great it was having sex with your elder sister. It made frank and feverish reference, dear God, to her torrential vaginal fluids. With the song 'Head', Prince enacts a scenario in which he diverts a female virgin on her journey to the altar. Flushed with mutual desire – and she, presumably, needing to keep herself intact – they submerge themselves steamily in the forbidden pleasures of oral sex. Prince makes a good number of his already familiar pre-emptive apologies, not least for his involuntary *faux pas* of (shall we say) exploding on to her bridal gown. A symbolic emission indeed.

84

But if this might be seen as Prince's lurid affront to the 'joke' described by Baldwin, some other words from the same writer – this time provoked by his relationship with big, butch, white Norman Mailer – make you wonder how effective a gesture it was: 'I think I know something about the American masculinity which most men of my generation do not know because they have not been menaced by it in the way that I have been. It is still true, alas, that to be an American Negro male is also to be a kind of walking phallic symbol: which means that one pays, in one's own personality, for the sexual insecurity of others. The relationship, therefore, between a black boy and a white boy is a very complex thing.'

With *Dirty Mind* Prince entered into the tortured territory of the relationship between a black artist and a black-and-white world. Was his celebration of abandon exposing the oppressive sexual neuroses of white power, or just pimping the licentious stereotype which was a central instrument of that oppression? That is, was he just acting like white racists say all blacks are? On the cover of *Dirty Mind* he gives us a good long eyeful of his new posing pouch look. Was the promise of Prince's penis part of the resistance, or part of the 'joke'?

But that is only one bit of the new rogue factor which Prince's *Dirty Mind* inserted into this nervous social equation of race, sex and class. Even as we try to see where he fits among a maze of evasive definitions, his music, his image, his half-imaginary milieu blurred the picture even more. *Dirty Mind* did not simply suggest that the shapes and signatures of rock – and in particular of New Wave pop – could survive in and contribute to a soul-funk environment. More than that, it went a very long way to executing a true hybrid, a new mutation from parents of many colours. If his underground sensual overdrive *did* fuel undesirable untruths about black men in the minds of whites, was he not also breaking spectacularly free from the restrictive, standard presentation of black entertainers?

As *Dirty Mind* began to earn one rave review after another, the black music monthly *Soul Teen* wondered about it all too: 'So what do all of these seeming contradictions mean?' they asked in a piece called 'Punk Funk: Gettin' Down And Dirty'. 'Are these black Punk Acts and New Wavers [Grace Jones and The Busboys were included] shunning their traditional black roots in favor of a little cosmic Uncle Tomming or are they merely climbing over the walls built by the white man and designed to keep black music microcosmic? Are they depriving their own people of the talent they lavish so freely on whites or is it all a shrewd endeavor to take a big chunk out of that lucrative white market, thereby creating a solid money base and a black musical force to be reckoned with?'

Dez Dickerson defines the attitude within the band. It was pretty basic: 'I think he, like the rest of us, just plain didn't care. You know, we really didn't understand why it had to be made such a big deal. So we just made every attempt we could to fly in the face of tradition.'

Cut it any way you like, *Dirty Mind* is a conceptually and musically convincing record, and part of what makes it matter is the way these awkward issues stake the enlightened listener out. It set its own targets and hit them. It was also a giant stylistic leap from the contemporary black pop orientations of *Prince* and *For You*, a leap into vivid darkness and light. It created and defined its own world.

The opening, title cut exhibits perfectly the completeness of Prince's marriage of punk, soul and disco with the sensibility of an infant debauchee. The drum thump is like a Giorgio Moroder machine beat. The low, pulsing keyboards are robotic pop à la Gary Numan; the cheapo organ, deliberate, like ? And the Mysterians, as revived and reinterpreted by Blondie and Elvis Costello. The guitar is tight, metallic R & B, sixties style. The voice, all angelic falsetto anxiety, hovers between confession and frenzy as this alarming baby libertine makes public his most powerful private desires. And it is a vision which is pure, vintage rock 'n' roll: he wants to do it to you in the back of daddy's car. Chuck Berry would understand. (Should we make that *black* rock 'n' roll? And shouldn't it always be thought of that way anyhow?).

Self-produced once more, the sleeve notes claim it to have been 'Recorded somewhere in Uptown'. This slice of instant enigma, as Prince himself uncharacteristically revealed in his interviews during the tour, simply conceals that *Dirty Mind* went out pretty much as demoed, not in LA, but in the relative solitude of Minneapolis. The spare, sharp, brittle sound lends it a spartan energy that is definitively punk in mood. So too does the unfettered lyrical provocation: the punk funker gets straight to the point. But where the New Wavers sang of sex in terms of domination and disgust, Prince invested crudity with something of the intense sensuality of which soul music is so blissfully capable. He is a long way from reality, yet aroused by the ideas in his head. The way he sings about sex is confrontational and fantastical, but for him it still has the magical allure of a Holy Grail.

'Do It All Night' is brash but so persuasive, helped by a proper funk bass-line that curves and flexes where 'Dirty Mind' 's just pumped. 'Head' is brickhouse funk as tense as a stripper's beat. 'When You Were Mine' is bubblegum envy, spiked with promiscuity, the perfect vehicle for a later Cyndi Lauper cover, just a dream of a *demi-monde* love song. 'Sister' is bare-faced punky taboo-baiting. It is the only track that a well-balanced individual could describe as 'irresponsible'. By the time you've heard the eight tracks out, there is only buggery left to the imagination. Perhaps you can't have everything, but *Dirty Mind* would be enough for most to be going on with – for some, too much.

Copies of the album were sent out to DJs, bearing the message,

'Programmers: please audition prior to airing.' The result was that *Dirty Mind* usually went straight back in its sleeve. 'We definitely ran into some raised eyebrows and some questions,' admits Russ Thyret, 'with a song title or the innuendo in a lyric; and as time went by there was no such thing as an innuendo! And in his packaging we ran into some problems. But I think that record probably was the one that got everybody's attention.'

Thyret's first exposure to this hot little number came when Prince showed up at his house one night saying he had some new music and would Russ and his girlfriend like to hear it? 'We sat and listened to it, and it just knocked us out. I mean there were a couple of things on there, you know, like "Sister" that took you aback a little bit. But I'm fortunate in that I work for a company that has a real basic attitude. If they believe in the artists and the producers that make the music, they don't sit back and try to make value judgements. Obviously we'd got an investment and we were concerned about him, but the guy's talent was there and you just had to believe that he knew what he was doing.'

Prince thanked Thyret on the record's inner jacket, and well he might. It is no secret that there were significant pockets of resistance within the company to releasing what is possibly the most sexually explicit long-playing record of all time. It was Dez Dickerson's understanding that there was a strong enough body of opinion at Warners to have had Prince effectively dumped: 'There was . . . one point where Warners offered him his contract back, but he wouldn't do it. They didn't know what to do with him. They didn't understand the record and they didn't understand him.' But lined up in favour were Lenny Waronker (now Warners' President), Mo Ostin, Thyret and, reportedly making an especially enthusiastic contribution, the late Bob Regher, then Vice-President of Creative Services.

The record went into the shops with stickers warning people about the F-word, and airplay was extremely thin on the ground, black stations or white. 'It wasn't as hard on the black, but it was difficult, yes,' says Thyret. And the white? 'Really not meaningful. I mean, I think it would be fair to say that, ah, the airplay was . . . not meaningful.'

It was the press, not radio, that backed the *Dirty Mind* project, and so launched Prince on the phase of his career that three albums later would make him the hottest property in the business. How ironic that the very people he now so steadfastly refuses to deal with are the ones who conferred legitimacy on an album that had everyone else quaking in their boots. Bob Regher was particularly active in encouraging the interest of journalists. And once again, you've just got to hand it to Howard Bloom. 'I want Prince to begin doing phoners with New Wave and rock publications around the country,' went his letter to Fargnoli. 'As you know, we're already getting coverage from die-hard New Wave publications like *New York Rocker*.' Bloom had views about the advertising budget too: 'Ads in publications like the *Prairie Sun, Night Rock News*, and *Oasis De Neon* are dirt cheap, and they reach a staunch record-and-ticket buying audience.'

What makes Prince's 'crossover' story different from the many others since was that he *had* to go underground to achieve it. He became a variation on a vintage rock figure, a rebel with a cause and a guitar. And whatever uncomfortable feelings crossover inspires, whatever hard realities a crossover star might encourage people to fudge and forget, it cannot be said that Prince – unlike some – bridged the market gap by blanding out. But more than that, this was 1980/1, and even Michael Jackson hadn't been properly reinvented yet. *Thriller* would be another two years coming, with its blend of MOR, hard rock and sparkling dance-soul. The radio category of Urban Dancefloor, where black and white pop were finally permitted to coexist, was still a long way off. To merge rock and black pop perspectives into so seamless, complete and singular an ideological position as *Dirty Mind*'s was, in market terms, almost unthinkable.

From a black artist, this introduced a whole new vocabulary into the border zone where black and white musics meet. It also suggested that the encounter could take place in a quite different imaginary environment to any cross-breed that had gone before. The dimensions of *Dirty Mind*'s world were encapsulated in the opening track on side two, 'Uptown'. This mythical location was not so much a physical place as a state of mind. To a terse, funk rhythm, layered with thin keyboards and some high, marvellously sloppy guitar fills, Prince describes his place among a gang of young social deviants, and the inability of society to understand them. It is a sub-culture with a simple philosophy – to let no one categorize or explain them. In his most innocently freaky falsetto, Prince describes an encounter with a girl who steps up to him on the street to demand if he is gay. Our hero's response is indignant, and he throws the question straight back. The message is, 'don't judge by appearances', and marks the most overt statement yet of his desire to escape labelling by others. It is a position partly at odds with that assumed by the prevailing logic of racial and sexual liberation in the preceding two decades. The need then was to close ranks around a shared culture, and to transform derogatory stereotypes into badges of pride. 'Uptown' articulated fully a preoccupation that drove Prince's work in the following years: to evade at all costs every semblance of an identity defined by roots in the real world.

The controversial nature of *Dirty Mind* turned Prince into hot copy as he and the band set off on their travels round America in the first six months of 1981. In the most intensive series of interviews he has ever done, Prince and the newsprint media added flesh and fantasy to the subterranean milieu he described on *Dirty Mind*. With the record barely making it into the *Billboard* Top 50, it was incumbent upon him to shrug aside his off-stage reticence to a degree that he has never had to since.

On 25 January the *San Francisco Examiner Chronicle* gave him a full-page spread, syndicated from the piece by Dennis Hunt in the *Los Angeles Times*. The interview was conducted over the phone: 'No one can see me on the phone,' ran Prince's quote. The article commenced with the famous tale of his reading soft-porn novels secreted by his mother under her home-maker journals. It went on to maintain the fiction of his age and provided possibly his first direct denial of a 'black' birthright.

Rolling Stone provided a further platform for the Prince philosophy with an interview placed alongside the album review of 19 February: 'I grew up on the borderline . . . I had a bunch of white friends and a bunch of black friends. I never grew up in one particular culture.' He explained the attitude that 'Uptown' was inspired by: 'we do whatever we want, and those who cannot deal with it have a problem within themselves.' The only thing he was sure of was his sexual orientation – not gay: 'I'm not about that; we can be friends, but that's as far as it goes. My sexual preferences', he said of his fans, 'aren't really their business.'

Not that this prevented the following revelation, as quoted in Calumet City's *Night Rock News*: 'They are all true stories', he remarked of 'Uptown', 'Sister' and the previous album's lesbian trauma, 'Bambi'. 'This album more so than anything I've ever done. It's basically about my life and the different things I've experienced.'

In *Night Owl*, a supplement of the *Aquarian Weekly*, he said that the sequence of tracks on *Dirty Mind* was in the same order they were recorded in, and added that the only compromise he had made with the content was in shortening some of the songs. ' "Head" was a lot longer. When I first cut it, it went on and on. I was trying to take a real life experience – there are parts of the longer version that are sometimes shocking to me.' Hey, some guy! He also expressed his satisfaction at the people who were getting into his daring new act. 'It's a free crowd . . . They're ready for a change, I can sense it. Change in music, change in lifestyle. They want to be open and they want to dress any way they want to at the gigs and stuff like that. Tradition at black concerts a lot of times was to wear your best clothes, to come looking really dapper. It's not like that at our concerts. There are a lot of black kids out there, but they're like open-minded and free, and they want to have a good time.'

The logic of *Dirty Mind*, then, was that attitude was everything, and all other potentially divisive factors were simply redundant. In the climactic party sequence of 'Uptown', Prince describes a unity of interests that cuts right across lines of race, a coalition intent purely on having a good time. To the *LA Herald-Examiner* he insisted that with his power as a burgeoning figurehead there came 'No responsibility. I think I'm only a conductor of whatever electricity comes from the world, or wherever we all come from. To me the ultimate responsibility is the hardest one – the responsibility to be true to myself.'

It was a persepctive which differed in important ways from earlier black manifesto-bearers whose sound and vision he admired. Through the seventies it was George Clinton and his cronies, doubling under the guises of Parliament and Funkadelic (not to mention a string of spin-offs) who expressed the temper of their times. As Funkadelic, this zany amalgam picked up the threads of Hendrix's freak-out guitar and the heavy-duty funk of James Brown (from whose band the JBs, P-Funk's horn and rhythm sections had come), and wove them into a framework within which was documented a fiercely parodic but definitively *black* political consciousness, which took much of its sound and presentation back from rock, but was, even so, rich in symbols of cultural identity.

Parliament's output tended more towards hi-tech, space-funk fantasias which proposed, with crackpot humour, allegorical solutions to the still blighted condition of the black American. Their most profound political statement remains the magnificent – and very funny – 'Chocolate City', where messages are not only delivered through Clinton's dark-brown rap in praise of black electoral successes, but in the cool and complex jazz workout that accompanies it. 'Chocolate City' makes connections across a range of styles which are united by their roots among black people.

But it was epic conceptual albums like *Mothership Connection* (1975) and its follow-up *The Clones Of Dr Funkenstein* (1977) which typified Parliament's work as the decade wore on. Clinton's surreal abstractions from black-American English created a true secret language which helped bind together a vast and committed cult of followers. And beneath the lunatic exterior of jabbering 'clones' and ludicrous platform boots, Parliament's rambling narratives were much more than just a lot of futuristic nonsense: the comedy was also a mechanism for affectionately satirizing such sagas of self-discovery as Alex Haley's *Roots*, or else indulging in utopian schemes for escape from the grinding realities of ghetto life. P-Funk's vision was political, cultural in the broadest sense, and quitessentially communal – and, as necessity had demanded, its identity was black without apology.

Black consciousness emerged in the sixties as a defence against the belittling, dominating consciousness of white society. But while Prince's idealism was intense, and inspired by dreams of liberty which were no less vivid, his 'Uptown' scenario comprises a rainbow coalition of diverse *individuals* whose minds had shed all shackles of class, race and sex. For Prince, to define himself as 'black' would be a restriction rather than a display of strength and pride. As such, it was a more escapist formulation than that of Clinton. But it would also enable him to conquer markets Clinton's embrace of his own 'blackness' caused him to be excluded from.

The famous *Dirty Mind* cover photo anticipates it all. Shot in monochrome by local commercial photographer Allen Beaulieu in his own studio, it implies a powerful sense of subterranean, downmarket decadence with very few obvious yardsticks to measure it against. Emerging eerily from the shadows, Prince's combination of open studded trenchcoat, black briefs, scarf, stockings and bare belly manages to indicate androgyny, depravity, sensitivity, alienism and rampant libido all at once. With his Rude Boy badge (appropriated from the British 2-Tone movement, where it carried its source meaning: a popular term for Jamaican delinquents of the sixties) on his left lapel, he offered himself to the public as the ultimate freak – a star.

Beaulieu says that Prince asked to be shot in front of bedsprings, but that the design trick of having them propped up as a backdrop was his. Beaulieu bought them himself at a junk yard ('They wanted five bucks. I said, "two fifty", and they went "sure." '), and probably has a point when he says that very few people would have immediately realized what they were. He also says that it was Prince's decision to use a black and white shot instead of colour. 'I think I fought for the colour shot because it was more shocking,' Beaulieu recalls, 'because you saw Prince way more than you did the bedsprings.' But Prince's thinking was to make the initial impact more low-key. Only closer inspection would bring the shock factor home, and that was right in line with how he wanted his audience to develop. Prince was turning himself into a cult. 'He wanted it to be this underdog thing that people would tell other people about,' says Beaulieu, 'not something that advertising would just kill.'

It was sound commercial logic. Black music had come to be promoted for the one-off dance-floor hit, but rock marketing sought to create loyalty to an artist and his or her wider perspective. Prince needed to cultivate a following that behaved like a rock one if he was to earn the creative freedom he sought. *Dirty Mind*, he explained to interviewers, was the album he wanted to put out for himself, not to fulfil his assigned pop-soul market role.

Packaging and debate were vital allies in breaking the mould, but the committed power of his concert performances was garnering impassioned support in its own right. The *Dirty Mind* shows used to open up with 'Do It All Night' played at high volume, setting the tone for a performance which would maintain a high velocity almost from start to finish. As with the album, one song would jump straight into the next with little explanation from the stage – another punk technique, as was the ensemble's commitment to manic, perpetual movement. This was a complete break with the traditions of even the grittiest street-funk acts. With them, catharsis came when the personnel slipped into a groove and stayed there. Prince's band picked up on the more belligerent conventions of rock, showcasing soloists (especially the dazzling Dickerson) and *driving* the music forward.

Dickerson considers the influence of the New Wave: 'There were some things about it that I didn't like. I was still a bit of a snob, musically, and I was put off by people with no intention of knowing how to play. Then after a while, the spirit and the attitude of it began to appeal to me. In the Prince thing I got into putting as many pins and buttons on my jacket as I could, and dyed my hair orange. I was impressed by the idea of scaling things down, and making them more simple.'

The crowd-pleasing highlight of the set at that time came with the strut and smut of 'Head'. Gayle Chapman's place had been taken by Lisa Coleman, a classically trained pianist and the daughter of Gary Coleman, a West-Coast session musican. Apart from Prince, she and Dr Fink are the only players credited with contributing to *Dirty Mind*. Fink played synthesizer on 'Head', and is also acknowledged as co-writing the title track. Ms Coleman's role was simply to deliver 'Head' 's single, heavy-breathing female line. Predictably, given its taboo subject-matter, the song turned into a celebration of solidarity between audience and band, which would segue into the frenetic 'Sister' and close with the anthemic 'Partyup'. Here was a true and cleansing unity of 'dirty' minds.

But there were tender moments too, and a smattering of moves from the classic soul conventions. 'Still Waiting', with its bar-room self-pity, and *Dirty Mind*'s one ballad, 'Gotta Broken Heart Again', were usually played back to back after the initial electric blitz of the first two or three songs. For these weepies, Prince would put down his guitar, and instead, cradle the mike in his hands to maximum suggestive impact. Elsewhere, his guitar-playing did not prevent him from exhibiting a repertoire of splits and spins in the manner of James Brown.

The videos of the album's title track and 'Uptown' give a dilute but realistic indication of the hyperactive eclecticism of the live show. What Prince does with his feet and body veers from crass thrusts of the pelvis, to Johnny Rottenesque glares into the camera's eye, to almost balletic leaps from one level of the four-tiered stage (the same as was used for gigs) to the other, the baggage in his briefs swinging pendulously as the flasher mac opened and closed. Probably the greatest performance for TV consumption, though, was their appearance on *Saturday Night Live*, where they turned out a frenetic rendition of 'Partyup', their demeanour wired-up and bug-eyed, aping punk's amphetamine energy. Bobby Z, behind the drum kit, looks like a Depression-era huckster. Dr Fink, in what soon became his traditional surgeon's mask and gown, looks like he had been watching the bizarre antics of Ohio new wavers Devo.

In concert, 'Uptown' would be delivered as a final, audience-binding encore. The shows are remembered as a complete, carnal *pot-pourri* of mutated pop sexuality with a real edge of hunger. These kids from the middle of nowhere were making people sit up and show provincial weirdness some respect. *Dirty Mind* was a mission, a pervert's crusade.

History eventually showed it to be an opportune time for such an irreverent cocktail of influences, though the new model Prince did not enjoy immediate widespread acceptance. It was a significant period in the evolution of pop culture, especially in Britain, where it had always been inordinately productive and intense. The nihilistic posturing of punk had burned out to reveal, quite logically, a knowing, ironic, wilfully lightweight, pop-art sensibility. Intense cults of androgynous vanity and pure fancy dress had emerged, ironically rehabilitating a long-standing affection in British youth culture's heart for dance-orientated music from black America. Soul was about to be hip.

But even with David Bowie and the Rolling Stones featuring heavily in its back catalogue, Britain offered only a luke-warm welcome to this bizarre night-creature in mirror shades, naughty knickers and woolly leg-warmers. His first album had not even been released in the UK, and his second had earned the serious attention of black-music papers only. For *Dirty Mind*, though, WEA (Warner/Elektra/Atlantic) made strenuous efforts to attract the serious weekly rock papers, at that time still a vital force in 'breaking' new acts. According to one commentator close to the scene at the time, they even gave away free Prince-style flasher macs to journalists, the studs arranged on a panel that could be easily removed later on. One way or another, when Prince and his band visited Europe in June 1981, all three of the leading papers – *New Musical Express*, *Melody Maker* and *Sounds* – ran faintly bemused pieces in the then dominant style of gleeful irreverence. Was this man a prat? 'Posin' Til Closin' ', said the headline in *Sounds*, taking the line from a vintage clubland soul hit by the English band Heatwave. 'Some Day Your Prince Will Come,' countered *Melody Maker* the same week.

Prince planted some more disinformation . . . or was it? He said he had a jailbird brother; that he'd seen a shrink as a child because he was obsessed with sex; that he was thinking of giving up making records altogether. He played his show at the Lyceum theatre to a rather thin audience – many of them the recipients of complimentary tickets from the record company – and went back home. Everyone noticed how strange and shy he was. He had started an on-off love affair with his British public that would continue for years to come. None the less, he had at least announced his presence to the international rock market. It all helped in the construction of a power base.

'I had put myself in the hole with the first record,' Prince said in a later interview with Robert Hilburn of the *Los Angeles Times*. 'I wanted to remedy that with the second album. I wanted a "hit" album. It was for radio rather than for me, and it got a lot of people interested in my music. But it wasn't the kind of audience you really want. They only come around to check you out when you have another hit. They won't come to see you when you change directions and try something new. *That's* the kind of audience I wanted."

With *Dirty Mind*, he got it.

8

Controversy

Allen Beaulieu

Marvin Gaye had some ideas about the relationship between religion, romance and sex. His biographer David Ritz reports the following remark from Gaye upon meeting the teenage woman who became his wife, and would obsess his work from the hyper-erotic *Let's Get It On* until the end of his life: 'I saw her as more than a real girl. She suddenly appeared as a gift from God.'

In some of his most emotionally candid music, Gaye articulated the idea of sexual fulfilment as a kind of salvation. The son of a preacher – who would eventually take his life – Gaye sang songs in praise of women in a voice that expressed ethereal certitude and honeyed earthly innuendo in equal parts. *Let's Get It On* made explicit the coded messages that soul had been sending out for years. Parallels between love, sex and a sublime state of spiritual connection had infused and dramatized the evolution of soul, a form born of the meeting of black gospel and black blues, the spirit and the body organically connected in the search for higher ground; it is there in the work of Sam Cooke, Bobby Womack, Al Green, Aretha Franklin and a million more.

Funk grew out of soul, a militant, arrogant, madcap and more worldly progeny that influenced a big part of Prince's seventies adolescence. It openly celebrated the physical aspects of black culture that had always been there, sublimated in dance; no big deal, but they had scared the hell out of those guardians of white morality who thought sex was only for making babies, and not for showing love and having fun. Funk was about The Body: how it looked, what it did, all the hot, nasty, lovely, smelly things about it. God would have to shake His ass, or just stay home.

What Prince did with funk was remind it, curiously, of the sacredness it had left behind. He reintroduced the libido to the Holy Ghost. The explicit nature of *Dirty Mind*'s material had, in a sense, been its own manifesto, contextualized by the celebration of the 'Uptown' community and anti-politicized by the sentiments of 'Partyup'. Here was free sexual individualism proposed as the solution to the warped mind-set of the authorities and masses alike. Sex was the essence of life, life was the antithesis of war, and God was the Lord of peace. Within Prince's sexual promise, he hinted, lay the salvation of us all; an alluring, if lofty suggestion. And with *Controversy*, he attempted to ensrhine these sentiments in tablets of stone.

It didn't entirely come off. Although carefully worked out, the ideas at work in *Dirty Mind* had *felt* instinctive rather than theoretical. Its central philosophies had been formed conceptually, in Prince's mind, but for the most part the album did not elucidate the theory – it just described the practice. An intense, vaguely animalistic advocation of carnal pleasure suggested its own context only in the rhetoric of 'Partyup' 's closing chant. Sex, lewd and feverish, was its own reward on *Dirty Mind*. This made the record – its hard sound, its provocative antitheses of Good Taste – complete in its own dissident morality. It didn't *need* to explain itself.

Controversy though, was pure justification. And pontification. And self-importance – a *statement*. Side one offers a three-part education in the World According To Prince, commencing with his defence, moving on to his diagnosis, and only getting down to the real business at the end. Side two is basically a muddle. Released almost exactly one year after its predecessor (14 October 1981), it directly addressed the mystique generated by the *Dirty Mind* album and tour.

The result is a musical curate's egg, and a lot of muddle-headedness. *Controvery*'s cover announced its constituency with a spread of mock newspaper headlines as the backdrop to a head and torso shot of Prince modelling his first, slightly shabby version of the Edwardiana garb that would become his trademark as a world star. It refers to the *Dirty Mind* look, half confirming and half contradicting it. The studded trenchcoat, this time of pale lavender, remained, as did the 'Rude Boy' badge. But now, underneath the coat, he is sporting a starchy, wing-collared shirt, a black waistcoat and a matching judicial tie. What seems to be implied is a bizarre conjunction of stiff moral conservatism with a more contemporary kind of sleaze. His hairstyle, meanwhile, had gone through a further metamorphosis. After the Afro of *For You*, the flowing pageboy cut of *Prince* and the lank, subterranean punk coif of *Dirty Mind*, he had now rearranged himself so that a wiry wave fell down almost across his right eye but was swept back over the left. With a dash of kohl black to accentuate what is at once a heavy stare and a prissy one, he actually looks rather untidy: not so much a style guerrilla as an uptight eight-year-old in fancy dress.

And so, with the stark, upright pulse of the opening title track – fanfare and square-bash mixed in equal parts – Prince commenced to inspect the boundaries of his own reputation. The song 'Controversy' is one of the album's best tracks because it streamlines and polishes the punk-funk hybrid of *Dirty Mind* with such high finesse. You can't complain about the grooves – if that is quite the right word for so unyielding a rhythmic base. The hectoring pump action of the drum brings out slivers of synthesizer in lean, constricted curves. It is a definitive example of how keyboards took the place of horns in Prince's sound. But as well as changing the instrument, he also changed the emotional implication. The brass on, say, a Stax soul record tend to provide either bulging, ostentatious punctuation, or intense melancholia. On 'Controversy', the 'horns' are slaves to the beat. This is nothing to do with spurious distinctions between 'real' and 'artificial' instruments – simply the way the rhythmic elements are forced together, emphasized by layers of chanted vocals where he drops his falsetto for the first time. There is a combative, almost oppressive tension to the thing, which only the delicious chatter of chicken-scratch guitar manages to alleviate. At one point in the track, Prince begins grunting in time to the bass drum, half work-out, half coition. It is, of course, entirely appropriate that he should spell out his indignation within an aural landscape which subliminally suggests him to be fucking like a machine.

This musical eloquence is not matched by the lyric. Rarely has Prince sounded so obviously petulant or devoid of ironic edge. Oblique self-reference would eventually come to lie at the core of his appeal as a beautifully elusive pop identity, but 'Controversy' 's grand denunciation of the excited speculation generated by *Dirty Mind* is the opposite of the nudge-and-wink role-playing to come. 'Controversy' is the sound of one foot stamping.

Prince informs us that he does not want people *thinking* about him. To be dissected is to become a corpse, and from his first flush of fame, curiosity – as opposed to admiration – had made him feel like a piece of meat. In 'Controversy' he spits fire at the questions being asked about him. But by declining to provide any answers, he back-handedly endorses those questions. Is he black or white? Is he straight or gay? What's with the fuss? he complains. We might ask him the same thing. The obvious conclusion is that he loves the attention of fame, but not the questions it raises. Prince, remember, is responsible to no one, except maybe to the Lord, whose prayer he enunciates in a flat, multi-tracked monotone before reverting to the perfect order of that humping beat. Sex and God, he insists, are the only certainties in a world full of people trying to push a million definitions down your throat. But Prince does not want to have to work these problems out. Instead he craves a sweet, carefree state of eternal evasion.

This purging done with, the album clicks into the uptempo 'Sexuality', with just enough of a gap to lull you into a false state of relaxation. Again, the back-beat demands our servility, and this time the keyboards are meshed into a pounding percussive effect. There is more of that taut, breathless guitar detail, a kind of fanfare motif in the background, and a fierce two-line chorus which is prematurely curtailed by the impetuous re-entry of the verse. 'Sexuality' is nothing if not dynamic, and it advances a resolution to the hang-ups Prince perceived in his pursuers in 'Controversy'. Sexuality' derides these people as 'tourists'. The sexual universe is a domain on a higher plane to the rest of life's experiences, and those aspiring to it are dubbed the New Breed. In 'Sexuality', the love-making he describes is undoubtedly aggressive. But the final part of *Controversy*'s side-one trilogy advances a mood of impossible, glutinous tenderness.

'Do Me Baby' is the ballad André Cymone considered to be his tune, back when he and Prince were learning their trade as teenage session men and André was still André Anderson. It is a grand seduction piece on the theme of making up after breaking up. Prince interprets it as pure soft porn. The piquant melody is picked out on a piano, which echoes like the cheap soundtrack to a video peep-show. Synthetic strings are unleashed in a cascade of plastic passion. You can bet your backside that the bedclothes are a livid shade of mail-order pink, and barely out of the wrapper. The song finally dissolves into a torrent of swoops, screams, graphic, orgasmic sound-effects and snatches of whispered dialogue which are genuinely funny, though the humour is something several reviews – including a particularly stupid one in *Melody Maker* – missed. 'I'm not gonna stop until the war is over,' swelters our protagonist, switching from active to passive mode and back again in a bewildering repertoire of roles. As a piece of sheer kitsch, 'Do Me Baby' is too delicious for words. And yet it was also his most believable love ballad since 'Baby', on *For You*.

Side one of *Controversy* prepared the ground for Prince's full emergence into a period of pop where gesture replaced 'authenticity', and all the action took place on the surface. In Britain, this post-modernization of great chunks of popular culture was already well advanced, anticipated by the mix-and-match stylizations beneath punk rock's 'street' realism, and given huge scope for expression by the emergence of the promotional video as the setting for a million hand-me-down Hollywood dreams. But as the juvenile indignation of 'Controversy' showed, Prince was better off going with the flow of his own fantasy. There was no point flaunting a badge with 'Rude Boy' written on it, then complaining when people lined up to agree. And anger got in the way of his enigma, betraying a set of political confusions which just made him look daft.

For a man whose blend of dirty talk and dandysim has earned him the wrath of the new American Right, Prince has expressed, more than once, an unlikely allegiance to the tenets of the American Way. In the Farfisa organ throwaway 'Ronnie Talk To Russia' he implores Mr Reagan to shift his ass to the negotiating table before the Commies come and blow away the Land of the Free. 'Annie Christian', stuck at the centre of the side two's disorder, is a kind of catalogue of headline horrors which makes mention of the Atlanta child murders, the shooting of John Lennon, and the then recent assassination attempt on the President. Prince intones the words in an odd, flat monotone which adds further disruption to an unsettling drum machine palpitation, some ruptured, whining guitar and a swirling synthesizer figure. Between them, they edge as close to anti-music as he has ever come.

The character of the title is a symbol for the spirit which Prince considers responsible for inspiring those famous acts of violence, and the nightmarish combination of sound and zombie enunciation are left to speak for themselves. But Prince's explanation for the Annie Christian character does not add up, and connects directly back to the neuroses etched out in the album's title song. The root of her evil, it seems, was not some cosmic devilry, but the fame syndrome. Reagan's would-be killer, John Hinckley, told police that he imagined his act as 'a movie starring me'. Prince equated his Annie's wickedness with her urge to hit the headlines. So what did that say about himself up there, moralizing in the spotlight?

Dez Dickerson believes that Prince somehow constructed in his head an elaborate set of rationales for all the contradictions that other people saw. 'To a high degree it was a mish-mash. We never specifically discussed this. I feel that at some unconscious level he was not comfortable. He knew some things were wrong, that he was influencing young, young kids, toying with some potentially dangerous stuff. In order to justify this, he created this sort of new religion where it's OK, and God smiles on you. You're pioneering something. Once again, this special dispensation – he and I pal around togther, he lets me do things that he won't let other people do. His theology accomplished that, and he's got a whole belief-system to back it up.'

The quality of Prince's work from *Controversy* onwards, throughout his rise to global glory, would often depend on the flair and wit with which he could detach himself from the rest of us, and conjure up his own dreamlike coalition of beautiful illogic, set his own moral guidelines, create and control a secret garden of his own. So the best moments among the erratic sequence of songs that comprise *Controversy*'s weaker half occur when he lets go of his indignation, or just *gets down*. The closing 'Jack U Off,' which, unusually, was recorded with all of the band except Dickerson, is a bit of teenage wanking rudery, virtually Vegas-style compared to the trash and thump of *Dirty Mind*. Not very good.

100

'Let's Work' is hand-on-hip, preening synthesizer R & B, an enjoyable, if very basic example of what would shortly become known as the Minneapolis Sound. But the highlight of side two is the first track, perfectly, symbolically entitled 'Private Joy'. An impossibly pretty piece of bubblegum with a ringing melody line, Prince delivers it in his daintiest falsetto. It could be about anything: a girl, an inflatable girl, his dick. It is incorrigible, irresistible, and sweet enough to eat. Prince is no deity. Prince is no politician. Prince is a flirt.

Shortly before the launch of the *Purple Rain* movie in 1984, Morris Day's mother, LaVonne Daugherty, decided that Prince Nelson was 'a devil'. Since her time as Grand Central's temporary manager, Mrs Daugherty had seen her son go on to make a success of himself, just as Prince and André Anderson had done. And yet, after two big-selling albums with a group called The Time, and his imminent introduction to an international audience as a gifted film comedian, Day, endeavouring to break out as a solo performer, had no money, no clothes, no manager, and no ticket for the première of the film he was in. This is the way Pepé Willie tells it. He says, 'Morris didn't even know where the première *was*.'

At this juncture in their relationship, Messrs Day and Nelson were not on the best of terms. Morris, out in Santa Monica, got on the phone to Pepé Willie. 'He called me up at home and said, "Pepé, come and help me out, man." He said, "I'll pay you. I won't do you like Prince did you." '

Pepé Willie flew out to California and 'arranged a meeting with Mo Ostin', at that time the president of Warner Brothers; 'I wanted to know if we could count on his support.' For a man about to become a star, Day's situation does not seem to have been too good. He was in financial difficulties, and embroiled in a dispute with Prince's management over money. For whatever reason, the atmosphere between the two of them on the set of *Purple Rain* had been, to say the least, extremely tense. Once the shooting was complete, Morris Day had had enough. Relocating to the West Coast, he began laying plans for a career of his own.

Prince took offence at Day's decision. According to Pepé Willie, Day had been paying the other members of The Time – a substantially revised line-up of the original band – eight thousand dollars a month for a whole year, without even using them. But by Prince's reckoning, Day was plain neglectful, the absentee landlord of one of the hottest funk bands in America. 'Him and Prince was arguing about something on the set', remembers Pepé. 'I don't know exactly what it was about, but Prince was saying, "you owe me, you *owe* me".' The Time, after all, had been Prince's invention.

101

It is now well known that the first album attributed to The Time was in all essentials recorded by Prince with Morris Day on voice. The songs were Prince's too, except for the bubblegum teen pastiche 'After Hi School', by Dez Dickerson, and 'Cool', for which Dickerson provided words and Prince music. Self-titled, and containing six lengthy tracks, *The Time* was released in the US on 29 July 1981, shortly before the appearance of *Controversy*, with production credits jointly awarded to Morris Day and one Jamie Starr. The latter, credited for the first time as engineer on *Dirty Mind*, has long been assumed – though never officially admitted – to be just the first of several pseudonyms Prince came to use. Warner Brothers in Burbank seem to have been fully aware that the song that Prince demoed for them, 'Get It Up', was to be used for such a dummy group. They ordered up an album's worth. According to Jimmy Jam, Prince and Morris put most of it together 'in about four days'. Then, as Jam remembers it, a meeting of the relevant personnel was called: 'Prince more or less said, "We've done the album, and you're the group." We did our first gig a few weeks later.'

Jam's fellow keyboard player in The Time, Monte Moir, offers a more detailed recollection. 'Everybody kind of contributed, but Morris and Prince did the bulk of it. Lisa Coleman, I think, did some of it. The record was kind of happening as the band was getting together. Some of the songs were cut. It was started elsewere, and we came in at the end.' There are a dozen minor variations in the several accounts of this whole saga, some of which date Jam's involvement from much earlier than his own (hurriedly related) account suggests. But whatever the minor chronological details, no one involved has disputed who was ultimately pulling all the strings – including the purse-strings.

The original line-up of The Time was Jam and Moir on keyboards, Jellybean Johnson on drums, Jesse Johnson (no relation) on guitar, and Terry Lewis on base, with Morris Day as singer and personification of the whole Time *spiel*. It was these guys who Allen Beaulieu photographed in black and white for the début album's cover, looking like a cross between the Harlem Mob *circa* 1945, and the most dangerous homosexuals on earth.

This pretty-boy hoodlum look (also being explored in the same period by August Darnell/Kid Creole in New York) was originally a thrift-store concept. Most of the threads sported by The Time on the sleeve of both *The Time* album and its follow-up, *What Time Is It?*, were purchased at a small, *outré* Minneapolis second-hand clothing emporium called Tatters, on Hennepin Avenue and 24th Street. Proprietor Marc Luers did a roaring trade with The Time before they existed properly as a group. 'They were way ahead of the white kids. They just *knew* it: they knew the stuff, the double-breasted fifties and forties suits. Everything on that first cover we sold them, except the shoes.' Ironically, it was

Jerome Benton, the stage valet who was not acknowledged on record covers as a Time member until their third album (when the band was, to all intents and purposes, defunct), who discovered Tatters in 1980. 'Then they used to all come in. I used to find those bright tuxedo jackets that Morris always has, and if it was an absolute killer, he'd want it. I guess the best customers of all were Jerome and Jesse. They had to kind of show Monte the way. He was the only one who didn't sort of know what he was doing. Back in 1980, no one even knew what pleated pants were. But these guys'd want them all. And that was what they'd wear, all the time. They'd buy and buy and buy, two or three hundred dollars' worth at a time. You just don't have customers like that every day.'

The nucleus of The Time was lifted directly from homegrown funk heroes Flyte Tyme: Monte Moir, Lewis, Jellybean and Jam. Moir recalls that Prince had already indicated an interest in the band three years back, when he was just starting out with Warner Brothers himself; his talk of record deals had come to nothing. Now the show was back on the road, but with Morris Day, rather than Flyte Tyme, as the main beneficiary of Prince's goodwill. The initial idea was for Day, rather than Jellybean, to be the drummer, and Alexander O'Neal, who was then Flyte Tyme's vocalist, to do the singing. But as O'Neal later put it, 'I didn't see no point in being a star with no money', and he declined to accept the deal Prince was offering. O'Neal, as his former manager Craig Rice points out, was a little older than the rest of the line-up, maybe too old to be running off on shoe-string adventures that would be directed, controlled and paid for by someone else.

But the bottom-line reason for O'Neal's non-membership was probably a plain and simple clash of egos. It is not hard to find people speaking highly of Alexander in the Twin Cities. But at the same time he is hardly noted for his readiness to dance to other people's tunes; as more former managers than Craig Rice could testify. And Prince's desire to direct the careers of his protégés would soon become notorious. Monte Moir remembers a discussion in a Minneapolis restaurant, well before any recording took place. 'Me, Terry, Morris, Alex and Prince were there. Prince and Alex clearly didn't see eye to eye on matters financial and otherwise. Prince wanted him to be in it, I think. But within about 45 minutes', he understates, drily, 'it was clearly established that Alex was not going to be in the band.'

O'Neal went off to exercise his superb romantic baritone in the supper-clubs of the north and mid-west. His ship would take a little longer coming in. But for the most musically accomplished manufactured group of all time, Prince's patronage was the start of something big. The album *The Time* became an immediate R & B smash. It stomped, it posed, it purred. Never mind that the ballads drag, exposing Day's voice in the upper registers (as a singer, O'Neal inhabits a different universe) and

103

disrupting the deadly serious, comic narcissism with an attempt at sincerity. At the guts of the record was a novel of streetwise cartoon chic: sharp, vain, arrogant and a little bit naff. 'Funky' is not quite the word. The music wasn't sweaty or domineering enough to demand rapid movement on the dancefloor. Instead, it just leaned up against the bar thinking how beautiful it was. The Time came up with a little-big-time spoof of ghetto pimp realism. Maybe it is a record the small-town Prince would have put his own name to, if he'd decided to be 'black'.

'Get It Up' became the first song released under the name of The Time, a single which rose rapidly in the black music chart to number six. It was the beginning of a success story that would swiftly threaten to eclipse the star (or Starr) who gave it life. 'They were, to be perfectly honest, the only band I was afraid of,' Prince admitted in a 1986 radio interview in Detroit. 'They were turning into, like, Godzilla.'

The roots of the fight between Prince and Morris Day might be traced right back to The Time's foundations. Prince fostered the deal with Warner Brothers to create a vehicle for Day, and part of his incentive – aside from their friendship – was to repay him for a 'business favour', as it has since been described by both Day and Jimmy Jam. This 'business favour' was Day's agreement to let Prince include a song he had written on one of his albums, and let him take credit for writing it. The song in question was rumoured to be *Dirty Mind*'s 'Partyup'. Dez Dickerson, and others, empatically confirm this rumour to be correct. It was scarcely a deal struck between equals, as the subsequent balance of power between Prince and his creation bore out. But on stage, The Time threatened to make the 1982 *Controversy* tour, to which they were enlisted as support act, their triumph as much as Prince's.

Locally, the band is remembered with awe. 'These boys were *bad*,' says Q-Bear Banks. 'They would go on stage, and by the time they got through, you bin and sweated enough just from sitting in your seat screaming, wishing that you were on the stage just so's everybody could see you, "Oh, boy, I'm on stage with The Time!" *That's* how funky they were.' Jimmy Jam says that The Time's renditions of the songs Prince put together for them blew the vinyl to bits. On both the *Controversy* and *1999* tours, they continually threatened to upstage the headliner. Jesse Johnson later told the *New Musical Express* (29 November 1986) that 'we used to royally kick their ass every night'.

The only member of The Time not long resident in Minnesota, Jesse Johnson would also turn out (with Jellybean) to be its longest-surviving member, and it was he who took on the mantle of temporary leader while Day was absenting himself in California. Yet since the final dissolution of The Time in 1985, he has been the most outspoken in his dislike for Prince, his one-time patron and employer. Having grown up with white foster parents in Rock Island, Illinois, Johnson learned his out-of-sight guitar style working with rock acts in biker bars, is rumoured to have put in some uncredited session work for more than one high-profile southern boogie band, and was wooed to Minneapolis in the aftermath of *Dirty Mind*, thinking it might be his town of opportunity.

He made the acquaintance of Morris Day, and worked briefly with a band Day was leading at the time called Enterprise. By this point, circumstances had set Prince and his former Grand Central sidekick several worlds apart. Enterprise was reportedly a proficient but unre-markable band, whose biggest success – a one-off gig at the First Avenue club – was unlikely to be much improved upon. Morris Day was washing cars to supplement his income, and refers to this on a later Time song 'Onedayi'mgonnabesomebody'. Back in 1981, The Time concept must have looked like easily his best shot at redemption. He was more than likely very happy to have Prince set him up. Like the other members of The Time, sick and tired of slogging round the same old dead-end Twin Cities circuit, Day was delighted to be on the high road out of town; never mind the price he might ultimately have to pay.

But maybe he could already have seen some of his troubles coming. Even as The Time was taking shape in Prince's mind, the uneasy liaison between his ambition and his personal loyalties had fractured. In the summer of 1981, shortly after the *Dirty Mind* tour returned from Europe, André Anderson/Cymone left the band. It was not a happy farewell. 'The personal side of things began to get strained over a three- or four-year period,' explains Dez Dickerson. 'Resentment crept in. André knows that he's a talented person. It hurt him a lot that he didn't get what he felt he deserved.'

The exceptional musical empathy between Cymone and Prince had welded their teenage friendship. But with cash, credit and acclaim suddenly at stake, this very closeness became a lever, prising them part. A dispute over the authorship of 'Uptown' finally signalled the end after a steady descent into antipathy. 'The bass line of that song is based on something André came up with in a jam that we did at rehearsal,' says Dickerson. 'I know that was the final straw for him.' Extended, not to say relentless, jamming was the cornerstone of Prince's rehearsal ritual. Grains of ideas would be communally worked into shape, and finally emerge on records as fully fledged songs, 'written, produced, arranged and performed by Prince'. 'We jammed so much', says Dickerson; 'and it's so easy to pick up musical ideas and not remember where they came from. [But] it did reach a point where Prince would do it knowingly, because he had stretched himself so thin having to be the main source for all these spin-off acts [he had planned].'

Cymone stuck it out till the *Dirty Mind* tour was complete, only to have his chagrin redoubled by the allged theft of 'Do Me Baby' for *Controversy*. Prince, reportedly, challenged Cymone to sue him, which might be construed as an act of bravado or one of righteous conviction. Whatever, it would be five years before the two worked together again, Prince writing and co-producing one track, 'The Dance Electric', for Cymone's third solo album, *A.C.* – and being properly credited for his work. Underlying this unequal battle between two considerable creative egos was a deeper dispute whose origins went right back to their child-hoods. 'André felt that Prince wasn't doing enough to repay a debt that he felt he was owed because his family had virtually taken Prince in,' says Dickerson. 'He'd lived under their roof. André just felt slighted.'

More unhappiness followed his split with Prince. Under the management of Owen Husney, who still seemed like the one man in the Twin Cities with the right connections, Anderson secured what was, according to Mrs Anderson, 'one of the largest contracts that CBS had given out'. Two André Cymone albums, *Survivin' In The Eighties* and *Livin' In The New Wave*, were released, though not to an especially warm reception. Husney and André fell out over them: 'At that time [André] was not doing the kind of music that I felt was his best,' explains Husney. 'He was being very experimental. We had a lot of discussion on those first two albums. I felt that he could be doing other music that would build a base and get him off the ground a lot quicker. We had major disagreements about his direction.' The dissolution of their partnership resulted, again in Mrs Anderson's words, in a hard financial period for her youngest son: 'I don't know how the money was spent. He was in debt when he left Owen . . . you wouldn't believe.'

For a while, the contrast between the two friends' fortunes could not have been much greater. Part of that was to do with luck, but a lot of it may have been to do with personality. 'Prince is very dominating, and André would not be dominated,' summarizes Mrs Anderson.

André Cymone has more recently found success as a writer/producer. His collaboration with David Z on Jody Watley's solo album put him right back in the public eye. Meanwhile, Prince and he have patched their friendship up. 'If they're both in town they usually get close,' says Mrs Anderson, 'and I'm glad of that. When they connect in the summer they go some place and play basketball. I'm sure as the years go by they'll get closer and closer. André is much more of a home person. He comes back from California even now at least once a month. I remember one day some girls came up to the house and André was mowing the lawn. They almost had a fit: "Why is *André* mowing the lawn?" I said, "better him mowing it than me!" Prince has come to the house to see me too, and I know if I ever needed anything, all I'd have to do is call. But Prince is more private. Just a totally different personality.'

9

Apocalypse

Minneapolis Star Tribune

On Friday, 9 October and Sunday, 11 October 1981, just before the *Controversy* album was released, Prince's dream that his band might become 'the black Rolling Stones' underwent an unnerving collision with Caucasian reality. At the specific request of Mick Jagger, they were invited to open the two shows of the Los Angeles leg of the Stones' record-grossing tour of that year. The promoter was veteran West-Coast entrepreneur Bill Graham, and the venue, the Memorial Coliseum, had an audience capacity of around a hundred thousand. It looked like the break the group had been dreaming of. But humiliation lay just around the bend.

Dez Dickerson: 'I had been trying to tell Prince for a few weeks going into this that we may see something from this rock 'n' roll crowd that we're not used to seeing.' For two songs of the first show, Prince and company survived intact. They opened with 'Controversy' and continued with 'a fairly metallic version' of 'Why You Wanna Treat Me So Bad?' 'I remember, after we finished that song,' says Dickerson, 'I'd never heard so huge an ovation in my life. That moment stands out in my mind. But the next song that we played – I don't remember what it was – was a bit too black for that part of the audience that harboured ill-feelings towards black people.' Dickerson's own experience as a spectator at rock shows had prepared him for what then occurred: a few paper cups began landing on the stage. 'I had seen many, many shows where the *headlining* act got pelted with things out of *admiration*. That's rock 'n' roll. Culturally it's a different thing. Black audiences generally don't throw things unless they don't like what's going on.'

But after a time it became clear that these missiles were not necessarily being delivered out of appreciation either. 'You've got to remember', explains Dickerson, 'that there was a hundred thousand people there. If only 5 per cent of the audience are lunatics, that's a lot of people – five thousand of them out there that don't want you alive. We had never played in even a remotely hostile environment up until that point. You could see the confidence starting to drain out of Prince's face. He started looking around for somewhere to go.'

Prince's response to these alien circumstances was decisive and abrupt. 'Something else came up that wasn't a paper cup, and that was the last straw. He left. At the Coliseum there's this long red carpet that goes up these rows and rows of stairs out to the exit. I looked back and I saw this solitary little figure going up this red carpet. I thought, "He's hung us out to dry! We're out here playing, and he's gone!" Prince not only left the Coliseum, he left the state of California altogether, and by the Saturday he was back in Minneapolis licking his wounds. Mick Jagger called him; Bill Graham called him; his manager called him. Then on the Saturday evening, Dez Dickerson, still in LA with the rest of the band, gave it one last try. 'I talked to him for forty-five minutes, and finally I convinced him to come back.' Dickerson appealed to Prince's pride. 'I said, "Let's not let some dirtballs throwing things at us run us out of town. Let's finish it up in spite of what they do." And I said, "Look, this could be the beginning of crossing over into an audience that we both want to have access to, the start of being all things to all people – a rock 'n' roll band as well as an R & B band." '

But as Dickerson puts it, 'the first show was a cakewalk compared to the second'. After Prince's early exit from Friday's performance, Bill Graham himself had come on stage and bawled the audience out. The resultant boos came across loud and clear on a couple of live radio broadcasts, and within twenty-four hours the story had been twisted to read that Prince had been effectively booed off the stage. 'To the moment that we stopped playing, there were only scattered boos,' insists Dickerson. 'For the most part the reception was good. But by the next day, the whole vibe was, "Well, we had gotten booed off stage, and hey, we'll really get 'em on Sunday." '

For Sunday's show, the neanderthals came prepared. 'The first thing I saw was a plastic bag full of old grey chicken parts. Someone had taken the time to take the chicken out of the refrigerator on Friday and let it sit out in the sun for two days . . . it was pretty disgusting.' They threw anything they could lay their hands on. They threw shoes. They threw big, full bottles of Jack Daniels. The LA shows marked the first appearance of teenage bass-player Mark Brown as André Cymone's replacement. 'He got hit by a half-gallon jug of orange juice. It was pretty wild.'

Dickerson's success in talking Prince round after the opening Stones show is an indication of their relative closeness in the first years of the band's existence. While Cymone started out as an intimate and ended up estranged, Dickerson became Prince's main confidant. But the following two years would see a change in Prince's relationship not just with Dickerson, but with all the musicians around him. The start of his rise to the top marked the beginning of his descent into the isolation of fame.

Talking Prince into coming back from Minnesota yielded one exceptional accolade for Dez Dickerson, not a man easily given to bitterness: 'That was the only time that I can remember Steve Fargnoli saying "thank you" to me.' With the best will in the world, it is not easy to find anyone claiming to actively *like* Steve Fargnoli. The terms of abuse employed to describe him behind his back are many and varied. It should be noted that big-time rock 'n' roll managers rarely win popularity contests judged by those whose affairs they run. Let us just say that more than a few who have worked in Fargnoli's proximity consider him the personification of one of chat-show host David Letterman's 'weasels' – his unflattering term for specious Hollywood operators. That said, Fargnoli has come to command the intense loyalty of Prince himself. The evolution of their mutual trust proceeded throughout the *Controversy* tour of 1981, and by the end of the following year Prince's removal from the bosom of his band to the bosom of his management structure was complete.

Controversy marked a major escalation of the Prince operation. *Dirty Mind* had not been a big seller – it did not even reach sales of half-a-million till after *Purple Rain* – but the enthusiasm of critics had created the possibility that Prince could become a serious contender for a vast 'crossover' audience, a kind of rock 'n' roll dream come true. *The Time*, meanwhile, had been a serious hit with R & B crowds. Together, Prince and The Time now amounted to a major draw, pulling together bedrock black dance fans, New Wavers, and many of those in between. And their cause was in no way damaged by the addition to the *Controversy* tour of Roger Troutman's splendidly idiosyncratic Zapp band, an Ohio-based operation which was mining its own eccentric seam of electronic funk. It was the first chance Prince had had to headline a tour from beginning to end. The itinerary was set to take in a mixture of theatres and indoor arenas chosen according to the strength of public support from region to region. For Prince's band, there was the promise of escalating success, a chance to explore the potential implied by the Stones support slot. For The Time, there was the thrill of breaking out of the Twin Cities at last. It was an optimistic party. 'Everybody was pretty cool,' remembers Monte Moir. 'We were just happy to be doing something after years of playing around here.' Flyte Tyme had progressed to opening Twin Cities shows for Cameo and The Barkays, 'kind of always on the verge of getting something going. So it was a big turn-on for us.'

In the classic rock 'n' roll fashion, The Time took their opportunity and worried about the consequences later. The band's initial work-outs together took place in the limited upstairs confines of Terry Lewis's house: 'real makeshift', laughs Moir. They threw themselves into the *Controversy* tour with no contracts, no job security, and a wage from Prince's organization of $140 each per week: a pretty meagre sum for an important support act on a full-scale, major-label tour. 'We asked to have something on paper very early on,' says Moir, 'when we first started rehearsing, and Prince said, "Oh, you don't need paperwork. You know, it's kind of a two-way thing. If you guys get pissed at me you could pack up and leave on the road, and I'm stuck." ' With hindsight, Moir thinks The Time were mistaken accepting these terms: 'In the end, financial matters were the main reason the group broke up.' But back then, Prince's favoured terms made a crude kind of sense. Moir's feelings on the matter are now rather mixed: 'I don't think we ever got the money we were due. So in the end it ended up just being a stepping-stone. In return we got the chance to get our names out there. It wasn't fair in that [i.e. the contractual/financial] sense. But what we got out of it as a learning experience was good. In other ways, we were helped very much.'

Plus, there was the management clout of Cavallo, Ruffalo and Fargnoli pretty much on a plate: 'Prince said, "I already made a bunch of mistakes. Now we know how to avoid it with you guys." ' It was a swings and roundabouts arrangement whose pros and cons would beome apparent, sometimes grimly, to many others in the following years: exposure and opportunity versus near-penury and subjugation to an artistic paternalism with an autocratic streak.

Meanwhile, Prince was shifting his stage presentation away from the spartan provocation of *Dirty Mind* towards something a little more plush, introducing props and choreography, and making the best use of the talents of his lighting engineer Brian Bennett. Through a combination of accident and design, the 'theology' Dez Dickerson described began to express itself in rock theatre. One of the most striking moments of the *Controversy* production took place during the performance of the song itself. For this tour, Bobby Z's drum kit was set up on a riser towards the rear of the stage. Gantries ran up either side, joined by a lateral catwalk behind the drums at the back. At the centre of this catwalk, forming a partial backdrop, was a mock-up of a stained-glass window – the same set-up featured in the videos for the singles of 'Controversy' and 'Sexuality'. 'He would go up on the catwalk', remembers Dickerson, 'and stand in front of the window with his arms out.' Dickerson is doubtful that this was originally intended to echo the crucifixion – 'it was never openly discussed as such' – but suspects Prince picked up the possible implication of the image he had created from another source. 'He would avidly read the reviews as soon as they came out the next day. I don't know whether someone read that into it, and he decided, you know. "Hey, maybe I'll do that every night." I do think that whole thing spawned something, whether he did do it on purpose or whether it was an accident. I think he definitely, purposefully started to go down that path after a bit.'

This 'crucifixion' ritual notwithstanding, the full-blown costume dramatics which became Prince's trademark were still in their infancy. But the *Controversy* tour's burgeoning sense of rock 'n' roll kitsch, mixed in with the raw punk-funk nerve, served as an overture towards the white audience. Steadily, it began to bear fruit.

'I would say the demographic began to shift towards, say, 70 per cent black and 30 per cent white,' remembers Dickerson. 'The reaction of the audience was beginning to resemble more a rock audience.' This gave the rock 'n' roller in Dez a kick. 'In my formative years I went to the Led Zeppelin shows and the Grand Funk shows and Deep Purple, and that was what I was accustomed to. So seeing that change, and seeing that that's what our audience was becoming . . . It was kind of neat to see that happen.' And that went for Prince as well. For Dickerson, this was the point where the band hit on the right combination of rockability and R & B style. 'There was still enough free-form stuff so that it didn't look like it was one tremendous Broadway play. The mixture of the two I think people found really interesting, before everybody on the circuit started doing little steps.'

As ever, Prince had rehearsed the band rigorously in preparation for the two month *Controversy* schedule. After such a punishing régime, the usual exhaustions of touring were a positive luxury. Dez Dickerson's Romeo days were not so far behind him that he couldn't appreciate a touch of class. 'At that time I guess I did enjoy it. Having come from a background of having to work real hard for eight or nine years for very little money, it was nice to travel comfortably, and stay in nice hotels. Being on the road was like a vacation.'

But by the time the *Controversy* tour was over, relationships at all levels of the Prince entourage had undergone substantial reorientations. Within his own band, there was the distinct feeling that their leader was becoming more and more remote. Dictatorship at first hand was one thing: emotionally wearing, perhaps, but to a degree understandable, and not without its creative rewards. Less easy to take was the feeling that decisions were increasingly being handed down from on high, heavily influenced by persons outside the band. Mark Brown, plucked from the Twin Cities circuit, where he led his own band, Fantasy, pays elaborate testimony to Prince's detachment from the other musicians. His closeness with Steve Fargnoli provokes Brown to particular abrasion. 'I never had too much time for him. We never really clicked. He never spent enough time caring about us. He only cared about Prince and his money.

He didn't care about nobody or anything else. He didn't care about anybody but himself.'

Brown's disenchantment was probably the greatest. But Dez Dickerson too was feeling increasingly isolated from Prince. Their relative intimacy was gradually becoming as much a problem for the ascending star as a blessing. 'One of the things within the whole organization is the definite distance that people that work for him keep from him in terms of what they are and are not willing to say. There was a lot of the yes-man syndrome that went on. Again, the relationship that he and I had . . . I *think* that he had a different kind of respect for me, because I would tell him what was on my mind, and my wife would tell him what she thought about things. On the one hand I think it was refreshing to him, and on the other hand I don't think he wanted to hear about it.'

Prince was becoming more and more cocooned within the superstructures that served his galloping ambition. As his power and success increased, so he retreated all the more from anyone or anything who might cause him to doubt his own convictions. As the logistics of career moves became more complex, and the possibilities of conquest soared, his erstwhile collaborators sensed him embrace the more closely those who seemed most able to sustain him in his dream. In keeping with this, Prince was able to let his antipathy towards the press off the leash. The town-by-town interviews which gave him such grief – and such mischievous gratification – on the *Dirty Mind* tour had been reduced to a trickle for *Controversy*, the most famous of which (with Barbara Graustark for *Musician* magazine) was the last remotely detailed explanation he would give of himself on any media platform for four years.

From now on, Prince would let his mystique generate its own set of explanations. His flight from the probings of journalists became complete after a brief, tense exchange with *Los Angeles Times* critic Robert Hilburn to promote the album which would finally fulfil his crossover fantasies, *1999*. 'Prince seemed to cringe as the door swung open at his West Hollywood hotel room,' Hilburn wrote. 'As an aide from [his] . . . management company ushered a reporter into the room, the young singer's doleful eyes suggested the sad resignation of a fugitive cornered after a long chase.' According to this piece, there were four interviews planned for the promotion of the record. But after his apparent ordeal with Hilburn, His Royal Badness blew the rest of them out. Perhaps he had already figured out that 'crossover' is not best served by the precise definitions reporters seek from their subjects. 'There's a certain type of people who may dig what we're doing, but won't even listen to it because of the stereotypes or whatever,' said Prince to Hilburn. 'I'm real proud of the new album, and I'd hate to have things get in the way of it.'

Steve Fargnoli and the management team were not the only important component in Prince's new inner circle by the end of the *Controversy* tour. Another was Prince's most famous personal bodyguard, Big Chick Huntsberry, a man destined for legend. Big Chick did not sing or play or know how to write a song. But his influence on Prince's state of mind should not be underestimated: Big Chick kept the world at bay. 'When I first met him, he wouldn't do *anything*,' explains Huntsberry, still incredulous after all these years, 'he wouldn't even walk out to the soundboard by himself.' For Prince, so Huntsberry has it, a trip to the local shops would have been a walk in the valley of the shadow of death. Chick became his guardian angel.

Huntsberry was originally appointed for the *Controversy* tour. He'd already accumulated plenty of experience at the head-banging end of the rock spectrum. After that, Prince's still predominantly black audience came as something of a culture shock. 'When I went to work for Prince, after all these hard-rock groups, it was like *church*. I couldn't believe it!' He got off to a bad start with his new employer. 'I was used to smacking people, you know. I thought, "Man, this is too easy. I'm gonna have to make some trouble!" I remember the first night. It was in Richmond, Virginia. I threw this curtain back, and there stood this black guy. He didn't have a back-stage pass or anything, so I started to take him off, like a gentleman, you know. The guy says, "Take your hands off me, you white piece of shit." ' Huntsberry went into action: 'I hit him. Down he went. I jumped down and kicked him about three, four times, rammed his head into the wall four or five times . . . The road manager walked in – a black guy named Hewitt – he says, "Tell you something, big man. You gonna have to change your ways if you wanna stay with Prince." '

According to Huntsberry, Prince had already made it clear that he didn't want the big man around: 'When he looked through the peephole [in his hotel room], all he saw was my big shadow. He says, "How can I tell this guy what to do?" ' The road manager, to whom the question was addressed, asked how exactly he was supposed to go about firing a man of six foot six, who looked like three Bible-belt farm hands welded together and weighed over 300 pounds. 'Prince said to him, "That's your problem." '

Big Chick hung on for about a week, and finally Prince had a change of heart. He attributes his reprieve to the adoption of a slavishly simple principle. 'Anything he would ask me to get him, or do for him, I would do it. It's so easy to say "No". So I figured, "Anything he wants, I'll do it." 'Cause at first, everybody used to say "No" to him. It would be, you know, "We can deal with that later on." But I babied him. I spoiled him, man.'

Huntsberry thinks it is no coincidence that with him on twenty-four-hour call, Prince put together the record that would make everybody

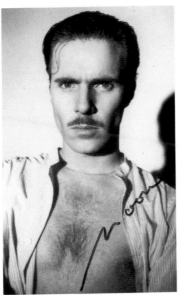

Crowd outside 1st Avenue club for one of Prince's 'secret' gigs. Whiteness of throng indicates this is post-*Purple Rain*. Black guy with burger is KMOJ DJ Walter 'Q-Bear' Banks. (*Minneapolis Star Tribune*)

Chris Moon, *not* as he is usually seen

Paisley Park studio complex with Minnesota foliage in foreground (*Minneapolis Star Tribune*)

Paisley Park mixing board (Tim Roney/Retna)

'No pictures . . .' London, BPI Awards Show, 1985 (Rex Features)

'. . . or else.' Big Chick leads the way. (Rex Features)

Big bad axe-man, London Lyceum, 1980 (André Csillag/Relay)
Black man in blouse and diamond necklace shock (Rex Features)
Working out on *Parade* tour, 1986 (John Bellissimo/Retna)
Sign 'O' The Times, Europe, 1987 (Erwin Gunter/Retna)

At Madison Square Gardens with
Sheila E, September 1986 (Gary Gershoff/Retna)
Inset: 'Excuse me!' (Gary Gershoff/Retna)

André, Prince and Dez, London, 1980 (Tony Mottram/Retna)
Parade soul revue, with Greg Brooks, Jerome Benton, His Royal Badness (Michael Putland/Retna)

Parade tour, 1986: Atlanta Bliss, trumpet; Wendy Melvoin, guitar; Eric Leeds,
saxophone; Prince, supplicant posture (John Bellissimo/Retna)

Parade finale (uncredited)

Fargnoli, Himself, and a red rose on *Lovesexy* tour bus, London, 1988
 (Mark Anderson/Retna)

The famous Steve Fargnoli (Mark Anderson/Retna)

Meet the press, London, 1988 (Mark Anderson/Retna)

else around him start saying 'Yes'. The double album *1999* was in most essentials recorded in Prince's own studio, located at his new home on Lake Minnetonka, out there with all the rich white folks Cornbread Harris talked about. This famous purple house, right on the waterfront, surrounded by an imposing black wire fence, was the secluded setting for his most impressive burst of creativity yet.

1999 was a record made in the image of Prince's 'crossover' dream. Musically, lyrically, conceptually, it loosed itself from the shrill indignation of *Controversy* and projected instead a profound abandonment to the extremes of his 'theology', in a manner which was more natural, more seductive and seemingly without further need for self justification. It was also the first record he put together from a position of relative autonomy and fame. It is rather a luxurious affair, simultaneously sexy and funny, and full of such spiritual indulgences as are often practised by those whose immediate thirst for attention has been quenched. Its whole sensibility suggests the product of a different emotional environment.

Released as a single on 22 September 1982, the title track remains one of Prince's fullest articulations of his longing to reconcile licentiousness and godliness under one hybrid groove. It was also his most programmable 45 yet. '1999' brings together the wipe-out bravura of heavy rock and the carnal sophistication of funk, and whisks them into the consistency of a driving anthem. Lyrically, too, the impulses of the two genres achieve a seamless blend. A generation of young white US males had soused their adolescence in the apocalyptic obsessions of heavy metal: implied in the screaming pantomime oblivion of everyone from Kiss to AC/DC was some death-and-glory vision of abandonment to Armageddon, or a metaphor for it. In '1999', Prince achieved a vivid fusion of HM cosmic destruction with the redemptive blend of physicality and spirituality which lies at the core of soul. The result is a thumping dance record which sees the final countdown as a stairway to heaven itself. Sex was a way of welcoming death.

Chick Huntsberry was particularly well equipped to nurture the confidence a man whose religious convictions existed within the perceived context of inevitable, ultimate violence. Earlier in his life he had worked as an evangelist, preaching door to door. On the other hand, he had, in his own words, 'been to hell. The devil took me over.' Huntsberry had bounced in biker bars, smuggled dope from Cuba, wrecked airplanes, been in shoot-outs, seen it all. He had lived his life on both sides of the Lord. On the *Controversy* and *1999* tours, he joined the band in their regular, ritual prayers before taking the stage. 'I'd always pray, "Protect the crowd, protect Prince, the band, myself . . ." I knew how to pray. I knew how to cover the crowd with the blood of Jesus.' Not for a minute does Huntsberry think Prince's devoutness was a stunt. 'Prince loves God,' he insists, seemingly as certain in this knowledge as of anything in the world. 'He believed in God, he loved God, and he prayed. That's still no excuse for going out and jacking off a guitar and all this kind of thing. But I don't think he really actually knew . . . he didn't think he was doing anything wrong. He didn't know no better.'

Whatever, in '1999', Prince's conceptualization of the Earth's destruction still manages to fall right into line with that of the new Christian Fundamentalists, who believe that it is the world's rightful destiny to be consumed in cleansing flame. It was at once a joyous and chillingly contemporary vision. The Lord's final solution was to be welcomed, for it would deliver us to Him. Party!

Heralded by this livid unification of the sacred and the profane, the *1999* tour was the one that finally bounced Prince across the race line, and turned him into that curious post-war animal, the rock messiah. And the key song in this was not the morbidly euphoric '1999' itself, but the track that follows it on the album, 'Little Red Corvette'. Released as a single in February 1983, part-way through the tour, the song moved swiftly into the national Top 40, bringing with it a fundamental change in the composition of the audience. '*1999* was 90 per cent black until "Little Red Corvette" came out,' remembers Monte Moir, 'and all of a sudden it shifted, drastically. It got to be half and half, if not 60–40 white. By the end of that tour, depending on what city, you could see that real crossover was possible.'

What set the *1999* LP apart from Prince's previous releases was his new-found comfort with his self-consciousness. The shift from the neurotic polemic of 'Controversy' to the exquisite fatalism of '1999' seemed to liberate a whole extra facet of his creativity. 'Little Red Corvette' is just one example of a dimension of sheer *playfulness* which had been only a submerged part of his work before the *1999* LP. Drawing directly from the rich motorvating history of rock 'n' roll imagery, Prince re-upholstered an established catalogue of car/girl/coital conquest metaphors to reflect his own all-concerning persona. 'Little Red Corvette' suggested the vision of Chuck Berry, focused through the false eyelashes of Little Richard; the swollen freeway romance of Bruce Springsteen, suffused with a parodic, purple braggadocio. He even smirks at his own history of sexual boasting as the music builds to a vintage teenage dream chorus, and Prince moves with blissful inevitability towards his triumphant score.

'Little Red Corvette' went out with a promotional video that aped the stage chemistry of the Rolling Stones, and was only the second to cross the informal colour bar of MTV. At each crucial moment, Dez Dickerson bounds over from stage left for a buddy-boy share of Prince's mike. The star himself hams it up a hundredweight, imperiously tossing an expanding crop of curls, sulking, pouting, playing the song's perfectly clichéd melodrama to the hilt. It was a 'performance' video – heavily mannered and extremely primitive when compared to the consummately design-conscious epics already flooding the market from the other side of the Atlantic – but no matter: it had a gauche good humour, and assisted the first rogue single Prince had released – the first, that is, not honed to the requirement of black radio – to make nonsense of racially defined musical categories, in terms of sales as well as style. It became a national Top 10 single in the spring of 1983, and catapulted him, mid-tour, into another entertainment universe. Prince's progress was begining to look like the latest American Dream drama.

Even the *1999* stage show metamorphosed into a ceremonial set-piece. 'He used the phrase all the time, "more like a play",' Dez Dickerson recalls, 'so the action would change from scene to scene.' *1999* hadn't started out that way. 'It was a bit more tightly rehearsed than the others but at the beginning we still had a little bit of the edge from the previous tours. However, we polished it off as we went along, so it became this really well-rounded, well-polished . . . *show*. It worked real well. People loved it.'

The flamboyance of Prince's aspirations had already been amply her-alded by the concept of the *1999* album. *Controversy* had consolidated his standing as a critical success. On top of that, he could now fill arenas in certain parts of the country, when topping the right sort of bill, proving he was developing into the kind of major black draw who could also attract whites. For one thing, *1999* was a double album, and it was highly unusual for a black artist to be granted so grand a platform for expression. The four sides of vinyl housed a mere eleven songs, but each one of them had the air of an epic about it. While 'All The Critics Love U In New York' seems a little *too* petulant, and 'Something In The Water (Does Not Compute)' is just plain obscure, 'Delirious' is a dizzy, silly little pleasure and 'D. M. S. R.' – Dance, Music, Sex, Romance – can only be described as an anthem. It was the closing track, 'Interna-tioanl Lover', which became the vehicle for Prince to make the most public exhibition yet of his blossoming iconic Self.

In concert, 'International Lover' turned into a set-piece of kitsch titillation, centred entirely on Prince's apparently limitless libido. But it was a song whose sensory impact was directed as much at the funny bone as the erogenous zone. On record, it is a piece of giggly soft-porn nonsense. The late-night cocktail-bar musical setting becomes increas-ingly surreal as Prince transforms into erotica's aviator and invites his chosen last dance partner to come into his cockpit. The routine safety-drill announcements of modern air travel are distorted into a kinky, murmured sweet-talk, interspersed with bursts of coital 'turbulence'. Prince performed the song on stage aboard a giant four-poster bed, hydraulically pumped up from underneath the stage. With screens and lights strategically positioned, a silhouetted Prince would ceremonially hump his invisible companion at an actual height of somewhat less than thirty thousand feet.

The transforming of the Prince show into a spectacle of bawdy narcissism complemented his elevation to major stardom. His resolution of the style-conflict between New Wave, pop, rock and funk was to dissolve them all in a grand exhibition of exotic absurdity: glam decadence as the complete panacea. And his new role of regal overseer was underlined by the full package of the *1999* tour. For this extended itinerary, both support acts were his own creations, and inspired the title of The Triple Threat Tour: The Time, and the newly-hatched Vanity 6, the ultimate in pneumatic female cut-outs.

The evening would commence with Vanity, Susan Moonsie and Brenda Bennett (Mrs Brian Bennett) panting, bending and flexing their way through about twenty minutes of low-grade vamping silliness, dressed only in their frillies. Behind a screen, members of The Time would churn out the music, some of which they themselves had written for the first, mildly excruciating, Vanity 6 album. A young singer from Ohio called Jill Jones (who also makes some memorable contributions to *1999*) was employed to soup up the vocals from the wings. Vanity 6 already had a smutty little R & B hit to their names – the anatomically specific 'Nasty Girl' – and their entirely ludicrous repertoire served well enough in scoring a few easy warm-up points before Morris Day and company took the stage.

By the time of this, their second full-scale jaunt with the Prince bandwagon, Morris, Jimmy, Terry, Monte, Jesse and Jellybean had really got their act down hard. Their second album, *What Time Is It?*, was a big improvement on the slightly stilted début, and enjoyed just as much consumer support. Tracks like 'Wild And Loose', 'The Walk' and the great '777 9311' - Dez Dickerson's phone number in those days, but not for long – became instant Time favourites, songs which helped develop Day's role into something considerably larger than life. Gradually, The Time's whole jive-ass charabanc built up such a head of steam that they began to threaten the supremacy of their creator himself. 'They got to the point where they were just really, really, making us look bad,' says Dez Dickerson – 'bad', in this sense, meaning bad.

The Time was taking on a life of its own. On their first tour, they had evolved sufficient chemistry and confidence to enable them to have a more assertive input into the creation of *What Time Is It*? 'When push came to shove,' Monte Moir admits, 'it was still down to Prince.' But the group was now tough enough in its own right to make their songs emphatically their own when they got in front of a crowd. What's more, they had an incentive: the whole situation with Prince and his inner circle was beginning to piss them off. 'Some of the reviews were starting to say we were doing better shows,' says Moir, 'and he hated that. So it

118

was like, he'd started this thing, and it had got to be bigger and bigger. He liked it, but he hated it. He'd done something good, but now he wanted to tear it apart.'

The *1999* tour audiences could not fail to get a kick out of the ultra-sheen spit and polish of The Time's cool funk, and Morris Day was the star icing on a very tasty cake. Rubber-faced, vain as hell, and perpetually primed for the main chance with the ladies, Day's projection of himself as the impossible essence of downtown ostentation was immaculate. The famous routine where roadie-turned-stage-valet Jerome Benton would smarm on stage and hold up a mirror so that Day could check his grooming was already passing into funk folklore. The Time's set even came to dictate the opening pace of Prince's. 'We'd come on and do forty minutes of just dance stuff,' remembers Moir. Three dance tunes, a ballad and then a hot-foot sequence to home. After Vanity 6, and then this, Prince inclined to featuring slow numbers like the rock ballad 'Free' at the beginning of his own set. 'People got a bit worn out,' says Moir.

As the tour continued, The Time set about their business with even greater gusto.'The playing was always fun,' says Moir, 'especially because there were so many other distractions and tensions building up. The stage was the one spot when there weren't any.' Maybe the decline was inevitable. Certainly Prince's relationship with the men of The Time seems to have been ambivalent from the start. 'I think he probably got on better with us than his own band in certain respects,' reflects Moir. 'He'd sometimes ride on our bus with us. In some ways he wanted to be one of the guys with us, I think. I think he envied us, 'cause we were always hanging out, and we were all real close. We were just friends.'

Moir says that in the final analysis, The Time was regarded as Morris Day's band. But that was more due to the way management would deal with him separately than a reflection of how the line-up saw itself. This was a very different set-up to that among the headliners. 'He [Prince] told Morris one time he felt that the only way to get people to do what you wanted them to was to put yourself *up here* and scream at 'em. Morris said to him, "Why? We're all friends. I don't need to yell at anyone. All we've gotta do is talk about it." ' Whatever, Prince might have found it hard-going, waving the big stick at The Time: 'It wasn't quite so much the case with us, I don't think, 'cause we were a gang of guys. With other people and with his band he was always very much the dictator. But he was threatened by us. He didn't want to walk into the middle of, like, ten guys, and start saying, "You do this".'

The Time's flourishing celebrity was becoming a mini-phenomenon in its own right. Their in-store promotions at the towns the tour visited would result in Morris Day being mobbed. Monte Moir remembers with astonishment the first occasion The Time went with Prince to Detroit, always a big town for both acts. 'Me and Jellybean, the two least visible members of the band, walked out the hotel to go to a McDonald's, and we just couldn't believe it. We literally had to get up and leave, 'cause there were just so many people coming up to us.'

The Prince roadshow was turning into a major event in a year yet to be seized by the dance fever of Michael Jackson's *Thriller*. His own promotional public appearance first came to require the support of elaborate security operations, and then eventually became completely impossible to conduct. Chick Huntsberry would have dummy limos set up out front, and a discreet getaway saloon parked outside some discreet side entrance. At one appearance in Atlanta, set up with no advance publicity, the crowd was proceeding in orderly file up one escalator to meet Prince, then straight down another and out of the store. Then Huntsberry heard 'a bunch of racket downstairs, and this police sergeant comes up and says, "Hey!, They're rioting. There's *five thousand* kids down there, screaming." I looked at Prince and said. "It's time to go!" '

While Prince and The Time turned up the heat for the ticket-buying public, relations back-stage came to crisis point. With their success, various members of The Time were beginning to speculate upon, and be offered, opportunities to build parallel careers outside the group, where their financial situation had improved only slightly from the *Controversy* tour's modest $140 a week. According to Monte Moir, Prince's response was decidedly cool. 'He didn't want anybody doing things outside. He wanted to keep control. He said, "You got all these opportunities here, right?" But everybody could see that the opportunities were there when *he* felt they should be. It was all his show.'

The story of how Jimmy Jam and Terry Lewis were fired from the band has since become a cornerstone of Prince mythology, a yardstick by which detractors measure the extent of what they see as his dictatorial paranoia. A business trip to the West Coast had given the pair the chance to write, play and produce a track called 'Lock And Key' (from the album *A Meeting In The Ladies Room*) for Klymaxx, a sci-fi chic girl funk group with Dick Griffey's popular Solar label. It was the first fruit of a partnership that would go on to rival Prince as the most powerful creative and business entity in the Twin Cities – Flyte Tyme Productions.

According to Jam, Prince expressed his displeasure to him and Lewis even at that first, fairly minor disobedience. But their best business contact in LA was one Clarence Avant, founder of the soul label Tabu, who had an international marketing and distribution arrangement with the CBS imprint Epic. Through Avant, they hit upon the chance to produce the SOS Band. A day off on the *1999* tour gave them the (probably welcome) opportunity to spend some time in the studio with Mary Davis and the boys. In order to get to the following night's show in Atlanta, they booked themselves on to the one and only connecting flight out of San Antonio, theoretically giving themselves plenty of time to make the pre-show preliminaries. But a freak snowstorm resulted in all planes being grounded for the day. That night, in Atlanta, Jerome Benton strapped on his half-brother's bass and mimed, while Prince himself filled the gaps in the rhythm section from the wings of the stage. When Jam and Lewis finally caught up with the roadshow, His Royal Badness handed them – metaphorically speaking – their cards.

Jam does not attribute this sacking to non-attendance pure and simple. 'Prince didn't want to break the group up, but the snowstorm provided the excuse he needed to fire us two. He thought we were off seeing some girls. The first thing that came out was, "Ha ha, serve you right for chasing women." Then he saw our picture in *Billboard* or something with the SOS Band, and all that changed. Seems like it was OK to be off seeing girls, but not OK to be furthering your own career.' But the twin pillars of Flyte Tyme Productions could be pretty hard-headed themselves. (When it comes to business, their reputation says they still are). 'We had already issued an ultimatum on the whole subject. I was nothing but a keyboard-player in The Time, and that was OK, but really it was Morris's group. We had a writing talent and we wanted to exercise it. We did different stuff on those outside projects anyway. We could never figure out what the big deal was.'

By this time, Cavallo, Ruffalo and Fargnoli had delegated one of their juniors, a Ms Jamie Shoop, to look after the immediate affairs of The Time. She was, in the opinion of Monte Moir, 'wonderful. Our relationship with her was great. But with the company as a whole, it was not so good. They mainly only dealt with Morris. To them, we were just the band, which didn't help any.' The attitude the band detected in Prince intensified after the departure of Jam and Lewis. His friendship with Morris Day was already strained, and if anything, guitarist Jesse Johnson was becoming the one Time member he felt able to communicate with.

The situation cannot have been helped by the increasingly hectic activity of the period. During the second half of the *1999* tour, various scriptwriters had been flown in to consult about a possible feature film to be shot soon after. Dancing and acting lessons were in the pipeline for many of Prince's entourage, in preparation for this latest, grandest scheme. But just when Prince most needed to keep his empire together, it showed signs of falling apart. 'After he fired Jimmy and Terry, he called me up,' remembers Monte. 'We talked for about an hour. He said, "Well, we're gonna do this and that. We're gonna do a movie."' But for Monte Moir, the story was pretty much over. 'My relationship with him was fairly distant. He was always giving people shit, a lot of times. That was kind of his way of communicating. He'd just walk in and start giving somebody shit.

'A few times there'd be instances, like, where he'd sit down and start talking about something. [It would be] like, "Hey, let's talk now." But he always had a little guard up for some reason. I'd talk to him a little bit, then all of a sudden he'd start making jokes. And then the guard would go back up. It's like he didn't want to let too much out. When he wanted to be a nice person, he could be a great guy, you know. But he always had this . . . *thing* going on. So after a while, I just kept my distance. Then, towards the end of the second tour, he started asking other people what I was doing. He would ask the person doing make-up and hair, you know: "What do you suppose Monte is thinking about?" '

When the embattled tour participants had completed their schedule and limped back home to Minnesota, Monte Moir took stock and decided to quit. Vanity, after participating in the acting and singing sessions which were the preliminary to what turned out to be the movie *Purple Rain*, also upped and left. In later interviews she attributed her departure to Prince seeing other women, though it is common knowledge that there was a dispute over money too. When Vanity left, she was replaced by Patricia Kotero, an actress from Santa Monica of very similar appearance. Prince picked her for the part and renamed her Apollonia after first making sure – so rumour has it – that she believed in God. She even went on to make a Vanity-style album with Bennett and Moonsie, the group being renamed Apollonia 6. Within Prince's band, meanwhile, it was also the end of the road for Dez Dickerson. He jumped, he reckons, just about soon enough to avoid being pushed. 'I didn't know it at the time we were out there, but when the tour was over, I was finished.' The bare essentials rock 'n' roll roadshow ideal had long since evaporated for Dez. 'The whole thing had grown, the number of people on the road, the entourage. It had grown from being six people in a basement to thirty or thirty-five people on the road. It lost something. All of a sudden, the people whose job it was to get the stage clothes dry-cleaned started having egos and attitudes.'

Dickerson's behaviour was, by his own admission, becoming less and less palatable, in response to what he saw around him. 'I didn't feel comfortable with myself anymore. Because of that I became very difficult to be around. I was pretty moody. Later, I realized that was just a by-product of not being very happy with what was happening, and where we were going; and at the same time feeling there wasn't a whole lot I could do to have any impact on it. I dealt with it by . . . being a jerk. I guess if I'd been him, *I* would probably have fired me.'

Where once he was a leader, Prince's success had made it possible for him to be a ruler: a fine, but crucial distinction. The *1999* album and tour had been the fulfilment of his quest for appreciation, and the beginning of his contemplation of the spoils. This opulent turning inwards, towards his own multiplying reflections, had already begun to generate some of his most alluring art. But all around him, his troops felt as if they were paying the price. As the unlikely pieces of Prince's transcendental sexual cosmos bonded together before his eyes, to Dez Dickerson it all began to look like the emperor's new clothes. Acclaim had bestowed a certain power – but what did that power mean? 'It was only the power to deceive. I just got to the point where I needed something real in my life. The thrust seemed to be to build a bigger and better illusion, and I wasn't sure that was a good idea. With hindsight, I can see so clearly how people become a slave to this entity they've created.'

The contradictions which Prince's ascending glory seemed to resolve so sweetly for him had, conversely, become too much for Dickerson to take: 'It was a very unsettling thing to try and reconcile. I was having enormous problems with going on stage in front of nine-, ten- and eleven-year-old kids, and singing about incest. I got to the point where I was mouthing the words and not saying them out loud to provide a balm for my own conscience. At first, I was able to say, "Look, I'm making money, I'm getting famous, and I don't care!" But as time went on, those other things weren't enough.'

Dickerson, like most of the rest of the tour personnel, came off the road prepared to get ready to play themselves – or approximations thereof – in the film project which had slowly fallen into shape during the long months on the road. 'But the way Prince envisioned the thing,' he says 'there would be at least a three-year time commitment. I had to be honest with myself, and with him, that I couldn't do that.' At close quarters, Dez Dickerson had been intimately involved in a three-and-a-half-year transformation in Prince's life. Their relationship had slithered backwards from one of friendship within a creative and business framework to one of almost complete non-communication. Still only twenty-four years old, Prince's world was turned inside out, relocating him in circumstances that effectively levered him apart from the emotional supports he had begun the journey with. To varying degrees he had become isolated from almost everyone around him. 'He seemed to have a sort of attitude that people in the band, people around him, always *knew* what he was thinking', says Dickerson, with regret. 'That caused some problems, especially with new people who got fired prematurely. He didn't talk, so nobody knew what he wanted. You know: he'd wave his hand, and the next day somebody's bed would be empty. People were walking on eggshells.

'Before the management change, where Prince was involved, there was a fair degree of loyalty. People became a part of what we were doing. I hesitate to use the word "family", that sort of worn-out cliché, but we would give each other respect and the benefit of the doubt, you know?

But as time went on Prince began to adopt more of the mangement's attitude, and their whole way of operating. They were just more cut-throat than we were. We were mid-western kids, and they were big-time LA managers, and their attitude was, "Well, if there's any problems at all, fire now and ask questions later." '

For Dickerson, his years with Prince had earned him a reputation, high professional visibility, and a wealth of experience, both good and bad. He finally got some credits on one of his boss's albums, and of those credits, the most prominent adorn the track which gave Prince his final breakthrough to the heart of young white America: Dez did guitar solos and additional vocals on 'Little Red Corvette'. By leaving before he was sacked, Dickerson also feels he was able to salvage something of their evaporating friendship.

But while others were feeling the strain, Prince just thundered on. He had already got himself on the cover of *Rolling Stone* after being voted Rock Artist of the Year in their Critics' Poll of 1982. *1999* was an artistic and commercial triumph, which showcased sometimes exhilarating new dimensions to his talent for parodic emulation, mischief, erotic role-play and widescreen vision. On the way to this status, he had lost three of his best friends, and several more once-valued acquaintances. What he had gained instead was an edifice of muscle – managerial and physical – personified by Steve Fargnoli, who no one much liked, and Chick Huntsberry, who everybody thought was incredible. In fact, Huntsberry was one of the few people who seemed to get on with Fargnoli. 'My relationship with management was good,' smiles Big Chick, ''cause as long as they had me they didn't have to do anything. I did it all. When I left Prince it took three people to replace me.' Huntsberry was vital to Prince. He held all the pieces together: running the tour, handling security, catering to Prince's every whim. 'He once said to some other fellas, "If I asked this guy to get me an elephant, it would be there in the hallway." ' Big Chick would run errands in the middle of the night, eat shit, punch people out, you name it. Chick cared. 'He's like a son to me. When you're with someone, like we were, twenty-four hours a day . . . I mean, I took *care* of the guy. I actually would have died for him. If a man would have pulled a gun on him, believe me, they'd have had to kill me to get to him.'

Chick parted ways with Prince two years after Dez Dickerson, in 1985. Both have since successfully endeavoured to reacquaint themselves with God, dropping out of the mainstream of Minnesota's entertainment scene in search of a greater spiritual equilibrium. It is ironic – though in no sense a source of sour grapes – that it was thanks to Dickerson's inter-vention that Chick got his chance to be one half of Prince's double buffer against the increasingly frenzied intrusions of the outside world. 'He'd only been around a couple of days, and he was pretty frightening. We were on the bus, and no one would even sit near him. So I went over and started talking to the guy, and that was when I discovered he'd had this incredible life. Later that day I went to Prince and said, "This guy's really all right. You just got to take a minute to talk to him." '

In the end, though, even the mighty Mr Huntsberry couldn't handle it. Prince, it seems, has outstayed them all. 'When I first started with him,' Huntsberry says, 'I remember being in hotels and stuff, and one time calling down for room service, and it was closed. I said, "Look, I'm with Prince. And if I have to pay extra, that's all right." The guy said to me, "What country is he the Prince of?" I said, "No, man, Prince, the rock star!" He said, "I've never heard of Prince." '

'I got upset. But I remember Prince saying, "Hey, settle down, Chick. Someday they'll know who I am." A short time later,' growls Big Chick, glowing with remembered, mutual triumph, *'we* was number one.'

Women

Michael Putland/Retna

Prince is a boy who quite likes to be one of the girls; he was even nice to the ones who worked for him. 'There was more of an intimate thing with them,' says Mark Brown, who says he found being Prince's bass player such a torrid experience he used to call his mother from the road, asking to come back home. 'He knew them better than he knew us [the men]. He would open up to the women. They would hang out with him, go shopping with him, and he'd spend his money on 'em. But with us, it was never like that.'

Intimations of femininity – a rather particular definition of it, that is – saturated the words, music, and imagery of *1999*. The most *knowingly* narcissistic Prince album yet, it underlined a public profile already loaded with enigma. As 'Prince' became a trigger word in the mass media dialogue, so attention became the more closely focused on the exterior he projected – that is to say, his entire performance as a star on the widest possible public stage.

1999 helped foster his rise to household fame partly because it teased the speculation surrounding him. The very nature of *1999* – the record, the tour, the *event* – inspired and stoked the sudden media fascination about what he *really was*. His anger and provocation were replaced by an urge to flatter and please, and yet stay firmly out of reach. Prince made the upscale move from black punk to untouchable Glam.

Women were a crucial component in Prince's expanding celebrity world. *1999* is suffused with songs of sex and romance where women characters are conjured up as foils in strange episodes of illicit game-playing, where no one stays in any one role for long. Ambiguity is the essence of Glam; self-love is its driving force. Prince certainly seems to be wild about women, as entranced by them as he is by himself. How better, then, for him to indulge both grand passions at once than by gazing at his own reflection and seeing a girl look back?

The song 'Automatic', which opens side three of *1999*, explores a range of the shifting definitions Prince hinted might apply to himself. Pulsing and juddering in a tight, constrained rhythmic pattern, it is, at its most literal level, a song 'about' sexual domination and submission. It is also a great comedy of innuendo, with the title, and the discipline of bass and drum machines, implying the subject matter with appropriate, rigid formality. At one level, 'Automatic' spoofs the idea that passion can be understood as a rationalized sequence of robotic stimulations and responses. Quirkily half-chanting the lyric as if in a mechnical trance, Prince declares his love to his partner with a slavish matter-of-factness that is beautifully absurd. The eerie, processed jingle of a synth line suggests a musical commercial for a service industry; burgers and bondage, all served up the same way. Meanwhile, the tantalizing beat repeats and repeats, clicked immovably into its cybernaut groove. The effect, conversely, is to set up a powerful erotic tension, which translates itself into a body language of short, contained physical 'phrases'. 'Automatic' effectively takes the body apart. It demands a dance style that is expressive, but with each movement self-consciously curtailed.

After a couple of these gasping verses and choruses, the whole thing swirls off into hilarious whispering dialogue, climaxing with a synthetic airplane 'take off' (Prince seems to get off on aviation), android voices, and the flat declaration by uniform(ed) female voices that, regrettably, it is time for them to administer some pain . . . (Is that seat belt tight enough, sir?) Then the sound is stripped back down to the weird rudeness of the rhythm, and the track pulses to its end. Nine minutes and twenty-four seconds of preposterous, parodic sado-masochistic sexiness.

A basic element in the chemistry of 'Automatic' was that its characters seemed to have inverted the conventional relations of sexual power: Prince played the faceless servant to a dominant (and equally faceless) mistress – or mistresses, for heaven's sake. And this was pretty much consistent with the way his whole look, not to mention his inventory of mannerisms, had taken on more and more of what are usually defined as feminine characteristics. Since *Dirty Mind*, his hair style had steadily come to resemble more closely that of Little Richard, the first black artist in the realm of rock to wave his 'deviant' sexuality like a semaphore flag. The former Richard Penniman was an obvious role-model for Prince. Not only was he a black artist functioning in a musical territory marketed at whites, but his entire life had seen him swing periodically between the sacred and the profane, alternately raising hell as a rock 'n' roll screamer, and putting himself at the services of the Lord (actually working seriously as a preacher). In Prince, we see both sides of Little Richard reconciled in sacred sin.

Little Richard modelled his outlandish, mile-high hairstyle on the bouffant favoured by fashionable young white women of the fifties. It is interesting, too, to note that Prince's natural mother, Mattie Shaw, and her sister Edna Mae have been described in their young days as 'wearing the Marilyn Monroe look *out*, even back then' (in Steven Ivory's biography, *Prince*). But for a man to ostentatiously pile up his hair did not only have a place among sexual non-conformists. It had also been utilized as a badge of black pride by the Godfather of Soul, the great James Brown. 'I used to wear my hair *real* high,' he explained to Gerri Hirshey in *Nowhere To Run*, her history of soul music. 'And people would ask, "Why you wear your hair so high?" And I tell 'em, "So people don't say '*where* he is?' but '*there* he is.' " ' For a whole mass of people dismissed as third-rate because of their culture – as signalled by their colour – to become so spectacularly visible was a subversive act indeed.

Part of Brown's power as a black cultural hero was tied up with his 'Superbad' heterosexual confidence. Prince, typically, played fast and loose with the alternative connotations of an elaborate hair sculpture. By having it teased into a mass of billowing ringlets, rather than tight curls, he found a new variation on the racial ambiguity he had actively promoted since *Dirty Mind*; and by crimping those billows into ever more blowsy shapes, he made a play of distancing himself from the regular conceptions of masculinity. He rearranged himself into a kind of universal hybrid. Or might that itself be yet another illusion? A disguise within a disguise? Whatever, Prince had found a knack of delighting the ladies, by rolling Brown's machismo and Richard's effeminacy up together. The songs on *1999* saw Prince skittering from one part of the sexual spectrum to the other, with plenty of stops in between, setting out his stall as a lover who offered an infinity of options. But as ever with Prince, there is never any doubt that the object of his display is to attract and captivate the girls. Nothing like wooing the women through the back door, as it were.

On 'Let's Pretend We're Married', musically a long, agitated throb from start to finish, Prince describes a scenario where his girl has left him, poor baby lamb, and the only thing to cure his pain is to find another girlfriend, and 'marry' her, fast. He begins his urgent seduction with a polite, 'excuse me' and completes it with the enchanting assertion that, though he isn't saying it just to be nasty, 'I sincerely wanna fuck the taste out of your mouth'. Such repartee! But don't fret – it's all in a good cause. After cheerfully admitting that's he's probably as mad as everyone says he is, Prince declares that he's on his way to heaven – and how about you?

In the epic 'Lady Cab Driver', a crackling street-funk workout, Prince takes us into the graphic heart of a bizarre urban car fantasy which boils up into a comprehensive blurring of the boundaries between anguish and exhilaration, almost as disturbing as it is alluring. Again, a sense of exquisite libidinal agony is communicated by the way his breathless falsetto clings on to the fine detail of the beat. In a style familiar since 'I Wanna Be Your Lover', he ingratiates himself to his lady chauffeur with a display of pain, penury and humility, before rolling her over on the back seat to administer a purgative, psycho-therapeutic, not to say socio-economic, bang.

It is an extraordinary piece of work. A squalling, delirious, convulsive, imitation of a female orgasm had enjoyed exposure in pop before – after 'Love To Love You, Baby', Donna Summer seems almost like a close personal friend – but not driven by so explicit a commentary from the male partner. To cut a long climax short, Prince dedicates his every pelvic propulsion either to some particular object of his love, or else some target of his revulsion. God, predictably enough, comes out on the credit side of this rabid coital appraisal. The real-life jealousy he has said he once felt towards his 'brother' – very possibly Duane, the tall half-brother on his father's side – gets a loathing shove. The extremely affluent, meanwhile, enjoy a carefully qualified damnation; the exemptions are selected with considerable strategic wisdom, given the rate at which Prince's own bank account would have been swelling at this time (it's only the greedy ones he hates!). As Prince pumps out this litany of moral ticks and crosses, a glut of ideological reinforcement and self-reference, the lady cab driver herself squeals and groans and probably makes a mess of the upholstery. Flipping over the coin of 'Automatic', it is plain that *she* is at *his* mercy. Is this a submission fantasy or a rape? Or are they just doing it right?

The cab driver herself is credited on the inner sleeve as being one 'J. J.' who is also one of the android torturers in 'Automatic' (Lisa Coleman is the other), and contributes backing vocals to 'Free' and '1999'. 'J. J.' is a thin disguise for Jill Jones, the concealed stage singer for Vanity 6, and one of the more interesting of Prince's lady confederates over the years. Soon to appear in *Purple Rain* as Prince's unrequited admirer, she and Lisa also act out their 'Automatic' roles in the long version of the video that went with it. This promo pulled a handsome range of deviant innuendoes out of the catalogue, with Prince himself appearing in a peaked cap, motor-cycle-cop-style – as favoured by the leather men of the gay underground – and his regular high-heeled boots. Jill and Lisa share a cigarette, and roll their eyes at each other from behind a bank of keyboards. With her bountiful blonde pompadour, stilettos, shades and minimalist black underwear, Ms Jones gives a fine impression of a blue movie Marilyn Monroe. The camera leers appreciatively. At the finale, this brace of simmering vamps take our hero aside, briskly remove his upper garments – very firm, they are, but fair – and tie him to a bed. Then, in a last descent into absolute stillness, they begin lamely lashing him with bits of left-over thong. It is a splendid piece of nonsense that has the half-hearted d-i-y look of a dirty home-movie.

Jill Jones has been a regular sparring partner in Prince's sexual phantasmagoria. According to an interview she gave to *Record Mirror*, he likes her because she doesn't take life too seriously. But she has credibility as an actress, bolstered by a solid knowledge of the theatre; Sam Shepard is a particular favourite. Her own, very creditable, solo album of 1987 was but the most ambitious of her many collaborations with Prince, the first in a relationship which began back on an early Prince tour, when she sang for the band of one of the support acts, Rick James' protégée Teena Marie.

But the first women in Prince's orbit to enjoy a really high profile were Vanity 6. It was not a promising start. As figments of a male imagination, the trio – Vanity, Brenda Bennett and Susan Moonsie – really just conformed to regressive, not to say adolescent, stereotypes. Clearly, they were intended as a female reiteration of the philosophy Prince was projecting through his own output. But as such, they betray a rather conservative dimension to what in his own work were hailed as subversive sexual messages.

The numeric component of the name Vanity 6 suggests a snickering reference to what tabloid newspaper editors describe as 'a nipple count' – a suspicion confirmed by observations from persons on the scene at the time it was coined. The trio faithfully reflected the trans-racial idealism of their creator. Known, like him, only by their first names, 'Brenda' was white, 'Susan' black, and Vanity herself a dark-eyed beauty of mixed blood. For Allen Beaulieu's album-cover shot they pose insolently among the rumpled bedclothes of what is actually the bedroom at Prince's purple house. With her two supporting players skulking in their lingerie, and the raven-haired Vanity smouldering in the foreground, it comes as no surprise that Prince had originally planned to call the girls the Hookers.

Vanity 6 explained the cartoon roles they were invented to play on 'Nasty Girls', their début album's opening track. Predatory, underful-filled, and with none of the normal conceptions of shame, they brusquely defined their qualifications for a lover's suitability by the dimensions of his member. By so gainsaying the overwhelming sexological consequences – that it ain't the meat, it's the motion – they made a play of rehabilitating the caveman stereotype of masculine potency which in other ways their mentor Prince *appeared* to be undermining.

The concept of the girls' sound and image seems based on the New Wave tendency to portray sexuality at its most tawdry and degraded: a shock tactic. So the way the liberation of lust is expressed by Vanity 6

132

is very much in terms of smut, rather than a more salubrious sensuality. As a stance, that is all very fine as far as it goes, and Vanity 6 was, presumably (let's give them the benefit of the doubt), intended as at least partially an in-joke. But so facile was the entire business, so predicated on old-fashioned ideas about sexually expressive women being 'bad girls', that they were hardly likely to overturn the predictable assumptions of a male audience, and Vanity 6 seem to have been taken pretty much at face value. 'Brenda', 'Susan' and 'Vanity' were 'shallow', 'duplicitous', 'dirty', 'bored', 'rude' – but even if people noticed the quotation marks, not many of them were impressed. Vanity 6's Bad Girl mannerisms ensured that their twenty-minute opening spot on the *1999* tour elicited a demeaning response.

The role of Vanity 6 in the Prince cosmos was to be, as it were, his harem, a throwaway threesome sufficiently 'free' to meet his requirements as a modern libertine, yet dependent on his patronage, and moulded by the assumption that any woman libidinally liberated to the same extent as he would have to resemble a tart. Compared to the polymorphous beauty he was making of himself, Vanity 6 are pretty much an insult to women. The sexual possibilities Prince set loose in his sound, his words and his looks could be plain parodic, but in their wit and subtlety, they did something approaching justice to the complexities of romance and desire. Vanity 6, though, had no redemptive cutting edge to counter their metaphorical opposite numbers, the underwear-fixated, male-chauvinist-pig caricatures who populated The Time.

The composition of the LP *Vanity 6* does much to back up Dez Dickerson's theory that one reason for Prince's invention of this side-project was to help ease the creative and financial disgruntlement of his road-show musicians. The playing is attributed to The Time, and various members of that band enjoy co-credits as writers. Dickerson himself is awarded joint authorship with Vanity for the closing track on side one. 'He's So Dull', which is also the highlight in this fairly facile exercise in stylized nail-paint 'nastiness', the entirety of which, one way or another, was still ultimately Prince's project.

In commercial terms, meanwhile, Vanity 6 ran into precisely the same marketing farces as Prince had done. Initially he hoped to break the group as a pop act. Several of the album's tracks fit either into the mould of Blondie-style Farfisa-driven pop revisionism ('Wet Dream', 'Bite The Beat'), or ride on the numb, synthesized pulse of electronic disco ('Make Up', 'Drive Me Wild'). Only the crude, *double-entendre*-laden 'Nasty Girl' had much to offer in the way of funk – yet the Prince connection seems to have assured that this was the song which enjoyed the full support of Warner Brothers.

The first Vanity 6 single was, in fact, 'He's So Dull', a genuine post-feminist skit which took the dreamy Chiffons girl pop standard 'He's So

Fine' and turned it inside out. 'She can't stand the guy', confirms its writer, Dez Dickerson (who, uncredited, also played drums and guitar on the record). 'She's saying, "Get him out of my life. I don't like him." ' The song should have been a novelty smash, but inter-departmental squabbles within the record company saw it die a quiet death. While the Prince camp saw it as a single to be aimed directly at a Top 40 audience, the Warner Brothers mind-set still insisted that anything to do with Prince had to be tagged R & B – and 'He's So Dull' was by no means an R & B tune. Instead, the lewd, if engagingly ridiculous, 'Nasty Girl' became a black hit, and, delivered in tandem with the visual impact of the unadorned camisole, assured Vanity 6 a raucous, if hardly respectful, reception wherever the *1999* tour went.

It was in the chemistry of his own group that Prince set a more genuinely challenging set of relationships circling around his own nebulous persona. The *1999* album had seen his band named as The Revolution for the first time, though this appeared only in tiny lettering on the sleeve, scrawled in amongst Prince's 'naïve' genital-suggestive lettering. But it was not till after the departure of Dez Dickerson, and his replacement by a white woman guitarist, Wendy Melvoin, that the sexual/semiological focus of the group changed its balance from masculine to feminine. The way it seemed to Dickerson, Wendy had appeared on the tour bus, apparently from nowhere in particular, as the on-the-road friend of Lisa Coleman. The two of them had actually known each other since early childhood in Los Angeles, where their fathers were – and are – highly accomplished musicians with some impressive session credits. Gary Coleman and Mike Melvoin have worked with Barbra Streisand, Frank Sinatra, the early Jackson 5, as well as the Beach Boys' classic 'Good Vibrations'. In 1971, the six Melvoin and Coleman children even made a bubblegum album together called *Geek City*.

Coleman was working as a shipping clerk in 1979, when a friend who worked for Cavallo–Ruffalo heard that Prince needed a keyboard player to replace Gayle Chapman. She sent a tape, was summoned for an audition, and Prince, as she explained it to *Rolling Stone*, was knocked out by her Mozart (both Lisa and Wendy have studied music in the 'serious' sense). They also shared a common enthusiasm for Joni Mitchell, first revealed by Prince in the liner notes of *Dirty Mind*: 'Special thanks to God . . . Joni and U.' Coleman, rather a poetic type, used to compose moody piano pieces with thoughtful lyrics, very much in Mitchell's introspective singer-songwriter mode. (In 1985 Prince told *Rolling Stone* that Mitchell's *The Hissing Of Summer Lawns* was the last album he had liked all the way through. He also explained to *Right On!* the influence she had had on his work – 'she taught me about colour' – and it is not hard to locate something of her blowsy lyricism in Prince's later music and words.)

Prince found out that Melvoin could play when he heard her practising down the hall in Coleman's room. Not only could she play, but she added to The Revolution's collective chemistry. After Dez Dickerson's unhappy departure, Melvoin just stepped into his shoes. From the *Purple Rain* movie onwards, the two women rapidly acquired a distinct joint identity within the band. 'Wendy and Lisa' became perceived as virtually a separate, inseparable entity. In the dramatic balance of the movie's screenplay, the pair of them represented the 'feminine' qualities of sharing and emotional togetherness as a moral counterpoint to Prince's 'masculine' hang-ups, manifested as selfishness, possessiveness and occasionally violent egomania. The special closeness between them, projected through their public lives with perfect subliminal tact, invited speculation that the girls *might* be something more than 'just' best friends. There is no direct signpost towards this, simply an undercurrent of possibility which Wendy and Lisa have sustained in their joint career since leaving Prince's band, notably in the cover photograph of their first album together as an independent unit. These tiny tremors of innuendo are sparked in particular scenes in the film where 'the girls' are portrayed as emotionally separate from all the men; also, on the soundtrack album's 'Computer Blue', where they share an oblique, anodyne spoken intro, much like Coleman and Jill Jones's contribution to 'Automatic'. The real cleverness of this sub-plot in Prince's multi-dimensional media performance is its deft tapestry of ambiguities. The very absence of clear statements of identity correctly suggests that there are no firm definitions in the sexual realm – and, as Prince's ideology patently insists, for outside forces to impose arbitrary standards of 'normality' upon them is an abomination.

It is precisely this conviction which fires the most immediately startling track on Jill Jones's album. The title 'G-Spot' refers to a massively publicized sex manual published in 1983 which purports to uncover scintillating new truths about the female physiology. The book is an excellent example of the tendency for science to reduce human sexuality to a question of pure mechanics. 'G-Spot' initially seems like a rather tiresome exercise in 'naïve' titillation. Dissect the song more carefully, and we find nothing less than a subtle critique of techno-erotic theory. 'I was kidding about, because you read this stuff in magazines, and I find it very funny,' explains Ms Jones. 'You know, they've found this G-Spot . . . and you think, "OK, where is it?" I think it's funny,' she resumes, 'that we don't like to make choices on our own.' Ms Jones explains that the rhythm of 'G-Spot' is deliberately hard and robotic, gently mocking the cold rationality of consumerized sexuality. 'It takes all the sensuality away from it,' she concludes. Her own delivery of the lyric trades on a parodic sense of puzzled wonderment. It is just one aspect of her several 'feminine' personae which, between them, comprise a kind of mirrored image of those assumed by Prince himself.

In keeping with Prince's own standard practice, the *Jill Jones* album sees its maker juggling with the myriad possibilities for inventing identity and yet eluding identification. It is an excellent modern dance-orientated pop album, in which the singer cleverly fits her phrasing to the tension of the rhythms, while the lyrics indicate a neat comic imagination at work, especially in the loopy suggestiveness of 'All Day, All Night', and the spoof stridency of 'My Man'. Seeing herself as an individual of infinite facets, Jill Jones expresses ambivalence towards the term 'feminist': 'I feel I am one to the degree that I make my own choices,' she thinks. 'But I still allow myself that certain bit of vulnerability. I'm trying to be very strong, but not lose the little girl.'

Jill Jones is the female Prince protégée who sounds most thoroughly like herself. Yet there is a distinct level of intrigue which depends upon our knowing that Prince is involved in the project, and also knowing – or thinking we know, or suspecting – certain things about him. Because he is a bigger star than she, this tends to result in Jones's appearing to exist not only within an agenda set by Prince but as a sort of prism through which his artistic personality is refracted and perpetuated.

Jones herself says that Prince offered to make his contributions to the album – sole writer of one track, co-writer of four, co-producer of two – anonymous, because 'people will say that I did all this'. She declined, insisting that she was secure enough with the balance of their collaboration to take such assumptions in her stride. And yet it might not have made much difference had Prince hidden behind a pseudonym, or anything else. With The Revolution, Jellybean Johnson and a new Paisley Park saxophone player Eric Leeds all enlisted as contributing musicians – plus production by David Z, and Clare Fischer's obliquely cinematic string arrangements – it is not surprising that the musical ideas and textures echo many of those on Prince's album of 1986, *Parade*. While it would do Ms Jones an injustice to say that all her album's roads seem to lead back to His Highness, it might be fair to remark that her overall sensibility is experienced almost indirectly – spiked by our image of him. 'Prince and I are like brother and sister,' says Jones, though media inference is that there was once a little more to it than that. Whatever, there are parts of *Jill Jones* which more or less subtly connect her with different phases of Prince's career, underlining the mood of spiritual intimacy with his muse. The plainest of these is her likeable cover of the ballad from his *Prince* LP, 'With You'. Less overt is her use of the title of her personal favourite song from *1999*, 'Something In The Water (Does Not Compute)', in the lyric of 'Baby You're A Trip', a song whose gospelish structure and use of metaphor also anticipates a Prince song to come on 1987's *Sign 'O' The Times* – 'The Cross'.

Part of why *Jill Jones* is such an enjoyable record lies in the way she marshals anecdotal detail. Her direct references to Prince are only one aspect of it. Rather, the whole *feel* is like that. Her tone slips from the declamatory to the private, shifting from the poetic-romantic dilemma of 'Violet Blue' to 'All Day, All Night' 's dizzily overstated symbolism. Captured on the front cover, she stands with her legs splayed, her toes turned in, and her cardigan buttoned up to the neck; with a disobedient look on her face, she swirls her short skirt up and around, to the obvious interest of a couple of male bystanders behind her. She epitomizes the deliberated contradictions which so-called post-feminism reconciles: here is a girl who plays dressing-up games, and flaunts her sexuality, but according to rules she feels she sets for herself. Jill Jones is, arguably, Prince's most complete and engaging female counterpart. Why, like Wendy and Lisa, she might even go on to sustain her artistic life independently from him. Imagine that.

By 1984, the libertine mutants described on 'Uptown' had been recast as a new celebrity élite. Prince being the phenomenon's leader and catalyst, we can have fun measuring his progress by the changing fabric of his studded trenchcoat. From the flasher's mac monochrome of *Dirty Mind* it had gone upmarket to the shimmering lurex number designed by Bernadette Anderson's daughter Sylvia and captured by Allen Beaulieu for the 12-inch picture sleeve of the '1999' single. From mutant outsider to glimmering star child in three easy moves. The '1999' 45 sleeve also graced the front of the album in its second, shortened, British incarnation. The original double-album format had met with a pretty luke-warm response in the UK, so it seemed to make more commercial sense shorn of three songs – 'International Lover,' 'DMSR' and 'All The Critics Love U In New York' – and repackaged as a single album, with a lower price and a stronger visual image, though it still didn't yield immediate results, either with the critics or the public.

By 1983, the British 'New Pop' convulsion was at its height, with acts like Culture Club, ABC, Human League and Eurythmics pulling together a similar range of influences as Prince, and turning the same kinds of gender tricks not only on stage and in photographs, but in the newly established medium of video. It was a pop sensibility which fed compulsively off the surfaces and iconography of the past – any bit of the past that took its eye. It was an instant, do-it-yourself *game* of celebrity, played with tongues in cheeks and eyes cast askance at every available mirror, yet at best, stiffened with a dissenter's irony. Prince's pose for '1999' (the entire session for which lasted a mere twenty minutes) taps directly into the heart of that cultural wave. With his rakish pompadour and Glam savage stance, he stands in a swirl of dry ice, every inch the alien presence. What were Hollywood's classic stars but fabulous humanoids from another universe? To each side of him there are 'windows' on the outside world. Through one we see a crescent moon in the sky at night. Through the other, clouds and the blue of daytime. It is a perverse, static celebration of inexplicable opposites, with an oddly dated, science-fiction-movie feel.

The cinematic penchant did not stop there. In 1984, just after *Purple Rain* propelled his success into hyper-space, Prince began a semi-public association with another woman performer who functioned within a parallel set of visual references. For the cover of her solo début, Sheila E – full name Sheila Escovedo – is captured wearing dangerous lace in a black and white photograph, frozen as if caught in the act of flight. Pinned in stylized shock against the wall of a litter-strewn, tumble-down tenement, she might easily have been employed to portray a revival of *film noir*'s greatest stills. The record's title, too, spoofs the conventions of forties' movie promotion: *Sheila E in The Glamorous Life*. Though ostensibly depicting a moment of rapid movement and high dramatic import, the shot is scrupulously posed. All that is missing from the subject is a knowing wink. Whether by accident, design or collaboration, Sheila E photographs like another girl constructed in Prince's mind's eye.

Sheila E and Prince really met because of Prince's guitar hero Carlos Santana. Ms Escovedo's father, Pete Escovedo, is a percussionist who worked with Santana for many years. It was this chain of acquaintance which led the pair of them to meet up in 1978, very possibly when Prince was working on his début album (it has been documented that a swooning Prince met both Santana and Sly Stone during this period). That Sheila E is herself a drummer and percussionist of high calibre should not be doubted. Though she is not averse to exploiting her novelty value as a female in a male preserve – for instance, during her support slot on the 1986 Lionel Richie tour – the fact that she became the full-time drummer in Prince's *Sign 'O' The Times* road band and stars in the subsequent movie adaptation speaks plenty for her ability. Nor did that credibility depend upon Prince's patronage in the first place. She had already proved herself capable of holding her own on stage with such weighty jazz names as George Duke, Billy Cobham and Herbie Hancock.

The *Glamorous Life* album, though, turned her from a musician into a 'star'. She took a sumptuous photograph, *la femme fatale* in peril, and the drum sticks shoved into the thigh pocket of her leggings became an 'innocent' phallic accessory. The music fuelled the same fantasy as the one constructed for the sleeve. All the 'hot-blooded' and romantic connotations of a Latin-American background are invoked – in the percussive structures of the dance material, or the goofy melodrama of a short ballad, 'Next Time Wipe The Lipstick Off Your Collar' (co-written by Sheila E and Brenda from Vanity 6).

Sheila entered the public domain as yet another sensual satellite with Prince as her centre of gravity. Behind the imprint of The Starr Company, he 'directed' the album's production. She shared the same management company and record label. Her costumes repeated the themes of lace and retrospective chic central to Vanity 6, The Time, and Prince's own latest look. Through Sheila E, Prince's lavish promises of pleasure found yet another mirror-image, this time a wilful woman of action who offered a further set of exotic cultural clichés to manipulate.

Prince made her the support act for his *Purple Rain* tour, and before that, teased public intrigue by making regular guest appearances on her own string of club dates. *People* magazine, the weekly Bible of star-struck America, stirred the pot in their cover piece on Prince and *Purple Rain*: 'If you pencil in a moustache and pour her vital assets into pegged trousers, Sheila E could pass for . . . Prince. She has his chilly eyes, sculpted cheekbones and pouty mouth. And if her own black curls weren't frosted, she would be his hair apparent.'

The most important songs on *The Glamorous Life* document a fictional-ized world of elfin naïfs, baby French kisses, dressing up in mummy's clothes and rolling around on the floor. Sex is the irresistible driving force, but its power is documented in fairy-tale whispers. Sheila slinks about in stilettos and furs, raising hell with her bells and timbals, but she and the boys in her song communicate like imps in the garden of Eden – a recurrent image in Prince's own work. 'Oliver's House' and the opening 'The Belle Of St Mark' speak of beautiful men-children who sin with the chaste eyes of cherubs. Sheila E presents lust through the idealized filter of vintage cinema and children's fantasy fiction. It is the glamour of pure escapism.

Subsequent adventures would see her reworking the formula and still keeping time with Prince's own stylistic evolution. Her next album again employed the movie-billing conceit for a work entitled *Sheila E In Romance 1600*. Released in 1985, in the aftermath of Prince's ascent to the very top of the rock pile, its cover imagery this time *precisely* echoed the florid blend of futurism and Regency employed in the *Purple Rain* movie. Featured among a feast of hennaed hair tints, whites, blacks and Hispanics, feathers and brocade, Sheila leapt from the mid-twentieth century to the onset of the seventeenth without putting a hair out of place. Prince's involvement in the project is, for once, openly acknowl-edged. He enjoys specific billings as Special Guest star for various vocal and instrumental contributions, plus a joint billing as producer, writer and arranger of 'A Love Bizarre'. *Romance 1600* did not just create characters within songs. It created them for the packaging too. Individual musicians are awarded suitably evocative positions in a mock *dramatis personae*, including Sheila's brother Juan Escovedo as 'Sir Dancelot on percussion (scenes 3 & 8)'. Musicians become actors, songs become 'scenes'. The songs also contain plenty of lyrical plays and innuendoes which reiterate the sense of spiritual communion with Prince: the racy 'Yellow'; the rude 'Toy Box'.

The whole Prince–Sheila palaver finally made the leap into showbiz reality when Ms E appeared on American network television to talk about herself and the single 'Sister Fate'. At the point in the song where Sheila makes reference to a secret lover, the video cuts to a fleeting image of Prince's head, which looks like it has been lifted from his own video for the song 'Raspberry Beret' (1985). 'So Sheila,' smarmed her interrogator, 'is Prince the mysterious lover?' Beaming and resplendent in her *Romance 1600* rig, Sheila confessed that indeed he was. This was what they call 'Great TV'.

The vagaries of Prince's personal life became, of course, a source of frantic fascination for a showbiz-besotted public – at least while the new sensation was 'hot'. Having his name linked in gossip columns with Vanity, Apollonia and Sheila E within the space of a very few weeks did nothing to damage Prince's reputation as a demon lover, a gigolo, even some unholy one-man casting couch. The truth hardly mattered. It was the craving for it that counted for most. So swollen were the ranks of his female protégées, past and present, by 1987, that *Ebony* saw fit to run a cover story dedicated to them: 'Prince's Intriguing Women'. All the girls were there, light-brown for the most part, slightly ravaged, and décolletée – including the Scottish pop singer Sheena Easton. The world had turned on to her and Prince's mutual admiration by white-hot tales of a million-dollar love-nest bought for her in Paris on a whim, and more explicitly by a song Easton recorded entitled 'Sugar Walls'. With authorship attributed to a transparently implausible individual named Alexander Nevermind, 'Sugar Walls' is not a hymn to a new era of soluble home construction materials, but a thinly veiled tribute to the interior pleasures of our Sheena's vagina. All told, the chirpy Top Shop type who so charmed the British masses with her 'discovery' through a BBC pop biz documentary, had become a very different kind of 'Modern Girl'.

From the moment of Prince's retreat from the publicity machine, the women associated with him became his connecting point with the information media, in some cases even after they had ceased to be on the team. Vanity herself, for instance, after signing a recording deal with Motown, garnered a clutch of high-profile publicity purely on the strength of her erstwhile relationship with Prince. 'When it comes to lovers, Prince is the best,' she purred to the *News Of The World*'s salivating *Sunday Magazine*. 'I've spoken to many women who've been to bed with him, and they all say the same thing. Prince is something different, something special. He's not like any other man on Earth.'

Wendy and Lisa, meanwhile, instantly became the most famous members of The Revolution, and went on to enjoy the weighty privilege of being allowed to speak to the press. When *Rolling Stone* did their cover story on Prince for his 1985 LP *Around The World In A Day* ('Prince's Women'), Wendy and Lisa were the interviewees, and shared the cover image with him. Once constructed for grand-scale consumption, his girls became his emissaries to the outside world. Through them Prince planted himself firmly at the confluence of contemporary squabbles about how men are, and what women want them to be. The different characteristics of those around him all found an echo in some compartment of his own composite persona: he could simmer like Sheila E, be 'innocent' like Jill Jones, nasty like Vanity, or introverted and a bit spacey like Wendy and Lisa.

And this 'feminization' opened doors. The flair with which he managed to reprogramme his sexual enigma to fascinate as much as shock was vital to his long-coveted deliverance to a mass audience. From Little Richard to David Bowie to Boy George, straight, white record buyers had fallen hopelessly in love with distant, fragile pop icons who broke the gender rules. It was his irresistible variation on this tradition that clinched Prince's grand metamorphosis from a star into a phenomenon.

11

Reign

Rex Features

The ingredients of a full-scale feature film production had been falling into place throughout the *1999* tour. An important figure in the process was the Hollywood screen and television writer William Blinn. It was he who first shaped the fragmentary ideas inside Prince's head into a script. The original psychological scenario was to have been a bleak one indeed: 'His initial concept, unlike the finished motion picture, was that his parents were dead,' remembers Blinn. 'They were the victims of a murder-suicide: his father had killed his mother, and then himself.'

In the finished product, the father of The Kid – Prince's character – tries to shoot himself in a pivotal scene near the end. Traumatized, The Kid sits in the family basement, his head swimming with visions of death: the temptation to bring about his own, and the hair's breadth by which his dad had avoided it. A chalk outline has been made where his father's body fell. It is a symbol Blinn originally wrote into the opening of the screenplay. 'The overview I had of the picture from conversations I had with him was that we were dealing with a character who had a moment of decision in his life. On the one hand what was pulling him was the trauma of this murder-suicide, and the magnetism of death, if you will. And life was represented by sex and music. It was a constant back-and-forth between these two things as to whether he was going to embrace life – in the form of the character of the girl, and the substance and form of his music – or whether, in essence, he was going to be swallowed up by the death that surrounded him.'

Blinn pulled his script framework together on the basis of an initial discussion at the office of Cavallo, Ruffalo and Fargnoli, followed by a dinner at a Hollywood restaurant with Bob Cavallo and Prince himself. On the strength of this he put together 'maybe twelve or fourteen pages' of an outline, in which 'the first third of the picture was represented'.

144

The task, as Blinn saw it, was not for him to *conceptualize* the film for Prince, simply to set it out for him in the form of a script. The psychological import of the story was not lost on Prince, but in conversation he just didn't have the language to communicate the messages that would pour from the songs he was writing for the film. 'The difference between what I just described and what he described to me is that his was a much more nuts-and-bolts description,' explains Blinn. 'Not the struggle aspect as such, but certainly the character of The Kid, that his father had killed his mother, and that he was attempting to deal with that. The germ of the story he was attempting to tell soon became evident to me. I wouldn't say it was hidden, I'd say it was inarticulated. I think it might have been something he was aware of, but he is not, ah . . . verbally comfortable. Certainly not with strangers.'

William Blinn's notion that Prince did indeed have within him a capacity for identifying the deeper significances of his creative impulses is well worth noting. It indicates a particular kind of intelligence in his work whose presence would be an intimidating one for certain agents of moral censure within America and its cultural satellite, the UK. *Purple Rain* would turn Prince into a superstar, but more than that, into a symbolic personification of a bunch of ideas about the world which were certain to polarize opinion. His eventual trivializing portrayal by particular bastions of reactionary thinking as nothing more than a deviant headcase is a clear indictment of the blind fear that the success of the 'wrong' kind of outsider can induce. Young, black, strong, prosperous, self-directed, unnervingly mute and sexually programmed to subvert – this is some people's recipe for hell on earth.

Not that some of Prince's personal idiosyncrasies and neuroses might not cause the most liberal sensibility to doubt his grip on any of the regular definitions of sanity. His erratic behaviour brought William Blinn to within an ace of dumping the movie project altogether. Committing a sizeable piece of his break from executive production on the TV series *Fame*, Blinn removed himself to Minneapolis with the intention of developing his screenplay in close collaboration with its star. After a string of cancelled appointments, the pair of them finally found themselves in the same party for dinner. Afterwards, they both went off to the movies together – some punkoid Australian comedy. Then, after about twenty minutes, Prince just upped and left.

'When I got back to the hotel, Steve Fargnoli was in the lobby,' recalls Blinn. 'I said, "Look, I want out of this. You've got a rock 'n' roll crazy on your hands. I know he's very gifted, but frankly, life's too short." If this was going to be some kind of ego nonsense, I didn't want any part of it.' It was a candid but, says Blinn, 'a very civilized conversation'. Thinking that was the end of it, Blinn returned to LA, where a couple of days later he received a phone-call from The Kid-to-be. 'He didn't exactly apologize, but he said he'd been under a lot of stress and tension, and he did want to talk.' This time, Blinn and Nelson enjoyed 'a very good conversation' in the purple house by Lake Minnetonka, and driving around in Prince's car. 'He had a wonderful sound system in there, and wanted to play some of the songs he had already written. They were wonderful, wonderful songs.'

From then on, things ran smoothly enough. A different aspect of Prince revealed itself. Blinn, echoing Chick Huntsberry's experience, reflects that their lack of immediate rapport was not altogether surprising. 'If ever there was a White Anglo-Saxon Protestant, I'm the guy. I was forty-six or -seven when we were doing the picture. I'm six two and I weigh about two hundred pounds. We were clearly not going to be instantly drawn to each other.' But Blinn was plainly impressed by what he saw once the frost had thawed: 'He was obsessively professional, incredibly disciplined, and absolutely could not be more serious about his music. There's nothing frivolous in his devotion. God knows, he's got his degree of pride, but that rock 'n' roll sloppiness is never there.'

From LA, Blinn put together full drafts of the script and sent it off in consignments of fifteen or twenty pages to Minneapolis, or wherever the Prince entourage was at the time. The response was, he says, favourable. To the disturbed interior text conceived for The Kid, Blinn added the comic input which would later be expressed so effectively on screen by Morris Day and his sidekick, Jerome Benton. Originally, though, it was to be a somewhat harsher, more disturbing humour than what finally emerged. In fact the entire chemical balance of the picture had been fundamentally changed by the time it was complete: 'I think once they resurrected the characters of the mother and father, they lost a little bit of the darkness that could have been portrayed.'

In the event, *Purple Rain* was far from the vintage rock 'n' roll movie a multitude of critics hailed it as at the time. This is partly a consequence of the changed position of the parents in the plot, but for other reasons too, the entire enterprise is ultimately far less a film than an essentially soap-operatic vehicle for celebrating – or rather, boldly anticipating – the advent of Prince's stardom. It is, finally, a homage, a glorified commercial for a tapestry of myth. *Purple Rain* is a sentimental melodrama. Beneath the libidinal frissons, the bursts of surface 'realism' and the odd forbidden expletive, the plot is maudlin and morally simplistic, more interesting for the manner of its execution than for its actual message. And a big part of that is the way its details subtly and suggestively vary from the biographical truth of Prince's life. It furnishes his legend even as it promotes it.

The basic storyline is this: Prince, 'The Kid', leads a band engaged in fierce competition with a rival outfit at an influential rock club called First Avenue. Back home, mum and dad are kicking and screaming their

146

way through a relationship blighted by the latter's failure to make a success of himself as a musician. The Kid's personal drama then unfolds according to the pattern of his parents' crisis, dictating the atmosphere within the band – or, crucially, the situation of the women in it, Wendy and Lisa (who play 'themselves') – and the path of his love affair with Apollonia, a new girl in town who dreams of being a star. Matters deteriorate to the point where The Kid is about to get purged from the First Avenue roster for transmitting his self-obsessive, self-destructive tendencies through his music – and hence, to the box office – and wrecking all his friendships to boot. Then daddy tries to blow his own brains out. After a short mental struggle The Kid sees the light, and demonstrates his new-found oneness with the world by performing a song – the title tune – written, for the purpose of the story, by Wendy and Lisa, something his ego had previously refused to countenance. Learn to share and ye shall prosper, reads the subliminal text. The crowd yells for more.

The glorification of Prince, the rock messiah, does not simply occur through this trimphant finale, or the fact that the narrative is shaped, sometimes clumsily, to showcase concert footage from The Revolution (as the band is simply called) at neat, regular intervals. The stroking of the star's beauty and importance proceeds unabated: in the way he is lit, directed and photographed; by virtue of the settings the camera captures him in; and by the fact that most of the supporting cast are reduced to two-dimensional signifiers for his dilemma – for his meticulously manicured pain.

Director Albert Magnoli played a crucial part in framing the Prince of *Purple Rain* into this perfectly tortured *object* of desire. And all reports suggest that Prince was a willing confederate in the venture. Certainly, there seems to have been a degree of communication between them which was unusual for anyone undertaking their first involvement with the star. In the aftermath of the movie's instant hit status, a famous quote emerged from Magnoli in a *Rolling Stone* cover story: 'Prince looked at me and he said, "I don't get it. This is the first time I've met you, but you've told me more about what I've experienced than anybody in my life." '

Magnoli reportedly got the job after a recommendation from the young director of the film *Reckless*, James Foley. Magnoli had edited Foley's movie, and enjoyed a reputation as a bright young thing after a film short called *Jazz* had won him a hatful of awards. Though committed to production of another of his screenplays, Magnoli breakfasted with Bob Cavallo, and, as he explained it to *Rolling Stone*, a revised version of the story 'just came out . . . all of a sudden the world was shaped. And within ten minutes I had convinced myself that this would be an extremely exciting film to make.'

In *Right On!* Magnoli is quoted explaining the flick as he claimed he had to Cavallo: 'There's music. That means there's night, there's bars, there are alleys. All of a sudden, a story begins to emerge. A girl comes into town to a club. She sweeps out of a cab in black. There's Prince – he's a dark figure. There's Morris – he's a light figure. There's the girl – she's mystery.' Magnoli is virtually describing the frantic sequence of collage and radical cutting which opens *Purple Rain*, and in just the right kind of language. It is a sensory grape-shot of stylized, audio-visual clichés culled from some imaginary auto-erotic TV ad. He characterizes the rest of the film in the same way: 'Prince is a powerful, magnetic force in the world of his peers, who becomes humiliated, frightened, damaged when he sets foot in the home he shares with his parents. His father and mother have a violent relationship that sends him inward, allowing him to express himself only in his music. But by the end of the film, he has learned to let others into his world . . . he has learned to love.'

It was precisely this litany of Day-glo corn that Magnoli appears to have superimposed upon the script of William Blinn, reportedly rewriting the whole thing in a three-week period in Minneapolis, after spending a month in the company of Prince and his, presumably strife-torn, entourage. In the true spirit of high-gloss soap, the upshot is a film more interested in the allure of Prince's image than in the complexities that image tries to suggest. As a result, it sells those complexities – and the potential for human drama – short.

The film's benign fraudulence is well illustrated by the disjuncture between the way the characters look and the circumstances they are supposed to be functioning in. Since the movie is really a commercial for Prince, the Crying Dove and Wounded New Age Video Sex Icon, we are allowed to see him suffering prettily, but never appearing to be plain, ugly or poor. For a large part of the proceedings, The Kid plays a mixed-up brat on the slippery slope, but even when Morris and First Avenue's feisty manager Billy (played by Detroit concert promoter Billy Sparks) are scripted to inform us that 'the place is kind of empty tonight', The Revolution look super-confident in their reading of the cryptic 'Computer Blue' and the lewd, nasty 'Darling Nikki'. Prince sports a taut, naked torso and a pervy black mask to show us how beastly and selfish he's being. But for a supposedly alienated audience, the punters seem enthralled. Morris and Billy might be at a different show. The Kid is not just Prince playing 'himself'; he is playing his *showbusiness* self. Even when Magnoli gets him off his phallic purple motorbike, or out of his stage costume, The Kid is never really anyone but the rock superstar Prince as his fans love to love him.

The direction is pretty literal throughout, and the action is paced precisely according to the need for crowd-pleasing signals to be transmitted. This creates the conditions in which Prince can appear at his most narcissistic, but not necessarily at his most interesting. Within the first five minutes we see him lasciviously fingering his tongue, and gazing at himself in his dressing-room mirror. Even when he bursts in on one of his parents' fights, the first scene in the film to occur outside the concert environment, he is togged up in his trademark regency ruffles. Slapped angrily to the ground by pops, he lies there, quivering, a tattered doll victim melting our hearts with those big Bambi eyes.

Magnoli's determined flattery of his star is beautifully illustrated in Prince and Apollonia's second courtship scene together. After Prince has eyed her non-committally at the previous night's show, and teased her mercilessly in one of downtown Minneapolis' famous Skyway shopping malls, she, fatally intrigued (this is *Prince*, after all), hops aboard his throbbing mean machine to go for a ride to the lakes. My, how fast and free he is, Apollonia's expression tells us as they roar through the outlying woodlands, backed on soundtrack by the coasting 'Take Me With U'. It's another cliché, but the loveliness of the song makes it work. Prince as the Lovin' Spoonful was certainly a first, and the melody, instrumentation, production and lyrics of the song add up to a feast of sumptuous romance. At the waterside, Magnoli frames our exquisite hero against the green of the foliage and the unbroken blue of the Minnesota sky. Longingly, the camera ogles his cheekbones and tumbling Dionysian curls as he shruggingly goads Apollonia into stripping off and leaping into the lake – an 'initiation' required to secure his professional help. It is scarcely an encounter between equals. The gauche Apollonia is made a fool of and rides home, suitably moist and ruffled, loving him for it. This is *not* a feminist film.

The great paradox, though, is that The Kid's emotional odyssey in *Purple Rain* might be seen as a quest to get in touch with essentially 'feminine' qualities. His problem is his inability to share his feelings, or allow the warmth of others to intrude into his private obsessions. His is a crushingly masculine isolation. It is the women in his life with whom he has no romantic involvement who provide a routeway out – if only he can make himself see it. Since the Apollonia character is so unfailingly puppyish and pliant, it is Wendy and Lisa who provide the only positive input into The Kid's perspective on womankind. Wendy, the more demonstrative of the special couple, enjoys the highest profile among The Revolution. She gets conspicously more lines than the others, and delivers them with an appropriately sullen disillusion. Lisa fits in as her other half. Matt Fink and Bobby Z play a minor deadpan double act, while poor Mark Brown is ascribed a bare split-second close-up in the entire 107 minutes. (Brown's virtual invisibility added to the 'whiteness' of the movie. Even the actors playing The Kid's parents were picked to confirm the party line on the matter of his ethnic origin – Olga Karlatos is white, the tortured Clarence F. Williams, black.)

But despite his masculine flaws, we are left in no doubt as to our Prince's spectacular powers as a sexual persuader. His seduction of Apollonia is carefully set up to capture the dim, sensual promise of his most exotic ballads. Literally beneath the shadow of a drunken parental reconciliation, he takes her down into his basement room, a humble setting transformed into a d-i-y den of strange, haunted opulence: porcelain ornaments and pierrot dolls glimmer in the low lighting; a curious piece of mood-music features the sound of a weeping girl played backwards.

'What did you do to her?' asks tremulous Apollonia, excited and a tiny bit scared. 'It makes me kind of sad when I hear it,' evades disingenuous Prince, as they reflect back the fire in each other's eyes. Within seconds we see him reaching from behind to run a lingering forefinger along the most intimate contours of her groin. It is a terribly sexy moment, but straining to be seen behind Apollonia's mountainous cleavage, he does look awfully small.

As an actor, Prince is most convincing in *Purple Rain* when stationary and admired. From this dominant position he gets his best chance to wink, nudge, and act all hurt. He injects a little life into some otherwise fairly inanimate settings. This is consistent with the way his most striking photo studies and album sleeves always find him still and stylized – a meaningful look is usually preferred to movement. The immaculately staged photo on the front of the *Purple Rain* LP is a perfect high-camp taster for the visual etiquette Prince imposes on the film. (Even Jeff Katz's great back-of-cover shot for the 1986 album *Parade*, which implies Prince has been caught in the act of dancing or stripping off, *feels* like a still-life study.)

But without the driving, motor compulsions of music, much of Prince's breathtaking fluidity is drained out of him, isolating the ironic distance he had learned to use so well, and leaving it to fend for itself. Once he is removed from the First Avenue stage, his coyness and love of throwaway gesture lose much of their spontaneity and charm. Paradoxically, his performance has most depth when he is at his most superficial, posing madly. He emits the artificial presence of an artful fashion model functioning in an otherwise naturalistic world. As a pop star, he invents his own environment and makes it tick. Magnoli, though, goes for a stunted literalism which is at odds with the chemistry of Prince's pop star 'act'. For this reason, Prince's instinctive displays of camp often seem incongruous, while conversely, his attempts at 'real' emotions – rage, for instance – look forced. So earnest is the film to conduct the coronation of Prince that it does not really play to his strengths. What emerges most clearly from the melodrama is not the old-fashioned rock 'n' roll realism

Magnoli seems to have had in mind, but the unspoken conspiracy between Prince and his fans, an in-joke which survives the film rather than being serviced by it. As Pauline Kael wrote in her *New Yorker* reviews, 'if he had performed the role more realistically, the picture would be really sodden'.

Prince has charisma, and he works at it. His allure, though impeded, makes its impact: those who come to drool get plenty of opportunity. But the character who really takes over the screen every time he appears is Morris Day. As a 'light character', Morris is encouraged to be a cartoon, and he pulls off the part with the supreme ease of a man who has been spoofing black pimp bravado since his days in the playground: kind of Don King with dance-steps. 'You ladies don't seem to realize how valuable my time *is*,' he exclaims with prim irritation to the two hard-pressed junior partners (Brenda and Susan) of what will eventually become Apollonia 6. He then turns tartly to his gofer Jerome for confirmation of this display of effrontery. 'Let's have some asses wigglin'. Ah want some perfection!' They slap five, and glide out into the street.

Morris's and Jerome's star turn revives a time-honoured convention, a Hollywood extension of a real-life syndrome, enabling blacks to satirize the stereotypes that oppress them. Together they are *playing* black. Specifically, they are playing ostentatious, bad manners, wanna-be-filthy-rich black, driving around in a big flash canary-coloured limo whose automatic windows don't work (the car actually belonged to Benton - a gift from Prince). Unlike Prince, who employs accent and idiom that are more racially neutral, delivered with breathy sensitivity, Morris talks 'black' too: lecherous, vain, nasty black, as his role requires. 'This just ain't happenin', man,' he declares to Jerome as the pair of them pace round the corner, dapper as could be. 'The bitches are OK, but we need something more exciting.' Morris already has his eye on Apollonia, who he reckons to have seen the previous night. He even has her details, though we never saw him notice her at the time – a technical clanger in the script. Jerome proposes they go and find her. But for Morris, this will never do: 'No, no, that ain't classy enough. I want this bitch to come to me. I'm the only star in *this* town.'

Virtually everything Morris Day does in *Purple Rain* is funny. The famous mirror routine translated beautifully on to the silver screen. In his leopard-skin jacket with lurex lapels, with his walking cane and neon-soled Stacey Adams shoes, he would be a hoot without even opening his mouth. He and Benton's fizzy repartee simply couldn't fail. Their jive variation on Abbott and Costello's famous 'password' sketch had reviewers howling for more.

The Time's stage numbers are also a treat. From their new album *Ice Cream Castle* they performed the jumping 'Jungle Love' and 'The Bird'. But by now, this was a radically different Time line-up from the one that had started the *1999* tour. Jam, Lewis and Moir had gone. Jellybean Johnson had been persuaded to stay on, but by the time the film came out, only Jesse Johnson remained as a seriously committed original member. When *Purple Rain* was set before the public, Morris Day had already effectively removed himself from the group, and was struggling to escape from the shadow of Prince.

Prince certainly intended *Purple Rain* to be a suitably touched-up and abstracted cinematic story of his life – an 'emotional biography', in Magnoli's phrase at the time. But as production proceeded, the sense in which characters in the film were relating to each other as extensions of their real-life situations was, in the case of Prince and Morris, translating itself back into real life rather too vividly. Day's circumstances were threatening to shaft his emergence as a star to a vast international public before it had barely started.

By Pepé Willie's account, Cavallo, Ruffalo and Fargnoli were effectively obstructing attempts by a salivating media to get hold of the triumphant comic turn of *Purple Rain*, by telling all those who inquired that Day was unavailable. Willie also maintains that Prince's managers had effectively ceased to administer Day's affairs, so he arranged for an attorney to dissect the contractual situation, and a new manager, Sandy Gallin, to take over.

Having made it to the *Purple Rain* première, Day spent the last two weeks of July and the first week of August 1984 doing a string of radio interviews, and making television appearances on *Entertainment Tonight* and the talk-shows of Merv Griffin and David Letterman. Day was learning that the comic persona he had developed with The Time served him equally well in publicity and business affairs as it did on stage and screen. 'You know,' says Willie, who supervised the entire Morris Day publicity blitz (and has the diary to prove it), 'we had fun!'

But this brief improvement in Day's career and business fortunes was not helped by the circumstances of his personal and domestic life. For one thing, he had acquired a dependency upon cocaine which went on to become a major problem in the following years. As one senior member of Sandy Gallin's management company (Gallin-Morey Associates) put it: 'we virtually saved Morris's life.' This did nothing to please Day's mother, Mrs Daugherty, who, Willie complains, was far too anxious to play a central role in her son's affairs, and did not approve of him [Willie] at all. 'She would want to be with us twenty-four hours a day,' he claims, 'and I could not stand it. She would get pissed off, and say, "Well, I can get Johnny Carson, I can call him up." I said, "LaVonne, we're in trouble right now, 'cause we can't get money to pay the rent. Can you get that?" We got money off of Letterman and Merv Griffin, and it helped pay off some bills.'

Bernadette Anderson (who, it is only fair to remember, maintains strong surrogate-maternal feelings for Prince) considers that the Daughertys had a little more money than the families of other Grand Central members – and the aspirations to go with it. Maybe Mrs Daugherty's sense of respectability was offended by the manner in which Morris, with Willie's encouragement, was playing the Hollywood publicity game. 'She did not like our attitude,' complains Pepé. 'I said, "But LaVonne, this is what they're *buying*. This is what they want to see when we walk into their office. They want to see the comedy, they want to see the chuckin' and jivin' or whatever you wanna call it." They wanted a *black, funny guy*.'

It should also be recorded that members of the Gallin-Morey organisation consider Willie to have been 'a bad influence' on Day, and that his account should be taken with 'a pinch of salt'. But Willie complains that Mrs Daugherty tried to make him the scapegoat for Day's nasal proclivities. His antipathy towards Mrs Daugherty has diminished little since. 'She was just really hassling us. We didn't feel free. She was calling us drug-addicts and stuff like that. I said, "If we were drug-addicts, we wouldn't even be able to *make* all these interviews." I told his mother, "Look, I didn't come here with a bag full of drugs in my suitcase. I did not come here with $2,000 a week in my pocket to buy drugs. I'm not buying it." *He* was doing all the buying! Every time he would want to do it, I would always tell him, "no". But what am I gonna do? Strap him down, and shit? He's a grown man. If he wants to do it, then he's gonna do it. I wouldn't let him go out on his own and do it. I was with him, because I felt I had to protect him. I was caught between a rock and a hard place. He would sneak out of his house, and, you know, I'd be sneakin' right with him.'

Whatever, Day's habit was not at that point debilitating enough to prevent him from fulfilling his publicity schedule, or from securing a new, solo recording deal with Warner Brothers, which would shortly yield his first solo album, *The Color Of Success*. On 11 September, with Day apparently considering his options for future movies, Pepé Willie flew back to Minneapolis, just to touch base and keep up with business. The next day, he called Morris's attorney: 'He said, "Oh, I heard you and Morris had broke up." I said, "Where'd you hear this from?", and he said, "His mother." '

Willie claims that he and Morris Day were all set to launch a joint production company under the name of MoPep, and that a sum in payment for his assistance had been agreed. But nothing came of either arrangement. 'Morris is a good person, he's got a good heart. But he screwed me over, because he would never back me up. He never even

153

called up to say, "Well, Pep, my mom did this, and here's your money." He just faded away. That's when I took out a lawsuit against him.' Pepé and Morris spoke for the first time since this episode at the 1987 Minnesota Black Musicians' Award Show, but at the time of writing, their legal malady lingers on. Day was approached via his current manager, Ron Sweeney, for his side of this story, but without success.

Morris Day's career scarcely blossomed in the ensuing years. As of spring 1988 he had not made any more films since *Purple Rain*, and it was not till February of the same year that the album *Daydreaming* was released to break three years of silence. But the 1984 *Rolling Stone* interview, and others with Day at the time, heralded him deservedly as a bright new talent on the entertainment scene. They also began to chip away at the careful fabrications surrounding Prince's empire, even as Day used the platform they offered to announce his intended self-exile from it. 'Quite frankly, nobody believed that I would take it this far,' he said to *Rolling Stone*. 'I think the whole thing was never expected to be anything more than an opening act.' In an evasive interview, which dodged precise descriptions of his own input into the band's records, Day was specific only about what he considered Prince's domineering ways, and the threat The Time had posed to Prince's supremacy. 'It created a tension between us, and there used to be some arguments before going on stage about things that I would do that were conflicting with things that Prince would do. I was told not to do certain things, certain dances.' Soon after, Prince and Day turned up at the same club in LA. Pepé Willie says he attempted to negotiate a reconciliation, but that Prince was in no mood for it. Willie recalls Prince calling Morris's mother something so terrible that he elected not to repeat it to her son till the morning after. 'If I'd told him right there and then, Morris would have jumped all over him.'

It is not inconceivable that Day's remarks as reported in *Rolling Stone* could have put him in breach of his disputed contract with Prince. Paul 'St Paul' Peterson, the white teenager who was among those recruited to the patched-up version of The Time, recalls having to sign a 'piece of paper' which 'said that I'd be sued . . . if I said anything bad or damaging about him.' There are former members of The Revolution, too, who seem to have signed agreements containing clauses to the same effect. One, preferring to remain anonymous, is happy to confirm it. And shortly before conducting an interview for *The Independent* newspaper with Wendy and Lisa, coinciding with their first album as a duo, this writer was advised by representatives of Virgin Records that the girls were 'contractually obligated' not to discuss Prince.

But whatever the state of contractual obligations – a vexed subject that recurs with torturous regularity whenever Prince's patronage is involved – *Purple Rain* effectively marked the death of The Time, even as they

154

strutted their funky stuff for their broadest audience ever. Following the *1999* tour, it was Jesse Johnson who basically ran the band after Day had absented himself to the West Coast. With Moir, Jam and Lewis gone, Johnson supervised a major reconstruction. Jerry Hubbard Jnr, from a noted black Twin Cities musical family, came in on bass guitar. Mark Cardenas, a white keyboard player said to be of Russian descent, stepped into one pair of synthesizer shoes, and Peterson the other. Or so they were billed on the *Ice Cream Castle* sleeve.

'St Paul', as Jellybean christened him, had only just graduated from high school when he got the call. He is the youngest of yet another large, singing, dancing, Twin Cities clan (this one Norwegian), and is related to the Rivkins through marriage. Consequently, Peterson was pally with them and some of Prince's other employees. 'We were all sitting around my mother's pool one day. David was over, and Matt Fink, and I said, "What the heck, give me an audition." ' The next thing he knew, his post-graduation holiday was interrupted by a phone call from his brother-in-law. ' "Get your ass back here. You have an audition with The Time." ' With Day away on the West Coast, the new line-up rehearsed for eight months solid. The plan was to undertake a major tour. In the event, rejoined by their leader, they played just one gig, at First Avenue. The two songs they performed on *Purple Rain* – 'Jungle Love' and 'The Bird' - were both filmed at this one-off show, and this live version of 'The Bird' also went straight on to *Ice Cream Castle* intact. Peterson, only seventeen, enjoyed his tenure with the dismembered band. 'We had a real good time. It was a real *disciplined* group. It wasn't the same for the original members, but it was sure a lot of fun for me.' He got on well with Jesse Johnson, to the point where 'we almost got a place together'. But just the same, Peterson's sole contribution to the album was the part he played live – the bass guitar (rather than the keyboards he is credited with) plus background vocals on 'The Bird'.

Ice Cream Castle was, in all essentials, a collaborative effort between Morris Day, Jesse Johnson and Prince. Day picks up all the songwriting credits on the album, save for the one he shares with Jesse Johnson for 'Jungle Love'. Production, though, is once again attributed to The Starr Company, and there is no doubt in Paul Peterson's mind whose final executive power this sobriquet concealed. He was even instructed as to what clothes he should wear for the *Ice Cream Castle* cover photograph. 'Yeah, the orange suit. That was Prince's thing. That one he said personally, 'cause I picked out a really cool-looking pattern, and he said, "No! No! I want you to wear this one." I said, "Oh, you are kidding, right?" He said, "No! Wear it! Trust Me!" '

The orange suit, as Peterson admits, 'worked out'. Another of Prince's bright ideas for a sartorial stunt never made it off the drawing board. 'You know, he wanted Mark Cardenas to wear *blackface*!' remembers an incredulous Peterson. 'It got to the point where it was almost going to cost Mark his job. He picked it out for him to wear in the movie, and Mark *refused* to wear it.' Prince had his reasons, though: 'He said, "If you wear blackface, people will notice you." Well, he would have been right there.'

In the event, the caricature 'blackness' of The Time hit home on a far healthier level: as a comic spoof of what whites think blacks are like, and, by implication, an in-joke with blacks themselves. In *Purple Rain*, Morris and Jerome carried off their double-act not only with pizzazz and aplomb, but also with the satirical detachment required to separate themselves from the stereotypes they were sending up. It was a vintage performance which distilled on celluloid the sophisticated essence of The Time.

It is a tribute to Morris Day and the original Time that they became perhaps the definitive post-disco, post-modernist eighties funk band, the get-down vehicle for a parodic celebration of black cultural archetypes. They could only have happened in an age of overpowering, eternally shifting mass-media images, where the meaning of every message is delivered in quotation marks. The Time underlined the fact that black kids of their generation grew up watching garbage television just like whites. The world of mass American culture was something they too consumed and were entitled to fool around with. They also illustrated that Prince, their secret Svengali, enjoyed a similar understanding of the new things that a black pop star could be, one that was as sharp as his talent to express them was vast. As a pop-art stuntman, Prince was a natural.

The success of *Purple Rain*, the album and the film, ensured the crowning of Prince as the main pop event of 1984. His ascent commenced with the release of the single, 'When Doves Cry' (16 May), a genuine 'cross-over' hit that went to number one on the American pop chart and stayed there for five weeks. It was supported by a perfectly awesome video, a triumph of kitsch. Consisting mainly of a collage of clips from the upcoming film, it commenced with a stark-naked Prince emerging from a huge purple bath and prowling across the floor on all fours. The *Purple Rain* album followed on 25 June, and occupied the top of *Billboard*'s LP chart for twelve weeks. The motion picture finally opened on Friday 27 July, and roared to the top of the box-office takings list. Pop is ever more pervasive, but it remains a relatively specialized field. The movies, though, are everyone's business. America's heavyweight media machinery cranked itself up to hail the latest rock 'n' roll sensation who doubled, as *Newsweek*'s headline put it, as 'The New Prince Of Hollywood'.

The elevation of pop stars into social phenomena is a process which, even as it increases the power of the celebrity concerned, occurs largely outside of his or her control. The mechanisms of deification require that the Chosen Ones be somehow *translated* for an audience which may never have heard of them before, and very likely will pay no serious attention to them in the future. Their presence is simply celebrated, then explained and presented in a manner which can be absorbed without too much intellectual effort. Any major artist becomes 'understood' in ways which he or she cannot reliably influence, magnified a million times.

Prince was presented as an icon who was, as *Time* suggested, 'a suitably odd one for these askew times'. His strangeness was becoming constructed as his entire substance, his mass-market calling-card. By November, with the opulent *Purple Rain* tour traversing the continent at full steam, that star-spangled bible of the personality cult, *People* magazine, had done its leg-work, and put Prince on the cover: 'For Prince, a playground is a place where the id runs free,' wrote Barbara Graustark, one of a fairly exclusive journalistic set to have *actually spoken* with the little big man; 'Prince's former manager one said that "his worst fear is being normal", and even the singer's friends admit he's weird.'

More sober publications went beyond explorations into the elusive 'personality', and commenced to probe the underlying patterns of the *Purple Rain* explosion. They came up, of course, with contradiction: godliness and promiscuity, machismo and effeminacy, spirituality and material ostentation, futurism and nostalgia, black rhythm and white rock. But beneath the surface, Prince's *Purple Rain* – the album, certainly – does more than impudently reconcile competing impulses, apparent polar opposites, in the soul of America's collective *mores*. While half-frivolously proposing a bunch of revolutionary liaisons, in a curious way it actually illuminates – and quite approvingly – the thought-processses of the American status quo. *Purple Rain*'s crucial tunes carry within them the bravado of cosmic certainty. Only the official Soviet newspaper *Pravda* seemed to catch on to this. In an article which accurately identified the glorious apocalyptic submission which lay beneath Prince's outlandish displays of impropriety, it noted with thorough disapproval that a large, demoralized section of American youth was beguiled by an icon who seemed to imply that a holocaust – nuclear or otherwise – was inevitable and desirable. The Soviets got it right. Everyone else was too busy being spooked, excited, offended or confused.

In *Purple Rain*, the guiding idea of '1999' is extended into an entire conceptual centrepiece. Why is Prince so excited in the opening, sheer rock 'n' roll, 'Let's Go Crazy'? Apparently because he knows that very soon *everyone* is going to die. Lyrically, four of the album's nine tracks feed, more or less directly, off this delirious conviction that the coming afterworld offers the promise of – and the excuse for – absolute liberation.

157

'Take Me With U', the duet with Apollonia that works with such corny splendour in the film, simply redeploys this yearning for abandonment as a romantic metaphor whose sensibility is no less celestial. He doesn't *care* about anything but his total capitulation to a greater power, a love beyond his control. The title track, which closes the movie and the album with a messianic pomp redolent of Dylan ('Knocking On Heaven's Door'), Lennon or Neil Young at their most transcendental, describes a kind of metaphysical promised land into which Prince offers to lead us. But most striking of all in its embrace of mortality is the torrential 'I Would Die 4 U', where the star defines himself as an entity incomprehensible in earthly terms, ready to give up his life for the greater good.

We all know Prince likes his little joke. But as the mulitudes flocked to hear his words from up on high, the little guy from Minnesota was making a pretty good fist of emulating the biggest box-office draw of all time. Certainly a Son of God revival was in the air, and there is no doubt that the fervour whipped up by rock stars can take on a distinctly religious character. Add this symbolic communion with the Lord to the other assets Prince could now boast in his armoury – sex, power and wealth – and he had all the main axes of the free-enterprise world not only covered, but implicitly glorified and endorsed. Not bad for a self-styled social outcast. But then, you know, they *did* say that about Jesus too.

This dazed ideological zeal was only the half of it. With *Purple Rain*, Prince put himself together as the cleverest rock-star collage since David Bowie's *Ziggy Stardust* had crystallized a totally new phase in rock. From the early seventies on, the most sophisticated artists were increasingly *conscious* of the culture they had inherited. This evolution was encouraged by, and followed on from, the disintegration of the so-called counter-culture with which rock was closely associated. The result was that the new rock icons became those most able to place a certain intellectual distance between rock mythology and themselves, even as they perpetuated that mythology. Artists like Bowie, like Roxy Music or the Velvet Underground struck audio-visual poses that were *about* rock stardom at precisely the same time as they enabled their creators to become stars. They were documentary *and* participatory at the same time. Prince became the first black performer successfully to employ that approach and make it work in commercial terms. With *Purple Rain* he celebrated the rock-star world to which he was simultaneously gaining the access he had long coveted.

Musically, it is an album of bold, brash strokes which embraced Prince's most radical range of styles yet. The idiom of the music, like the symbolism of the words (and the movie), had shifted distinctly into rock, with no one song answering with much conviction to the descriptions 'soul', 'R & B' or 'funk'. And the centrality of the colour purple, of course, just underlines parallels with the definitive ecstatic black rock hero, Jimi Hendrix. 'Baby I'm A Star', which provides the crotch-fingering finale of the film, was pure grandstand rock 'n' roll, a slamming confirmation of Prince's arrival in the heart – and at the head – of the superstar mainstream. Add to this full-tilt boogie finale the grinding sexual hatefulness of 'Darling Nikki', the Glam, subterranean desire of 'The Beautiful Ones', and the oblique two-part 'Computer Blue' (co-written with Melvoin and Coleman), and the result is an album which pulls together shock tactics, audacious musical variety and an over-arching, personalized mysticism as different dimensions of a fantastical, self-defined world. It is not as good as *1999* or *Dirty Mind*, but it thinks itself more important.

Purple Rain proved that Prince could hone Hendrix, hard rock and psychedelic pop whimsy to fit both his own sensibility and the more disciplined musical dictates of his time. But the album's real masterpiece was the extravagantly sensitive 'When Doves Cry'. In contrast to the guitars-and-drums assault of the more anthemic tunes, the emphasis here was on a quite radical rhythmic economy. The trick was simple enough, but its effect was startling: the song has no bass-line. In fact all the usual rhythmic components have been completely stripped out; a drum machine carries the beat, with *staccato* keyboard figures used pretty much like percussion to augment it and add a spartan detail. Otherwise, the song is carried along on Prince's voice: a cracked, piquant delivery of a lyric whose florid language did not detract from the timeless appeal of what 'When Doves Cry' really is – a classic pop cry for help. The beautiful boy was hurting. He was on top of the world.

12

Fallout

Rex Features

One night in 1986, Big Chick Huntsberry came face to face with his moment of truth: 'I found myself at four in the morning, stoned out of my mind, looking into a mirror, with a cocked .44 Magnum to my head. I was gonna kill myself.'

Two months before the end of the *Purple Rain* tour, Huntsberry had walked out on his boss. 'We just had a little falling-out. I was on drugs, bad, but Prince never touched 'em. He was clean. I lost everything I had because of drugs. I even sold my lawnmower one time to buy drugs. I couldn't take the pressure. If I wouldn't have been on drugs, I would never have left him.' Huntsberry estimates that at one time he was spending $1,000 a week on cocaine. When he breached Prince's strict gag rule against talking to the press, and sold his story to the *National Enquirer*, it was to get money to buy more. For the time being at least, that was the end of a beautiful friendship. 'I really had a love for Prince,' he explains. 'Not, you know, *queer* or anything, but a son love. It really hurt me when we split up. I started thinking things that were probably not happening. I started thinking he was doing me wrong, which he wasn't. Prince begged me to come back. He called me from New York and said he needed me. I wanted to go back and help him so bad, but because of drugs I didn't. As long as I was doing them, I couldn't even think.'

As the *Purple Rain* hullabaloo hollered on, Big Chick had become more and more a part of Prince's off-stage act. A walk-on part in the movie hadn't hurt his visibility, and his ferocious devotion to duty soon made him a notorious figure in the whole media furore surrounding Prince. It is something he is perfectly conscious of. The first thing Mr Huntsberry asked when approached to assist with this book was: 'You're not one of those reporters I smacked over there, are you?'

Prince's flying visit to England to collect the British Phonographic Industry award for Best International Artist has gone down as a classic in the pantheon of camp. Perched on his highest heels, hair swept up into a sculpture of waves and curls, and clothed in his snazziest brocade, he looked a complete and utter tart. Behind him, all biceps, beard and braces, was Chick. As a ploy, it turned on a brilliant display of clashing clichés. Rather than trailing in Prince's service, Huntsberry looked like the kind of redneck psycho who should be stringing up little black faggots (*sic*) from the nearest tree. But of course, at 6 foot 6 and 320 pounds, Huntsberry's intimidating presence amounted to a lot more than a stunt. 'The thing that amazed me about the British press is that they actually *like* pain,' he says, really quite impressed. 'I'd smack 'em once, and they'd come right back so's I could smack 'em again!'

For three American photographers, though, one smack was more than sufficient. After being vigorously dissuaded from trying to snap His Royal Badness at a Los Angeles club, Carlos and Charlie's, they filed a $15 million lawsuit against Prince, Warner Communications, Huntsberry, and three other named bodyguards, claiming they had been 'wrongfully, maliciously and violently' assaulted, and that the heavies, including Huntsberry, had later returned to the same venue with the express purpose of repeating the performance.

This story is but a fragment of the legend surrounding Prince's security arrangements, and the extreme methods by which they have been enforced. One of the best bits of nonsense, as reported in *USA Today*, concerned a visit to the Bel Air home of the actress Elizabeth Taylor, apparently a big Prince fan. While one of the goon-squad stood guard inside Ms Taylor's house, three more combed the bushes in the garden. 'You'd have thought it was [President] Gadaffi,' she reportedly remarked afterwards, irked by this massed intrusion of muscle.

Prince's dogged silence within his security citadel fuelled a burgeoning media image as a paranoid madman. Huntsberry's *National Enquirer* exposé was the single most dramatic example. 'Recently Prince told me, "I've always wanted to be really famous – but now, like Elvis, I'm a prisoner. My life's dream has turned into a nightmare," ' ran the testimony of Big Chick. Then there were tales of the hate mail: 'The letters object to Prince's mention of God in his songs, and some letters are filled with racist rantings. The biggest complaint is that Prince dates white women.' And so it went on. The man who would shortly win in five categories at the 1984 Grammy Awards Show was portrayed in the *Enquirer* text as pathologically fearful of attack, hounded by death-threats, girls and reporters, and protected by armed guards twenty-four hours a day; he had an explosive temper, and was painfully sensitive about his height; he was an insomniac workaholic, obsessed with inspiring the same sense of mystery that surrounded Marilyn Monroe, believing himself to be the second Mozart. 'One thing's for sure,' said Big Chick to the notorious gossip rag, 'when they made Prince they broke the mould.'

The *National Enquirer* splash defined the tone for most subsequent down-market coverage of Prince from *Purple Rain* to the present day. The idiosyncrasies of his personal conduct were seized upon as the key issue, and sensationalized to create an image of lunacy in action. It marked the beginning of a backlash against Prince's popularity whose character tells us a lot about the aggressive conservatism of modern times.

In Britain, the tabloid newspapers, increasingly dependent on pop for their showbiz shockers, have perpetuated the *Enquirer*'s school of ridicule, gift-wrapping it in a selection of alliterative epithets. If it's not 'pompous Prince', it's 'potty Prince', 'prancing Prince', or just 'Ponce'. On the face of it nothing worse than moderately pathetic examples of old-fashioned irreverence, these caricature portrayals actually mask a powerful urge to demean the more revolutionary possibilities suggested by his appeal. Prince's BPI Show performance, and the fuss that surrounded it, drew plenty of flak from the ligging correspondents in the next few days. 'It was the Purple Pain himself . . . who took the trophy for Idiot Poser of the Year,' sneered *The Sun*. 'Not only did he fail to crack his face even once, he didn't even move a muscle without the assistance of his heavyweight bodyguards.' The *Daily Star* had its twopence-worth too: 'When it came to his acceptance speech he seemed to be speaking gibberish . . . Of course . . . poser Prince only agreed to appear on condition he won [an award].' So, an egomaniac nancy boy and a retarded one at that. Worst of all, not prepared to make public property of himself – not one of the lads. Obviously, he must be mad. It didn't even matter what country he was in. 'Pop superstar Prince's wacky behaviour reached a new high at a top New York nightspot,' chortled *The Sun* a few days later; '. . . The singer arrived at the Limelight Club . . . posted two bodyguards at the door and ordered the other six to surround his table. Later all the beefy escorts were instructed to surround him as he boogied under the flashlights.'

Behind their snickering triviality, these reports, and others like them, strike an ideological tenor in keeping with the editorial positions of these varyingly right-wing publications (and that includes the ostensibly socialist *Daily Mirror*) that dominate British newspaper sales: broadly, anything or anyone not conforming to traditional ideas and demarcations with regard to race or sexuality must prepare to be mocked and marginalized, under the guise of good clean fun. In the ensuing years, more and more frantic in their construction of Prince as a living, breathing loonytune, pop gossip journalists have worked hard to taint and undermine his reputation as a winner with the girls. It is as though they simply cannot contemplate the notion of a short, slight man who dresses and moves like a popular (mis)conception of a homosexual being attractive to millions of women. Even when his talent as an entertainer is grudgingly acknowledged (after all, the public buy his records and can only have their predilections insulted so much), his caricature camping is demeaned as 'mincing' (*The Sun*, 16 June 1987), while his uncontrollably skittish sense of humour is explained away as arrogance or insanity ('weirdo pop star Prince staged a crazy £7,000 game of hunt the egg on Easter Sunday as he played Lord of the manor in a quiet English village' (*The Sun*, 22 April 1987), and his portrayals of the sinister side of humanity inflated into ludicrous, subliminally xenophobic claims that he is obsessed with 'the black arts' (*Daily Mirror*, 18 June 1987).

The myths of black sexuality linger on, to be gawped at and feared. Any opportunity to lampoon Prince as being sexually ineffectual is seized on as avidly as the chance to describe him as sexually depraved. There is nothing quite like a mad black dandy to bring out the bigot in a self-styled True Brit. Within the space of a year, *The Sun*, almost surreal propagandist for a particularly repulsive school of right-wing extremism, had splashed reports of 'Prince's Fear Of Naked Girls', only to inform us later that he was 'turning his European [*Sign 'O' The Times*] tour into a non-stop love marathon with a different girl in every city.' Prince projected attitudes and celebrated sensations which were, for all their ultimate superficiality, undeniably disturbing to a whole range of conservative interest-groups. He stirred disapproval from the guardians of all the social taboos which, after all, he had taken such pains to offend against.

On the religious front, much of the opposition to Prince was, coincidentally, coordinated in the Twin Cities. Since late 1979, Dan and Steve Peters, brothers in arms at the Zion Christian Center in North St Paul, have produced a number of books, and enjoyed widespread publicity for their work in – to quote the cover blurb of their *Hit Rock's Bottom* – 'Exposing To The Light, The Real World Behind The False Image Of Rock'. Enjoying the support of fundamentalist preacher Pat Robertson, who ran for the Republican Presidential nomination in early 1988, the Peters Brothers organize seminars where young Christians are encouraged to talk about, and preferably disown, rock idols who preach or practise immorality as their religious perspective defines it. After their first such gathering, the Peters brothers even gave Twin Cities youngsters the chance to burn the offending vinyl: 'A lot of the kids wanted to get rid of their material,' explains Dan, 'and we said, "Well, you bring it back tomorrow and we'll provide a bonfire." We burned about $11,000 worth of rock music that first night. The media heard about it, and that's how we got started.' And when Prince's *Purple Rain* tour came to Minneapolis, the Peters Brothers led a protest demonstration against the man whose work is seen as typifying what Dan Peters describes as 'the heavy promotion of the sexual experience to young people'.

The Peters brothers once debated with Gene Simmons of Kiss. 'He found it incredible that we believed in a literal devil,' says brother Dan. 'I believe the whole movement in the area of loose moral standards, immorality or fornication, is all a master-plan of the devil.' And one whose principle purpose would be to threaten the institution of the conventional nuclear family, something Prince's intimations of promiscuity and sexual 'deviance' did not support. Not that Mr Peters necessarily considers every rock musician to be possessed by a demon, His Royal Badness included. 'We continue to pray for Prince. We'd like to see the guy who claims to have a great relationship with God [and] have an ongoing relationship with the living and breathing God, Jesus Christ. But I'm afraid at this point, as far as I can tell from Prince's lyrics, the God he serves has to be his genitals.' Peters says that many young people are genuinely confused by Prince's apparent implication that overt, unburdened sexual expression and Christianity can accommodate each other, a conviction dramatically underlined by the insertion of a secret message in the closing instrumental section of *Purple Rain*'s 'Darling Nikki'. Listen hard, and it is possible to detect human speech proceeding in the wrong direction. Play the record backwards, and discover Prince uttering the following: 'Hello, how are you? I'm fine, because I know the Lord is coming soon, coming, coming soon.'

The various controversies revolving around Prince often manifested themselves as basic silliness. But there is no doubt that on the surface his vision ran deeply against the grain of what many would perceive as the natural order of things. The clearest proof of this was the predicament in which his approach continued to place even his closest and most trusted friends. Proximity to Prince's 'theology' was still more than some of them could handle.

Big Chick's solution was to follow Dez Dickerson and Gayle Chapman in forsaking the fame, glory and sex-ationalism, and snuggling closer into the arms of God. His decision not to pull the trigger on that .44 Magnum marked the start of a new phase in his life, together with a militant anti-drugs posture: 'I said to myself, "What are you doing? What *is* this?" And I haven't touched drugs since. Now I'm going back to the Lord. I'm going to start working for him, trying to help others so they won't go down the same road I've bin down. And I'm telling you,' he says, shaking his head and beard with Old Testament *gravitas*, 'I was in *hell*.'

Huntsberry has maintained to stay friends with his former boss in spite of everything that came to divide them. A year after the split, he, like Dickerson, was still on the payroll, even though he had left the team. There's no doubt that this seemingly odd couple were very close.

166

And the next record Prince made after their split only confirmed the unlikely extent of their common spiritual ground.

It was spring 1985 when Prince released *Purple Rain*'s eagerly anticipated follow-up, *Around The World In A Day*. With no particular marketing ceremony, the album was trailed as a Personal Statement, a treat for the converted, rather than more manna for the masses – and eventually its sales bore that out. In fact, the distance this new music put between Prince and the expectations of his new global audience could hardly have been greater. Lunacy? Brilliance? Caprice? Probably a bit of all three.

Prince presented the completed music to Warner Brothers in New York with a ceremonial panache in keeping with the album's muse. The event was reported in *Tiger Beat*: 'Employees scurried to ready the fourth floor conference room and decorate it with purple, lavender and white helium-filled balloons. Then, they covered the floor with flowers . . . Finally a limo appeared and first Prince's attendants emerged . . . Suddenly, the rear passenger door of the car popped open and Wendy, Prince's guitarist, garbed in gold silk pajamas and a black robe stepped out on to the kerb. She was followed by John L. Nelson, Prince's father, who was dressed in grey pajamas and a silk paisley robe . . . Finally, Prince made his grand entrance. Dressed in white pajamas, a purple silk robe and white high-heeled boots . . . Without uttering a word, Prince and Wendy sat on the carpet. Somebody turned on the reel-to-reel and the songs on Prince's new record began to play.'

The guiding spirit of *Around The World In A Day* is anticipated by Doug Henders' cover art, a kind of idyllic surrealist portrayal of the band's members and others gathered near the edge of a pool from which protrudes a ladder stretching right up to the clouds. In the background, a hillside traces the outline of a prostrate woman, disguised by a multi-coloured collage decoration. The imagery is derived from the hippie notion of a Utopia where people would retreat from the logic of the industrialized world and revert to a child-like wonderment at the simpler pleasures of nature. It is a fantasia whose suggestion of an Eden-like purity would have appealed to the part of Prince that believed – and, according to the testimony of those around him, believed sincerely – that he was especially close to God.

The album was Prince's most collaborative effort so far. Like *Purple Rain*, it was credited to Prince and The Revolution, which comes close to describing the way things actually were. In fact it was substantially recorded after rehearsals for the *Purple Rain* tour. But there were others involved as well, notably Prince's father. The two of them had repaired their relationship, and now Mr Nelson Snr was enjoying co-writing credits on two of the new album's songs: 'The Ladder', a quasi-religious

167

fairy tale on side two; and the opening title track, whose authorship is attributed three ways: Lisa Coleman's brother David is credited an equal share with the father and son team.

For some members of The Revolution, this was probably the happiest of the three albums they had any substantial input into making. The communal concept Prince was abstracting the music from actually reflected his approach to recording it, with several additional players, and a cast of engineering staff including long-standing assistants, Peggy McGreary, David Leonard and Susan Rogers. The first two tracks capture the air of familiarity extremely well. 'Around The World In A Day' is built on a stumbling, cyclical percussion pattern, and features David Coleman on cello, fingercymbals, and two middle-eastern instruments, the oud (or ūd – a plucked lute) and the darbūka (a vase-shaped drum). Tambourine is added by another of the Melvoin siblings, Jonathan. The song commences with a whirring, careering solo from some kind of high-pitched flute, slips with a screech into a jangling, staggered momentum, and climaxes with shards of what might be treated guitar, and Prince's euphoric yelps and exhortations. Throughout, a loose vocal line-up chants the words of the title. 'Paisley Park', which follows, employs a similar mantra-like method, handclaps and tambourine following a bumping drum march. A see-sawing performance by violinist Novi Novog further heightens the prevailing giddiness.

Lyrically, both songs take up the transcendental promise of 'Purple Rain', but express them with the naïve moral certainty of psychedelic nursery rhymes: lots of primary colours and holding hands and believing in the promised land. The obvious, and most regularly cited, inspiration for all this is the Beatles' *Sgt. Pepper's Lonely Hearts Club Band*, made in 1967, though an infatuation with the mystic power of the East was a general feature of that period. With the Joni Mitchell influence apparent too, somehow, Prince seemed to have absorbed an entire sensibility whose heyday had been past nearly twenty years before. The language he employs is so florid that it strays into the parodic, but then Prince's sense of parody seems so utterly compulsive, whatever the context, that pretence and sincerity can be just two parts of the same thing for him. With *Around The World In A Day* he contrives yet another unity of artifice and spiritual conviction. Just because his tongue is never far from his cheek, it does not mean that his theological streak is any less earnest. And *Around The World In A Day* is stuffed with philosophical convictions. He's goofing around with God.

This becomes more bizarrely apparent on the second side, with the tracks 'America', 'Temptation' and 'The Ladder'. This last song briefly became the centre of attention when Prince announced, completely out of the blue, that his Easter Sunday (7 April 1985) concert at the Orange Bowl in Miami, closing the massive *Purple Rain* tour, would be the last

168

from himself and The Revolution for the time being. Steve Fargnoli offered an explanatory remark to the *Miami News*: 'I asked Prince what he planned to do. He told me, "I'm going to look for the ladder." So I asked him what that meant. All he said was, "Sometimes it snows in April." ' This last utterance, as time would reveal, was the title to a song from the forthcoming soundtrack album of his second movie, *Under The Cherry Moon*. In the meantime, everyone shrugged and scratched their heads. Everyone, it would seem, except the band and Prince's immediate circle. For them, this kind of stuff went on all the time. If Prince said he was retiring, well, he meant it – at least until tomorrow afternoon, by which time he would probably have changed his mind. But for the world at large, all this was just another pirouette in the subtext it consumed with his records. That is to say, not Prince's real life, but his *pop* life.

As if there wasn't already enough fuss. The build-up to the Miami gigs had been dominated, locally at least, by objections to Prince on grounds of taste. Since it was Easter Sunday, the church was involved; that is to say, the late Reverend Donald Connolly was, then fifty-two and a senior Roman Catholic. 'To schedule this [concert] on the most sacred of sacred holy days is a slap in the face,' the Reverend Connolly told the *Miami News*. 'It's sacrilegious.' Shortly afterwards, the mayor of Miami, a Mr Maurice Ferre, said his piece for the benefit of the same newspaper: 'I am personally offended by some of the songs Prince sings.' Reportedly, Ferre went on to claim that Prince's show contained a simulated sex act with a boy – something nobody else ever seems to have noticed – and all this shortly after giving away free tickets for the show to students of two high school basketball teams, procured because the Orange Bowl is owned by the Miami City Commission. It was not an especially dignified performance by Mayor Ferre, who preferred not to elaborate on the episode when approached to do so three years later.

Miami, Florida, in the heart of the sun-drenched South, had been the site of unpleasant experiences for the Prince roadshow before. Chick Huntsberry recalls when Dez Dickerson was in the bank seeing him and his wife, a white woman, threatened and abused by passing racists in a pick-up truck as the pair of them walked down the street together: 'I said to Dez, "Hey – this is the South." ' But the Orange Bowl fuss was a storm in a teacup. Suggestions of widespread public protest amounted to nothing, and seventy thousand tickets were sold – a box-office record, completing a total *Purple Rain* tour take in the region of $22 million. Even so, the period marked the beginning of the end of Prince's spell as the biggest rock 'n' roll money-spinner in the world. The off-beat qualities of *Around The World In A Day* guaranteed that those who had embraced him as the new sensation the previous year would be disappointed with the more esoteric directions his artistic development was taking. And there was no shortage of strangeness to put them off.

'The Ladder' was the penultimate cut on side two, the title being a metaphor for the route to a higher spiritual plane. 'Temptation', which follows, is a mad bit of cod electric theatre where Prince appears to engage in a summit meeting with the Lord – or with a very deep voice suggesting itself to be His. The result of this audience-on-high seems to be that His Royal Badness is condemned to death. His crime? Liking sex more than he loves love. And as our narrator resigns himself to oblivion, he quails that he cannot say when he will be coming back. 'Temptation' and 'The Ladder' fit together like customized bookends, framing the controversies Prince had created for himself, and making great play of a recurring rock idea, that of a symbolic death. 'The Ladder' offers gospel according to Prince. That is, the structure, chorus and build-up ape the style of black church music, with Prince half-preaching his lyric as a full-blown choir stirs up the heat behind him. 'Temptation' follows this celestial reverence with a corrupting physical raunch. A far-out, hard-rock blues guitar grind defines a deliberately crass aural bordello, whose subject-matter is familiar, but whose gonzo execution is designed to suggest gluttony more than satisfaction. Then comes that little spat with the One Most High.

Around The World In A Day presents a kind of gift-wrapped purple cosmos, the most perplexing Prince album in many ways, but in others a quite logical fulfilment of the spiritual promise enshrined in *Purple Rain*. Here was the secret garden Prince had talked of leading his disciples into. The distinctive feature of the instrumentation is the use of 'real' instruments – that is to say, synthesizers play a marginal role compared to the various acoustic and percussive combinations featured on the album's definitive tracks. It underlines the idea of pastoral simplicity he is trying to evoke. And look, folks! No drugs! It is a tribute to Prince's unerring capacity for absorbing musical styles and related cultural philosophies, then recasting them to fit his own quirks and convictions. The imagined state of paradise he was borrowing from had been organically linked to the psychedelic drug-culture of the late 1960s. But in the track 'Pop Life' there is a clear, disapproving reference to the things some people – and some of Prince's lost best friends – liked to put up their noses. Is *that* where all their money goes? Was Morris listening? The relevant lines are even picked out in white where the lyrics are reproduced inside the album's gatefold sleeve.

'Pop Life' is a rather ambiguous song. An oblique, vaguely insouciant piece, its words might be interpreted as faintly mocking of the ways and means by which the masses struggle to soup up their mundane lives, although a derisory attitude to such a subject would be out of character for Prince. Its intention may well be to praise people's quest for satisfaction outside material life. But there is a certain resignation about the music, with its leisurely funk bass-line and drum thump. The message seems to lie in the assertion that everybody needs a thrill, but not everybody can be on top. Some are born to create and others to blindly consume? This is either very patronizing, or a very accurate examination of the eighties pop environment, depending on your point of view.

But even if 'Pop Life' *is* open to interpretation, Prince has hardly gone out of his way to suggest that the politics of side two are intended to be ironic. 'America' is a galloping alternative hymn to the American Way, and its message *seems* to be perfectly candid – better to be dead than red. And around a year later, soon after the track was released as a single in his homeland (with a self-directed video) Prince would state, in an MTV interview later published in *Right On!*, that the song was indeed 'straightforwardly patriotic'. It certainly is a strange one. The American magazine *New Republic* noted this apparent ideological quirk with some delight: 'Conservatives were happy to embrace Springsteen. But what will they make of this?' The answer is, they never really noticed.

As if to take some of the steam out of the wilder media speculations about his sanity and style of life, Prince finally granted a press interview. It appeared in *Rolling Stone*, to coincide with the release of *Around The World In A Day*, and was reproduced in that tone of muted but unadulterated adulation which the *Rolling Stone* of the last ten years unfailingly employs for its superstar interviewees:

Question: 'Why have you decided that now is the time to talk?'

Answer: 'There have been a lot of things said about me and a lot of them are wrong. There have been a lot of contradictions. I don't mind criticism, I just don't like lies. I feel I've been very honest in my work and my life, and it's hard to tolerate people telling so many bare-faced lies.'

Question: 'What picture were you painting with *Around The World In A Day*?'

Answer: 'I've heard some people say I'm not talking about anything on this record. And what a lot of other people get wrong about the record is that I'm *not* trying to be this great visionary wizard. Paisley Park is in everybody's heart. It's not just something that I have the keys to. I was trying to say something about looking inside oneself to find perfection.'

Question: 'Sounds religious.'

Answer: 'As far as that goes, let me tell you a story about Wendy. We had to fly somewhere at the beginning of the tour, and Wendy is deathly

171

afraid of flying. She got on the plane and really freaked. I was scared for *her*. I tried to calm her down with jokes, but it didn't work. I thought about it and said, "Do you believe in God?" She said yes. I said "Do you trust Him?" and she said she did. Then I asked, "So why are you afraid to fly?" . . . It's just so nice to know there is someone and someplace else. And if we're wrong, and I'm wrong, and there is nothing, then big deal! But the whole life I just spent, I at least had some reason to spend it.'

The *Rolling Stone* article contains a description of the inside of Prince's purple house which suggests it to have been considerably less exotic than painted in the *National Enquirer*'s Huntsberry exposé. A single picture of Marilyn Monroe is mentioned, which is a lot less than the candlelit roomful we had read about in the *Enquirer* account. One security guard is noted in front of the big black fence instead of a posse of tooled-up meatheads. The feature effectively gave Prince a nice, sanitized platform from which to rehabilitate himself as at least a semi-regular human being. 'The only thing that bothers me is when my fans think I live in a prison. This is not a prison.' The other thing that Prince seemed at pains to emphasize in the *Stone* Q and A was his wilful sense of the ridiculous: 'A lot of my peers make remarks about us doing silly things on stage and on records . . . the music, the dances, the lyrics. What they fail to realize is that is exactly what we want to do. It's not silliness, it's *sickness*. Sickness is just slang for doing things somebody else wouldn't do. That's what I'm looking for all the time.'

The sheer wackiness of *Around The World In A Day* is its greatest strength. It is fruitless to try and decide how seriously to take the album, as opposed to how frivolously. The urge to be just *totally* off the wall is the most powerful component in Prince's monstrous drive to produce. This maniac means business, you might say. Consider, for instance, the curious bunch of characters described on the ballad 'Condition Of The Heart'. A shimmering, meandering butterfly's wing of a thing, Prince's voice clings to its mellifluous melody, dipping and floating through the octaves in its quest for the essence of emotional despair. Fanciful, incredibly mannered, maybe just utter tripe – but 'Condition Of The Heart' is rather lovely, however you care to hear it.

There are also two tracks which customize Prince's loopy sexiness in keeping with the album's overall mood. 'Tamborine', with its juddering backbeat and manic singing, is another nudging, winking wanking tune. Just as naughty, but nicer, is the great 'Raspberry Beret'. Also released as a single, this impossibly pretty song is a worthy paisley inheritor of Prince's tradition for flirty, forgivably untrustworthy compositions about girls, not to mention his interest in the sensual possibilities of fruit. It is a very much a *pop* song – the plainest example of a polished Top 40 craftsmanship which runs through more of *Around The World In A Day* than is immediately apparent. 'Raspberry Beret' is vintage Prince. Though filled with misty adolescent images of motor bikes and losing his innocence in the hay, he still has the front to describe the over-ripe apple of his eye as basically pretty dumb. But the wistfulness was convincing enough, and he had more of it up his sleeve. He gave a song in a similar flower-power mould to a girl group after his heart (long straggly hair, very short skirts) that he met on a plane one day. Shades of 'Automatic'? Whatever, 'Manic Monday' (which Apollonia 6 also recorded) was a hit for The Bangles on both sides of the Atlantic. The name of the credited composer was Christopher Tracy, a pseudonym soon to experience wider exposure.

'Raspberry Beret' also spawned one of Prince's surprisingly few outstanding videos, and the very first he directed himself. With the band perched on podia surrounded by a crew of very funky technicolour dancers, Prince trips up to the mike in a baby-blue suit printed with cotton-wool clouds, the one he is portrayed wearing on the album sleeve. The video features an extended instrumental intro, in the course of which he is handed his white guitar – the same one purchased for him by Apollonia in *Purple Rain* – by a peach-skinned naïf, and is briefly, suddenly, convulsed in a cough. Really 'sick'. And it works.

But the cleverest thing about this spinning, pastel-shaded production are Prince's facial stunts for the camera. It is a better piece of acting than anything he did in *Purple Rain*: just smirking and swooning, pulling faces and fluttering his lashes, sharing the mike with Melvoin, but never actually *looking* into the lens at all. It is a beautiful spoof of an innocence he would struggle to sustain in his work, never mind what kind of chaotic worldliness went on around him.

13

Cherries

Retna

A record as successful as *Purple Rain* confers upon an artist a potential for creative independence that few pop performers are ever allowed in the rigorously market-researched environment of the modern music business. The fact that Prince had enjoyed some fairly major freedoms from the start of his recording career did not lessen the quantum leap represented by his multi-platinum record and award-winning film: the *Purple Rain* LP had sold around seventeen million copies worldwide; the movie grossed over $65 million before the end of the year of its release. He now possessed the resources, and the industry clout, to pursue pretty much whatever options he liked. Success has a way of breeding fear – particularly the fear of losing that success. Given the extent of Prince's urge for acclaim, the determination with which he had worked towards it, and his sometimes demagogic desire to control his immediate environment, he might in some ways have seemed a likely candidate to put safety first in his work from *Purple Rain*, or indeed from *1999*, onwards.

It is, then, to his eternal credit that he has done precisely the opposite. *Around The World In A Day* sold well at first, but it was simply not conceived as a blockbuster follow-up – just the unleashing of another aspect of his hyperactive imagination. *Purple Rain* was dense, strident and inherently cinematic. *Around The World In A Day* was woozy, inter-stellar and weird. Prince had it planned long in advance. As he told his *Rolling Stone* interviewer, 'I think the smartest thing I did was record *Around The World In A Day* right after I finished *Purple Rain*. I didn't wait to see what would happen with *Purple Rain*. That's why the two albums sound completely different . . . You know how easy it would have been to open *Around The World In A Day* with the guitar solo that's

176

on the end of "Let's Go Crazy"? You know how easy it would have been to just put it in a different key?'

Fame, far from stifling him, seemed to encourage Prince to liberate his most irreverent and whimsical ambitions, but without any slackening of his creative discipline. The result was twofold: on the one hand, a blithe foray into milieux in which black artists had rarely, if ever, functioned *positively*; on the other, the first serious reverse in his popularity since the steady upward climb from *Dirty Mind*.

Under The Cherry Moon was a movie project conjured straight out of left field. In a radio interview with the famous Detroit disc jockey the Electrifying Mojo, conducted between the film's completion and its release in the summer of 1986, Prince seemed to anticipate the possibility of a certain audience resistance: 'All I can tell you is that you'll have a good time. I'm hoping that everyone understands where I was trying to go with it. It is like an album for me, and I put my heart and soul into it . . . There's a message behind it all, and I'm hoping that people think about it when they leave.' Sadly, the main problem Prince had with *Under The Cherry Moon* was getting people to turn up in the first place. In the States, the film opened in over two hundred theatres, but reportedly earned only $3.2 million in its first week, compared to a figure almost four times as great for *Purple Rain*. This was a very unhappy return on a picture which cost around $12 million – approaching twice the *Purple Rain* budget – to make.

It was hardly a failsafe project from the off. Shot on the French Riviera, it eventually came out in black-and-white, though it was actually shot in colour. Prince had favoured monochrome from the beginning, but Steve Fargnoli considered that to be an unacceptable commercial risk. They compromised: the film would be made in colour, and they would make a final decision later. In the event, Prince won the debate, and the footage was reprocessed into black-and-white.

The film was modelled on the vintage romantic comedies of the thirties and forties, and although *Cherry Moon* appears to be set in the present day, it contains a generous smattering of references and representations which seem to have escaped the updating process. The result is a temporal muddle which though probably the result of incompetence, is actually quite engaging. From these details alone you can spot the serious risk of culture-shock to a mass audience many of whom had discovered Prince, the rock star, sitting square-eyed in front of MTV. Projecting an important part of his musical persona onto celluloid, he plays a gigolo who goes by the preposterously goo-goo 'Manic Monday' name of Christoper Tracy. As the movie's opening commentary tells us, Christopher was 'a bad boy', who 'only cared about one thing – money'. Though working as a bar-room pianist, Christopher really makes his living by dipping and rolling his big doe eyes at rich and beautiful ladies (such as

177

Mrs Wellington, played by Francesca Annis) from behind the keys until they invite him to brighten up their lives – especially in bed, and all at their own expense. His partner Tricky is played by Jerome Benton. Together, they have come out from Miami in the hope that Christopher can marry a fortune. The potential pay-off soon shows up in the person of Mary Sharon (English actress Kristin Scott Thomas), daughter of a multi-millionaire businessman (Steven Berkoff) who has set aside a huge trust-fund, due to become Mary's when she and a suitable partner embark on marriage. Domineering daddy has someone in mind. Restless, over-protected daughter is none too happy about his choice.

Christopher and Tricky move in on their target at her twenty-first birthday party, where she makes a grand appearance dressed only in a bath towel – and momentarily, not even that. It immediately becomes clear that Mary is a thoroughly snooty English rich girl, and that slippery Christopher is going to have his hands full. And so the romantic action unfolds around this clash of cultures: slick US crooks try to re-educate Miss Upper-Crust Snob, a kind of *Pygmalion* in reverse – with, of course, an original Prince And The Revolution soundtrack thrown in.

The critics absolutely murdered *Under The Cherry Moon*. *Variety* called it 'an example of ego gone amuck . . . Even rock stars' adoring fans have some standards.' *Hollywood Reporter* described the Prince character as 'a wimpy ninny'. In one major American newspaper, a reviewer even advised the public to avoid any *continent* where the film was playing.

There is no doubt that where *Purple Rain* was a dull melodrama enlivened by camp, *Cherry Moon* was an exercise in full-blown camp with its battery half flat. This time, the whole production was built around Prince's sense of cute, comic narcissism. But from his very first scene, posturing rapturously behind his piano, his humour is outstripped by our embarrassment. Of course, mannered exaggeration is essential to camp, but good camp also has a sense of its own absurdity, and a cutting, subversive edge. Ultimately, Prince's self-love overwhelmed his critical faculty. Although his humour is at work throughout the film, it is too often swamped by displays of vanity which are inept rather than disarming. Little looks and pouts that might work well in a photograph, a four-minute video clip, or on stage – where he has a certain knack for appearing to make eye-contact with individual punters – can soon become tiresome in a feature-film of ninety minutes plus.

Just the same, the invective hurled at *Under The Cherry Moon* seems rather excessive; the film is not without its compensations. Despite the irritating aspects of Prince's performance, and the fact that Ms Scott Thomas's role never quite allows her to shake the nasty smell out from under her nose, a lot of the comedy works well. This is primarily down to Prince and Benton managing to work up some genuine rapport on screen. And it is in their scenes alone together, or bouncing off Mary's prudishness, that the most interesting moments occur.

The hoodlum twosome's patter is stylized, badass, smartass black. They slap five; they imitate their mothers' downhome indignation; they answer the phone by saying 'What it is?' When Christopher juts his chin out and calls Mary a 'cabbage head' in a memorably half-cock sparring tango scene, it is an insult delivered straight from the North-Side streets. Prince, who commandeered direction of the film from an early stage, makes the most of the incongruity created by these culturally alien infiltrations into a formula-genre where blacks had previously existed only as freaks, menials and Uncle Toms. The script is full of jokes which turn on the disrepute whites associate with black-American mores: in sexuality, musical taste, and most of all in language. Quite a lot of the exchanges between Tricky and Christopher would be almost impenetrable to unhip whites, although these gags feel more like entourage in-jokes than 'realism'. ('Only confused men wear loafers'. Great line. But *what*?)

The best verbal exchange of all takes place in an expensive restaurant where Tricky and Christopher have plans to lower the tone and free up a few tight asses. Just to wind Mary up, Christopher jots down a phonetic spelling of the place where, as he describes it, you would go to buy a Sam Cooke album: the 'Wrecka Stow'. Lofty Ms Sharon, totally bemused, is momentarily knocked from her perch. Then, in a sudden explosion of eighties technology, out comes Tricky's giant ghetto-blaster, a string quartet is brushed aside, and suddenly all is forgiven as the house gets down to the great, dizzy funk of 'Girls And Boys'. It is interesting to note that in the very first piece of work where Prince uses accent and idiom to define himself clearly as a sharp 'black' trickster making fun of a prim white world, he also hints at a revival of the 'half-caste' profile that emerged from the press during his *Dirty Mind* tour. In one scene, the naughty boys discuss whether they can pass themselves off as brothers. Christopher decides not, because while Tricky's colour is 'chocolate', his he describes as 'butterscotch'. It hinted at a distortion that the black *Village Voice* writer Greg Tate would later put down as pandering to a taste for 'mulatto exoticism'. By the end of the movie, of course, Christopher and Mary have fallen in love, daddy is outraged, and the plot concludes with him having our reformed hero gunned down before his daughter's eyes. The emotions have been so shallow throughout that there is no feeling of tragedy, just a faint recognition that we have seen all the right conventions slightly improperly observed. Otherwise, *Cherry Moon* is just extremely tipsy, a fluffy bit of self-indulgence. So *weightless*, in truth, that it does not really warrant being loathed.

Like *Purple Rain*, though to a lesser extent, *Under The Cherry Moon* plays to Prince's home crowd. It looks to confirm and glorify his trademarks as a rock superstar with little winks and nudges like the Prince-speak spelling of the messages Tricky passes to Christopher at his piano – 'she wants U – Ask 4 The Moon'. The whole Christopher role is like a persona lifted out of a Prince song and reassembled in pictures – or at least, as a sequin-encrusted cardboard cut-out. Christopher Tracy was not a proper acting part for Prince to try and play, just another costume for him to throw on and animate. The conjuring tricks Prince plays with superficiality are, paradoxically, what give depth to his best creative efforts. It is the brilliance of his illusions that keeps you listening. The trouble with *Cherry Moon* is that, even at its most charming, its superficiality is just . . . not very deep.

In the London listings magazine *Time Out*, Steven Berkoff wrote a short, rather cryptic account of his involvement in the picture. Berkoff was drafted in to replace Terence Stamp, who had dropped out at the last minute. 'One glance at the script offers me a clue as to why I am in Stamp's cast-offs . . .' revealed Berkoff, clearly unimpressed. Further, he seems to have a rather ambivalent relationship with his employer, and eventual director.

Prince took over from a young American named Mary Lambert, who hung on to a place in the credits as 'Creative Consultant', but was actually fired from the picture because the star was not satisfied with her performance. It was her first major film – she had previously directed pop videos, including the one for Madonna's Monroe parody, 'Material Girl' – but, according to one insider, Lambert approached the project with 'this real Hollywood attitude. I'll never forget this one time when all the actors were busy preparing for a scene, and she was lounging around in the pool having her secretary read her her mail.' Ms Lambert has continued her directing career, notably with an 'erotic thriller' called *Siesta* which features a soundtrack by one of Prince's most illustrious admirers, Miles Davis. But she is not prepared to discuss her experiences with *Under The Cherry Moon* – she is not even prepared to discuss *why* she is not prepared to discuss them.

Berkoff, who reputedly did not really feel at one with an ambience defined by the closeness of Prince's 'family', offered the following observations: 'Curiously, he directs really well, in a quiet and authoritative way . . . He watches the scene off-stage on the small screen monitor. If the shot is good I hear nothing . . . but if Prince doesn't like it I can always tell. I hear the clattering of high heels on the marble floors, followed by this perfectly formed figure, clutching the script.'

Berkoff declined to contribute any fresh reflections to this book. Perhaps it is a project he too would prefer to forget. 'He [Prince] has some time for me and we get on well because I can always manage to squeeze some juice out of what on paper is as dull as a British Sunday. This is the craft of most stage actors for whom nightly repetition has loosened the improvisational spirit, but Prince now wants it exact and has a curious regard for the text . . . We do the take over and over until we get it right, and the tapping of the feet becomes my torture . . . "You missed a word out here," Prince says patiently.' This rather laboured directorial precision comes across as you look at the film, with everyone taking great care not to get in the way of each other's lines, and noboby generating too much electricity for long. Visually, the pleasure really lies in basking in the Art Deco ambience, and taking the laughs as they occasionally come. It really is a rich boy's private party, great fun for avid fans and some of those involved, but pretty thin going for everybody else. As Berkoff put it, 'I admired Prince's ability to combine acting with directing and even composing the music, but of course, with such responsibility, one does need smart and helpful colleagues . . . And who tells the truth to a star?'

It was during the filming of *Under The Cherry Moon* that Prince did an interview with MTV, a transcript of which appeared in the American black music publication *Right On!* In the course of it he passed a few guarded comments on the nature of his new Paisley Park record label, named after the song, and in anticipation of the studio complex to come. *Around The World In A Day* had appeared under this imprint, and there was more on the way. 'Paisley Park is an alternative,' Prince decided. 'I'm not saying it's greater or better, it's just something else. It's multi-coloured, and it's very fun.' In the recording studio, Prince's output continued apace. During his radio interview with the Electrifying Mojo, just prior to *Cherry Moon*'s release, he was asked exactly how many songs he had in cold storage. 'Three hundred and twenty,' said Prince, 'to be exact.'

As before, some of Prince's material went into his own albums, and some surfaced in disguise. His main front operation through late 1984 and 1985 was a 'band' called The Family, a name which, as Sonny Thompson is quick to point out, has seen usage in Minneapolis music circles before. Thompson considers this revival of his old band's name to be a joke by Prince at his expense. So far as the sleeve notes and photographs of their self-titled album of 1985 are concerned, the Family comprised 'St Paul' (Paul Peterson), 'Jerome' (Benton), 'Jellybean' (Johnson), 'Susannah', who is Wendy Melvoin's identical twin sister, and 'Eric' (Leeds), a saxophone player up from Atlanta, the brother of Prince's then road manager (and now an administrator with Prince's company PRN – Prince Rogers Nelson) Alan Leeds. In reality though, the band was basically Prince on most of the instruments, with Paul Peterson handling vocals. 'After The Time broke up,' St Paul recounts, 'Prince had a little meeting with all the sidemen that were left and said,

"We're gonna put another band together . . . and *you* are gonna be the lead singer." I said, "I am?" '

At that juncture in his career, the idea had some appeal for Peterson. He wanted to show what he could do with his voice, an attribute he fancies Prince might have become aware of when they had adjoining dressing rooms during the filming of *Purple Rain* – Peterson and Morris Day used to sit around and jam. But not every remnant of The Time's personnel could see anything to be gained from this latest Prince scheme. 'Jesse [Johnson] said, "No, I'm gonna leave." So Jesse left at that meeting, and that was the last time he was ever seen or heard from at the Prince camp.'

Still, the project proceeded, and on what was by now a time-honoured basis. Never mind that he only credits himself for 'Nothing Compares 2 U', Prince was the main compositional force behind all the songs on the Family's LP except for 'River Run Dry', which really did come from Bobby Z like the label says. Recording took place in Prince's facility of that time, a warehouse in the Minneapolis suburb of Eden Prairie, later to be redeveloped and become Paisley Park. As credited, David Z helped produce and arrange, while the gifted Clare Fischer made a significant contribution, organizing strings on a number of cuts as well. Leeds provided the excellent saxophone parts, with Melvoin and Johnson doing some vocal back-ups. Jerome Benton was, in Peterson's words, 'basically there for moral support'. For the most part, says Peterson, 'He [Prince] recorded all the tracks, everything, and I just came in and sang on it all. When I went in there he would say, "Well, you've gotta do this", or "You gotta do that . . . No, you can't go to lunch yet. And don't make any plans for dinner, 'cause we're gonna be here till late." They billed me as the leader of the group, but I tell you, I certainly wasn't. I was told every move to make by Prince.'

The Family was a pretty good album, and its hyper-tense funk outings like 'High Fashion', 'Mutiny' and 'Yes', anticipated the newly stripped-down dance material Prince would soon explore, starting with *Parade*'s sensational 'Kiss', and continuing with large parts of *Sign 'O' The Times* and the aborted – but much-bootlegged – *Black Album*, which was to have been released just before Christmas of 1987. But for Paul Peterson, what *The Family* project might boast in artistic quality it lacked in terms of pay, prospects and promotional support. The story has a rather familiar ring.

'I was getting paid a very small weekly wage, compared to the amount of work I was putting in: $250 a week, minus $50 or $60 in tax. And I didn't sign anything [relating to The Family]. They [Prince's managers] issued contracts, but they were unacceptable.' The group's members were advised by attorney Dan Brennan not to sign, and to 'seek individual counsel', since the precise circumstances of each was slightly different.

Jellybean and Benton, for example, were already in the employ of PRN, and would, according to Brennan, have actually taken a cut in pay had they signed the new contract relating to The Family. The main sticking-point, though, was the restraints Brennan considers these contracts would have imposed on the future artistic and financial autonomy of each member. 'We attempted to negotiate a few points. I had made a suggestion that instead of getting weekly salaries that if they were going to be an entity, that they get their money once a year or twice a year, so that they could set up their own corporation as The Family or whatever.' In other words, they should be paid in such a way as to enable them to enjoy the appropriate independence. 'In the case of Paul, I always felt that they would have to deal with him a little bit differently, because although he didn't do much on that album, he was a writer and a [multi-instrumental] player as well as a singer.'

Peterson was not feeling especially well disposed towards his former employer when these conversations took place. Having resigned from the semi-dormant Family some time after the album came out, he severed his connection with Prince, and eventually signed a solo deal with MCA. In response, Prince's lawyers drew up lawsuits to the tune of $5 million apiece against Peterson and Brennan (who also represents Monte Moir), to the effect that Peterson had breached a verbal agreement, and Brennan had advised him to do it. At the time of this interview (early 1988), the suits had not actually been filed. But they were hanging there.

'I had a ten-thousand-mile showdown on the phone with him,' Peterson recalls. Prince was in Nice, becoming an instant film director. With him were Benton, and also Susannah Melvoin and Leeds, each of them fulfilling one role or other in the *Cherry Moon* entourage. Peterson was in LA, taking acting and dancing lessons at Prince's expense, apparently in anticipation of a third feature film for which, according to the 'Prince's Women' piece in *Rolling Stone*, Wendy and Lisa had already begun composing. But Peterson felt out on a limb. 'The single "Screams Of Passion" was out, and there was no promotion, nothing. We didn't have any idea what was going on. It was just so unorganized. I said, "If you're gonna be in charge of this band, you can't do four million other things at the same time." He said, "Yes I can! I did it with the Time, didn't I? I did it with Sheila E. I did it with Vanity 6." '

Peterson concludes that the main reason he left was simply that after around five years of being told what to do, he wanted to be his own boss creatively. 'I'll never forget the time when he was pointing out a certain thing to the band, and I wasn't needed at that point, so I went and shot some pool on the table he had out the back. And he went, "All right, Paul, come here and tell these people exactly what I just told 'em to do. You're supposed to be in here listening to everything I play and everything I do." He made me feel like a two-year-old, like I was back in school all over again. That's like any boss, I suppose. But it was, like, totally stifling.' Peterson remembers the first time Prince ever spoke to him. It was just his third day in rehearsal with The Time, and Prince came up to him with something written on a piece of paper. The ensuing exchange turned out to be a dry run for *Under The Cherry Moon*'s funniest scene. 'He said, "Say it, say it!" I said "Wrecka Stow" . . . Here I am, nervous out of my ass. He said, "Say it!" . . . "Wrecka Stow" . . . He said, "Where do you buy your records? . . . Wrecka Stow." That's how I met him. Strange.'

And yet, struggling hard to be objective, Peterson had some positive observations too. These also sound pretty familiar. 'We had some fun too . . . once in a while. Hey, I remember that time we had fun! But let's be realistic. I am deeply grateful for the amount of exposure I got through him. I have to be. And I will say this for the guy, too: he's an absolute musical genius. He's got a great mind for pop music, and he excels on so many instruments, it's sickening. He creates a lot of stuff right on the spot. A lot of it's just, bang, right off the top of his head. That's just pure creativity, and it's very much to his advantage.'

The ability of Prince to conjure up an air of spontaneity about his records, even though they are often created one painstaking layer at a time, became increasingly apparent from *Around The World In A Day* onwards. But where the hallucinogenic looseness of that record was often arranged within the crafted confines of the pop song, *Parade*, a collection of tracks featured in the soundtrack of *Under The Cherry Moon*, juggled influences from half-a-dozen different directions at the same time to result in Prince's most radical-*sounding* music yet.

Parade made it three times in a row that members of The Revolution played a significant, collaborative part in the creation of a Prince album. And by this time, the ranks of the band had swollen to include several fringe contributors and supplementary players besides the *Purple Rain* nucleus of Coleman, Wendy Melvoin, Bobby Z, Brown and Fink. The additional full members enjoyed exposure to a mass public during the memorable closing titles of *Under The Cherry Moon*, where Prince/Christopher Tracy leads the new, full complement through 'Mountains' (a song which *Rolling Stone* reported was one of two co-written with Wendy and Lisa, the other being 'Sometimes It Snows In April' – the women are not, however, credited as composers on the album). There's a black rhythm guitarist called Mico Weaver (whose Christian name was subsequently spelt 'Miko'); there's a couple of really meaty-looking dancers, Wally Safford and Gregory Allen Brooks (who wears a fur hat mountainous enough to give Dave Crockett a complex – apparently it is known as 'Frank'); there's a white trumpet-player going by the name of Atlanta Bliss; and then there's Eric Leeds, honking on his sax.

184

Of these, all bar Safford and Brooks are individually billed for their musical contributions in the small print of *Parade*'s inner sleeve, and the whole lot, plus Benton, are credited at the end of the film as being Revolution members. All eleven assorted singers, dancers and players took part in the 'Hit And Run' concerts supporting *Parade*, a dance-oriented stage show whose blend of *outré* theatricality and new-fashioned R & B revue captured precisely the mixture of moods portrayed on the LP.

The record starts off not with an overture but a fanfare, 'Christoper Tracy's Parade', which fills the bill almost as well. It introduces a new dimension of Prince's musical imagination, but also something of his father's; John L. Nelson gets a joint writer's credit for this track (and later for the lurching ballad that is the movie's title song). 'Christopher Tracy's Parade' also relies to great effect on Clare Fischer's string arrangements, which sweep the song's marching beat and striding chorus along, after a traffic-jam burst of backwards noise and a drum-beat that jars deliberately against the grain of our expectation. Together with its children's-verse lyric, the track recalls the brilliant vertigo of the Beatles' *Magical Mystery Tour*, rather as the paisley pop of *Around The World In A Day* had *Sgt. Pepper*'s.

Parade borrows freely, but manages to go beyond pastiche into moments of genuine invention. Each side (the first called 'Intro', the second 'End') is stylistically episodic, almost chaotic, with a succession of impossibly varied musical confections jumping into and out of each other in rapid fire. The opener's fairground chorus subsides, relaxes and suddenly pops into 'New Position', the first of three pieces which persuade fresh and radical textures out of the chemistry of funk. 'New Position' 's rhythm is put together with an almost brutally sparse combination of the tightest of drum sounds, a Caribbean clink of metallic percussion, and a burbling bass-line; there is nothing else but Prince's voice, almost frantic in its urgency to save a fading sex life. This notion of a madly libidinal sonic austerity had already débuted in the collage of steel and self-pity that was 'When Doves Cry'. This time, Prince eased back and let it swing on the compulsive 'Girls And Boys', with its leap into a froth of giggling French bawdiness, and a repeating hand-clap pattern that somehow manages to recall the Top 40 prime of T. Rex (though it is hard to explain quite why).

But most stunning of all *Parade*'s dance-floor pieces was the breathtaking 'Kiss'. It really is a *startling* piece of work, a distillation so pure that, in the words of *Rolling Stone*'s reviewer Davitt Sigerson, Prince had 'achieved the effect of a full groove using only the elements essential to the listener's understanding – and so has devised a funk completed only by the listener's response'. In 'Kiss' we hear Prince's R & B technique pruned back tight to the root, but done so with the expertise of an artist who has taken funk's mechanisms apart in his head a million times. So assured is he in his grasp of what made James Brown's get-down formulations work that he is able to build 'Kiss' around nothing but the most spartan of drum-machine shuffles and the tightest coils of electric guitar. David Z – a frequent collaborator in the editing of Prince's singles – is credited as arranger of the track, but the way he tells it, the skeletal tension of 'Kiss' was really down to its composer: 'he gave me the song in a very rough acoustic guitar version form. I cut the track with a couple of guys from [Paisley Park artists] Mazarati, and the next day he put his lead guitar and a voice on. We originally had a bass part and a snare-drum sound and a clapping sound and acoustic guitar things, and Prince just hauled it all out – "We don't need that!" He has a very radical approach to things.' Prince's reversion to his falsetto voice for 'Kiss', together with the dramatic emptiness of its noise, recalled superficially the sexually ambivalent, punky rawness of *Dirty Mind*. But the light-headed good humour of the song's lyric has a warmth that underlines how pornographic – to use the word in its correct sense, as in depersonalizing – those early efforts were.

In contrast to the movie they decorated, the resonances of *Parade*'s best songs run deeper than the seductive surfaces they project. 'Sometimes It Snows In April' – in the film, Christopher's swansong – is a melancholy epic constructed from lilting piano and acoustic guitar, and no percussion at all. Lavish in its poignance, it tends to drag over six minutes and fifty seconds; but Prince's delivery actually sounds straightforwardly *sincere*. 'Anotherloverholenyohead', meanwhile, has a genuine dramatic desperation to it. There is also a mature confidence about his sense of texture and timing that enables him to bounce the album from dense, pounding discordancy – as in 'Life Can Be So Nice' (Beatles-ish again) – to the looping, Euro-continental ostentation of 'Under The Cherry Moon', or the piano instrumental 'Venus De Milo'. Each one is put together with the same easy control over the way different sounds can be made to flower and interact. Even a ghostly reverie like 'I Wonder U', which fits between 'New Position' and 'Under The Cherry Moon' almost like an interlude, feels totally fresh and is executed with blithe assurance.

It is not that all the material on *Parade* is sublime beyond compare – indeed, Prince has since declared himself dissatisfied with it. But all of it is at the very least unorthodox and diverting, and illuminates some aspect of Prince's emergence as a truly innovative songwriter, musician and producer. If the music often feels frivolous, its execution is never trite. It makes a vivid contrast with the rhetorical exertions of *Purple Rain*. 'Mountains', which opens the album's 'End' (second) side, soars with an ease that renders its visual representation at the film's close dottily appropriate: Prince, half Tracy reincarnated, half 'himself', leads the augmented band through the song, dressed like a Spanish troubadour, with the whole lot of them 'floating' like angels in the stratosphere, perched on a cloud.

'Mountains' was one of four singles released from *Parade*, along with 'Girls And Boys', 'Kiss', and 'Anotherloverholenyohead'. They yielded some of Prince's more sophisticated videos. For 'Mountains', the closing sequence from *Under The Cherry Moon* simply doubled as a promo. For 'Girls And Boys', the band plus Susannah Melvoin form a whole alternative cast of slapstick characters edited into the appropriate piece of footage from *Under The Cherry Moon*. The video concludes with a completely mad trick-ending, with Jerome Benton sprawled across a chair, racked with uncontrollable laughter. Another Prince-directed promo, it also sees him make the most of the potential for identity-confusion provided by the presence of the Melvoin twins.

But the outstanding video of the *Parade* period is, appropriately, the one for 'Kiss'. Filmed in a virtually bare studio, and with plenty of bare skin, it interprets perfectly the constrained fizziness of the music. Only three people appear in it, using the absolute minimum props: Prince himself, in the button-studded, belly-baring tunic-top of the *Parade* album sleeve, complete with tight matching pants; Wendy Melvoin, smirking and smiling on a stool, duplicating the record's sparks of rhythm guitar; and a dancing partner in black underwear, a lace shroud and shades.

The 'Kiss' video is basically a dance set-piece into which all the ripples and shimmers of body language Prince knows how to use are condensed. His dancing is a delight, his moves fluid, witty and sharp. He pursues his enigmatic partner round the floor, spinning, shuffling and daringly planting his lips on the base of her belly. In the name of 'sickness', he leaves the miming of the title-cum-punchline to her. The clip concludes with the pair of them framed by a mock TV-screen, pressing forward like zoo animals, wondering whether to try stepping out of the set.

'Kiss' made number one in the US national chart for two weeks in March 1986, earning a gold disc for sales of over one million copies. It was Prince's third American chart-topping single in two years, and his ninth Top 10 entry in just over three. But while his knack for reeling off successful 45s seemed undiminished since 'Little Red Corvette', album sales had failed to come close to those for *Purple Rain*. Compared to the US figure of around ten million for the latter, *Around The World In A Day* only amassed two-and-a-half, and *Parade* marked a further decline (if that is quite the word) to around one-and-three-quarter million copies sold. With 'Kiss' being the album's biggest hit, and in the context of an apparent retreat from the album and movie by a large slice of the mass market, a Prince hardcore seemed to be identifying itself. That hardcore was looking at least as black as it was white. And whether by accident or design, Prince's work seemed to be tilting back towards the traditional black music market. It was not simply the strong funk element in *Parade*'s many and varied tunes that creates that impression, but the generally improvisational ambience, and the stage show Prince worked out to promote the album.

These were concerts that drew strongly on the time-honoured conventions of live soul troupers: full of dance-action and loose rhythm jams, with Prince conducting the ebb and flow, often hand-cueing the different musicians in. The repertoire pulled together material from *Around The World In A Day*, as well as *Parade* and a few old favourites including the crowd-pleasing 'Head'. Prince would emerge in his *Parade* cover get-up, strip to the waist, and from there go through a series of costume-changes, taking in a smart white, yellow or orange zoot suit, the studded, over-size leather jacket he sported in *Under The Cherry Moon* for a fragment of 'Whole Lotta Shakin'', and – to close the proceedings – a long, fawn topcoat. Aside from the wardrobe activity, though, it was a show that ousted ostentatious production in favour of movement, economy, and images that floated, shifted and changed. Prince was modelling an assortment of personalities, musical and visual, setting up an ironic buffer between his performance and himself, playing off the cartoon qualities of his three lumbering back-up men, Benton, Safford and Brooks. It was, put simply, very *sharp*, a genuinely eclectic modern pop-and-soul show, which accentuated every little tremor of Prince's outrageously flirtatious charm.

And yet the communal buzz from the stage did not sustain itself for long after all the dates had been played. Before the end of 1986, Prince was back to making records in the studio on his own, and the core of The Revolution was no more.

The way some of its members tell it, The Revolution's old guard were not exactly fired. They just sort of ran out of reasons to be there. The most bitter about the affair, indeed, about his entire tenure in Prince's group, is Mark Brown. He had filled the bass-player's post vacated by André Cymone after getting a phone-call from Prince out of the blue, asking him to audition for the role Sonny Thompson thought was his. Brown knew about Thompson's situation, but believed he had to put sentiment aside. 'I said, "I'm not going to ruin my chances to make it because of Sonny." I'm sorry it had to be that way. I guess Prince was looking for someone a bit younger that he could control more. Sonny was uncontrollable. Sonny's one of those guys, if he got mad at Prince he'd bust him in the mouth. Prince knows I wouldn't do that.'

Brown was another Central High student, another graduate of the

Jim Hamilton Business of Music class. His band, Fantasy, had swung themselves a few First Avenue gigs thanks to slotting some Top 40 material into their act. Prince, in those days still a relatively small-time figure, used to watch them there. 'Evidently he'd been spotting me for, like, nine months,' says Brown.' Once into the band, Brown had his name reversed, creating a typical racial pun, Brown Mark, and suddenly understood he was entering another league. 'I realized this was going to be a learning experience for me. I didn't know Prince was that famous. The opening night [of the *Controversy* tour] he had fifteen thousand people out there.' The way Brown tells it, his baptism of fire at the Rolling Stones shows was just a warm-up compared to some of his experiences with Prince: 'Sometimes we would get to be really good friends. We would laugh and giggle. But then he would just jump into a whole different mood. He'd turn into a demon. The way the guy treated me when it was [out of] the business [environment], he was just my friend. He was nice to me. But working? Hey, he'd kick my butt. He'd say, "Hey, you do it right." Man, he beat me up. Not physically but mentally.

'He told me when I first joined the band. He says, "Don't ever argue with me. Even if I'm wrong, I'm right." Those were his exact words. I went through a lot of head-trips and heartaches. I got brutally, mentally mutilated by things that were done to me with no explanation. They left me behind once [on the *Controversy* tour] 'cause I was a minute late for the bus. I came down the steps with all my bags and everything, and all the fans down there. One of them said, "Yo, man, I think they left you. They forgot you were here . . ." I called my mum. I said, "Will you get me an airplane ticket? I'm coming home." ' Eventually the bus returned. 'When I got on I was pretty pissed off. They were all on there laughing. I said, "I don't see nothing funny." I was almost ready to bust the road manager in the mouth 'cause he was laughing, and he docked me $200. I went to Prince about it, and he said, "You shouldn't have been late." '

Still only eighteen, just a year out of high school, Brown says he found the pressures close to impossible. 'I was unhappy, and it started showing in my weight. I started gaining weight and I started drinking. I used to get drunk every night. There were times when I cried. I'd call my momma and say, "I wanna come home." She'd tell me, "Hang in there." Once I broke a guitar string on stage and he cussed me out in front of fifteen thousand people. I remember once we had a head-on collision on stage. To make him look good and to play it off, he pushed me down on my back. I got up and he pushed me down again. He drop-kicked me three times; the last time I ended up half over the drum riser.'

Brown accumulated a litany of resentments which culminated in his resignation from the group. He says that Prince wanted him to continue, but Brown had had enough. He even claims he was broke. 'I didn't have

189

a penny, man. I didn't have a cent.' A big part of the problem was the relationship between the band Mazarati and the Paisley Park label. Mazarati were Brown's own side-project, something he says he kept secret from Prince for as long as he could. Fronted by an ebullient young singer and fashion designer called Sir Terry Casey (his full, real Christian name, it was transformed to Sir Casey Terry on the record sleeve), Mazarati were a young, mainly black Minneapolis band playing a blend of rock and funk. Brown wrote all of the songs but one, and arranged and co-produced (with David Z) their self-titled début album, released in early 1986. The odd track out, '100 MPH', was contributed by Prince himself, and the band's florid, ambi-sexual appearance carried more than a tiny echo of the Purple look. It is Brown's contention that Prince imposed his own stamp on Mazarati, and then his company failed to give them adequate support. 'He let them go downhill. He made 'em wear those clothes, he made 'em look like that. [Then] they [Paisley Park] held me responsible for . . . a whole bunch of things.'

Contractual disputes added to the tension between Prince and Brown Mark. Eventually, according to Brown, he committed himself to the *Parade* tour 'out of the goodness of my heart. They guaranteed me a figure that was insulting.' Brown claims that he was offered $3,500 a week to work with the Fleetwood Mac singer Stevie Nicks, at a time when he was earning close to a third of that with Prince. 'He [Prince] talked me down. He gives me all these hopes: "You're gonna be rich next year." I believed that. I went on and on believing that, but it never happened.'

Both Brown and Mazarati have since signed to Motown under the managership of Craig Rice, with Brown enjoying a growing reputation as a producer of black pop hits, as well as being an artist in his own right. The sleeve notes of his début solo album, *Brownmark* (now one word), thank almost the entire Minneapolis black music hall of fame, but one name is conspicuous by its absence: Prince. In his 1985 *Rolling Stone* interview, Prince is quoted as saying 'Mark Brown's just the best bass player I know, period. I wouldn't have anybody else. If he didn't play with me, I'd eliminate bass from my music.' But if that was the esteem in which employer held employee, Brown does not seem to think it was reflected in the status he enjoyed in the band. On previous tours, Brown's positioning had guaranteed his visibility: up front, stage right. For *Parade*, though, he was stuck behind both Matt Fink's piano and the new trio of singer–dancers, Benton, Safford and Brooks. And this was in addition to what Brown felt was already a demotion on- and off-stage in favour of Wendy Melvoin, who did not join The Revolution till two years after him. 'I believe in seniority, but I believe in not taking favourites. I don't believe in segregating your band, but that's what he did. Wendy comes in the band one year, and she's famous, because he

190

makes her famous, while you've got guys that have been hanging around with him for years. It's not fair. But it makes him bigger.'

By Prince's own testimony, Melvoin and Lisa Coleman had come to be closer musical confidantes than most. 'It is true I record very fast,' he told MTV/*Right On!*. 'It goes even quicker now that the girls help me. The girls meaning Wendy and Lisa.' In the April 1986 *Rolling Stone* cover piece on Wendy and Lisa, Ms Coleman said, 'We don't want to leave and start our own thing because this *is* our own thing. I don't feel like we're just hired musicians taking orders. He's always asking for our ideas.' As for Ms Melvoin: 'We tell Prince we love him all the time. He always gets all embarrassed and doesn't know what to say. We tell him to tell us the same thing, so he goes, "Uh, OK, yeah, I love you too." It's silly, us being all so intense about it and swooning over each other, but it's meaningful. Not that the rest of the band doesn't understand Prince – they do. We're just a bit more spiritual with him . . . I'm sorry, [but] no one can come close to what the three of us have together when we're playing in the studio. *Nobody!*'

The precise circumstances of their departure so soon after these expressions of warmth and intimacy remain unclear. Since striking out on their own, the pair have sheltered, understandably, behind verbal smokescreens about the need to move on, explore new worlds, and so on. Both they and drummer Bobby Z – who had been there in Del's Tyre Mart with Prince and André Cymone from the very beginning – are bound by contractual agreements not to talk about Prince in public. But there is enough testimony from inside the business to suggest that, without overstating the point, Wendy's and Lisa's leaving was not undertaken entirely as they would have chosen at the time. Once adrift on their own, they put their talents out to tender; rather than simply stay on with Paisley Park, they eventually signed to Virgin.

As for Bobby Z, it seems he was just about ready to move on anyhow. His reputation, like that of his brother David, is for having a more phlegmatic attitude towards the way the rock industry works, ego trips, power games and all. For him, the bullshit is just part of the deal, and to expect anything else is naïve. He is not a cynic, just a realist. Prince once described Rivkin as 'my best friend. Though he's not such a spectacular drummer, he watches me like no other drummer would.' But with his music assuming more and more of a free-form, almost jazz orientation, Rivkin's sturdy rock approach, with its emphasis very much on anchoring the beat, was becoming less appropriate than that of Sheila E, at that time waiting in the wings, ready to take his place. And he had other options too: he had already produced a rock band, the Suburbs, for A & M in the States; he put his studio expertise directly at the disposal of Wendy and Lisa once The Revolution had disbanded; and soon after, he set up base in England to produce and co-write an album for Boy George. For Rivkin, the parting with Prince was an amicable one, even though the termination of his contract entailed PRN paying him a substantial sum in compensation.

Bobby Z's friendship with Prince appears to have lasted through thick and thin: his whims and eccentricities, his erratic scheduling of 'emergency' rehearsals that could be just as suddenly postponed, the calls made in the middle of the night to fly to LA and participate in the recording of 'Jack U Off', the fawning and crawling, his gradual isolation from the rest of the band, his exercise of a God-like prerogative to nurture, punish and forgive. Rivkin spotted Prince's special talent at an early stage. His admiration for it remains undiminished, and also for his sheer dedication simply to getting things done. Even the most resentful of his former musicians has to hand that to him: 'He'll pay for all the damage he's done to people,' says Mark Brown. 'But maybe that's what he chooses. Maybe he chooses not to have friends over fame and success. That's his trip and it's none of my business. I still respect him, though. I respect him because he wouldn't be where he is now if he hadn't had that attitude.'

14

Black

Michael Putland/Retna

Detroit, Michigan, is the coldest, toughest, blackest blue-collar city in America. It has also been a big town for Prince Nelson, ever since his star really began to rise with the *Controversy* tour. And when, after the (probably unrepeatable) peak of *Purple Rain*, sales of his records began to fall off, Detroit's special passion for Prince lived on. For Prince's twenty-eighth birthday show, only Detroit would do. And it was directly after leaving the auditorium that he called the Electrifying Mojo from his hotel room to do a live interview on Radio WHYT. 'I want to thank my little Motor Babies,' he declared, all hot breath and limpid humility. 'It's a fine way to spend my birthday to be sure.'

Mojo had played a significant part in elevating Prince to his special place in the hearts of the Detroit audience. Born locally, his career as a DJ had been dogged by much of the same conservative thinking about what a black performer could and could not do as had troubled Prince himself – and like Prince, Mojo had battled hard to overcome it. For him, market-format programming is the bane of American radio. Determined that there was an audience for a show that pulled together adventurous musics from every different school of pop, he has even been willing to fill late-night slots for no pay, often being obliged to go round drumming up advertising revenue in person in order to support himself. That was Mojo's deal: you buy me, you buy the show. No compromise.

As a result, Detroit has made Mojo into a cult figure. Falling out with a succession of different stations, creating a Clintonesque space-age mythology around himself, and never showing his face to the public, Mojo has also, from 'Soft And Wet' onwards, championed the cause of Prince. Mojo helped bring the sound of big, small-town Minnesota to the big, bad Motor City.

'It was pretty different, kind of sad to be exact,' said Prince, reflecting with Mojo on his Minneapolis childhood, ten years after his horizons had begun rapidly to expand. 'The radio was dead, the discos was dead, the ladies was kind of dead. If I wanted to make some noise, if I wanted to turn anything out, I was gonna have to get something together . . . which was what we did. We put together a few bands and turned it into Uptown. That consisted', he resumed, getting into his stride, 'of a lot of bike-riding nude . . . but, you know, it worked. We have fun. That's why I wanted to come here on my birthday, 'cause I wanted them [his 'little Motor Babies'] to have a little taste of where we live, and get a little taste of where y'all live. To me, this is like my second home.'

Eddie Murphy once went on record saying, 'Prince is *bad.*' Prince agreed: 'In people's mind,' he had told *Rolling Stone*, 'it all boils down to, "Is Prince getting too big for his britches?" I wish people would understand that I always thought I was bad. I wouldn't have got into the business if I didn't think I was bad.' And if Detroit didn't think Prince was bad, he would never have been their sweetheart.

Long before Michael Jackson set about reacting to the taunt that he was, in Black Moslem leader Louis Farrakhan's word, 'cissified', with his 1987 *Bad* album, Prince was secure in the hearts of his black audience as possessing the qualities Jackson was having to work so hard to assert: that combination of brazen certitude and ultra-cool demeanour, a combative display of pride. He might have been a dandy, but he could still kick your ass. So as the bulk of the great white mass moved on after *Purple Rain* to whatever Big Thing came next – Madonna or Oliver North or computer games – the black hardcore, the radio stations, the club DJs, the black public itself, stayed pretty firm. Prince's subsequent works did not let them down, or the reputation they conferred upon him.

Sign 'O' The Times was released worldwide on 2 April 1987, with a peace sign in the middle of the "*O*" and two long-playing records inside the sleeve. It is Prince's most opulent album, his most free and eclectic, and, culturally, his most black. *Sign 'O' The Times* had a portion of almost everything he had to offer in the past, but all delivered with a feeling of total self-assurance, the sort which often marks the difference between defensive arrogance and a deeper, healthier confidence. That is what is, if you like, 'black' about *Sign 'O' The Times*. It is not simply the fact that the bulk of the songs draw from each of a half-dozen relatively uncolonized Afro-American styles, but that Prince seems so at ease with himself – and no matter how many white friends he made, or white rock groups he listened to, or records he sold to white kids, that Self, surely, *has* to be a *black* Self. Until the wider world permits it, there is no complete excape for anyone from the strictures imposed by 'race' – not even for Prince Roger(s) Nelson, the crossover king of his own private paisley world.

Some of the songs on *Sign 'O' The Times* may have come from Prince's giant vault of reserve material. A few certainly involved a degree of collaboration with Wendy Melvoin and Lisa Coleman. Their musical contributions are duly credited on two tracks: 'Slow Love' (Wendy, guitar and backing voice; Lisa, backing voice); and 'Strange Relationship' (Lisa, sitar and wooden flute; Wendy, tambourine and congas). And in the course of the interview they conducted for *The Independent*, Melvoin and Coleman indicated that they had originally contributed to other tracks, but that Prince had subsequently re-recorded them. In addition, the complete *Purple Rain/Around The World In A Day* incarnation of The Revolution, plus those who augmented the line-up, as well as Susannah Melvoin and Jill Jones, are credited on the live Parisian party piece. 'It's Gonna Be A Beautiful Night'. But for the most part, *Sign 'O' The Times* saw a return to the one-man show. The only other musicians to contribute very audibly were the trumpet-and-saxophone team, Atlanta Bliss and Eric Leeds. Their input is fairly crucial. Chick Huntsberry says that Prince used actively to *hate* the sound of horns, but on *Sign 'O' The Times*, the synthesizer swathes and punctuations with which Prince had replaced them on his early albums were in turn displaced by brass.

Eric Leeds provided an unlikely connecting bridge between Prince and one of the blackest and baddest of his musical and iconic influences: James Brown. At thirty-five Leeds was the oldest member of the band to undertake the *Sign 'O' The Times* European tour in the summer of 1987, and the only one permitted to preview it for the press. Leeds's brother Alan had been Brown's road manager before he became Prince's for *1999*, and Eric, tagging along, says he had come pretty close to actually being enlisted in JB's band. Brown's legendary saxophonist Maceo Parker was a very big influence, and Leeds's ineffably fruity playing brought the Brown legacy right back to the centre – or one of the centres – of Prince's sound. 'I think he has always considered himself a black artist,' says Leeds. 'His music is a product of his background, and, if there is such a thing, a black outlook on life . . . though he might disagree with that. He is a black artist with success in crossing boundaries.'

Sign 'O' The Times skipped back and forth across boundaries to unleash a benevolent poltergeist of pleasure. And yet the initial sound we hear is a howl of pain. The title track was the first social-comment song Prince had released whose impact was truly *sobering* rather than petulant. Initially, coming from Prince, such a direct lament for the plight of the species was an odd, alien concept. To be purely subjective, it hit an emotional blind-spot – but one which was swiftly illuminated as the sheer cleverness of the spare, popping percussion sank in, and the forbidding rasps of guitar gradually convinced you that this time Prince's agony was not centred purely on himself. 'Sign 'O' The Times' was modelled after the tradition of the talking blues. It is not a polemic or a critique, just a testament to a troubled state of mind. Prince intones the words with a flat, weary quality he had never utilized before, detailing a modern world of AIDS and gun-lust, poverty and bomb neuroses, and, crushingly, the springing of eternal, farcical hope. Lyrically, it is not astounding. But as a vision of utter bleakness it is extremely eloquent. The odd thing about 'Sign 'O' The Times' is that although its title doubles as the album's masthead, its terse realism does not typify the collection as a whole. As a launching-pad for the abundant indulgences to come, it comes across like a preliminary word of caution before the fun begins.

'Sign 'O' The Times' was an opportune departure, in that it kept Prince in step with a pop environment where 'concern' had become a key idea, with the Live Aid famine appeal as its grand global expression. Prince had been the target of some disapproving noises when he failed to add his famous face to those who got together to record 'We Are The World' as USA For Africa. He made some atonement soon after, contributing '4 The Tears In Your Eyes' to the ensuing album. But there were other critics for him to appease. Never mind the attempts to condemn or belittle his artistry from moral custodians of the Right, Prince had also come in for some stick from quarters more deserving of his respect. From Los Angeles, the National Association for the Advancement of Colored People had issued condemnations of Prince, Michael Jackson, and other major black stars for not employing more fellow blacks within their organizations. And the ripples of disenchantment from the black music press were turning into sizeable waves of indignation.

In Britain, *Black Echoes* had not been slow to express its irritation at the way muck-rakers from the tabloids had been ushered into the post-*Parade* shows party, while the papers covering black music, who had supported Prince when no one else wanted to know, had been ignored. In the States, meanwhile, *Right On!* ran an opinion piece as its cover story, entitled 'Is Prince Getting Too Big For His Lace Britches?'. It criticized his apparently studied isolation from the 'real world', the bruising notoriety of his security entourage, and the arrogance they perceived among those who took care of his business. 'By continually refusing to talk for himself,' wrote Paul Lamont, 'by dodging interviews that would set the record straight on his actions and the meanings in his often confusing lyrics, he risks the possibility of a backlash to his impressive success so far.' Perhaps it was in response to this that Prince, in his MTV interview reprinted in the same publication, denied that he had ever abandoned his 'funk roots', putting his non-attendance at USA For Africa down to shyness, insisting that 'I'm not afraid of anything', and talking about James Brown: '[He] played a big influence in my style. When I was about ten years old, my step-dad put me on stage with him and I danced a little bit until the bodyguard took me off. The reason I liked James Brown so much is that on my way backstage, on my way out, I saw some of the finest dancing girls I ever saw in my life. And I think in that respect he influenced me by his control over his group.'

On *Sign 'O' The Times*, Prince mustered a dance song that might almost be a direct tribute to Brown. 'Housequake' is simply one of the funkiest and funniest things he has ever done, a firecracker of a party track with a bunch of sidekicks hollering and hooting back-ups, and Prince exclaiming squeakily in crackpot jive aphorisms. The breathless horn motifs are pure Brown, a delicious pastiche of the brass on his classic 'Papa's Got A Brand New Bag'.

In his autobiography, *The Godfather Of Soul*, Brown described a concert at the Beverly Theater in LA in 1984, where Prince *and* Michael Jackson joined him on stage: 'Michael sang "Man's World" and sounded fantastic. When we broke into "There Was A Time", it blew his mind. He sang and danced, and the place went wild. Prince played some guitar, but I think he was a little nervous because Michael fit into my thing a little better since Michael had been studying me for years. But later on Prince practised, and he got into it real good. When I was in California later, he came to a show and lay on the floor back-stage and watched my feet. Afterward, he asked me if I had roller skates on my shoes.'

Brown, Jackson and Prince stepping the same boards would amount to a real summit-meeting of black pop icons, but also a confluence of very different life experiences. With *Sign 'O' The Times*, Prince indulged all the musical and spiritual riches that Brown's upbringing in the rural south of the forties would have made socially impossible, and Jackson was just too neurotic – too star-spangled – to try. Brown's bullheaded talent had created the potential for someone like Prince to sidestep the racially defined rules imposed on Afro-American music. As for Jackson, well, Prince had been to his shows too, and watched with the proper respect. But the differences in the responses of the two of them to the demands of celebrity hint at completely contrasting conceptions of what show-business glory might be worth.

For Jackson, only the biggest could ever be the best. After 1983's *Thriller* had turned into a tearaway sales phenomenon to beat them all – forty million albums sold worldwide – it was as if he had become beached on the sands of his own success, swamped with family obligations, besieged by critics from all sides, but, most of all, stymied by his own conception of what constituted a good record. The child of a father fired up by the American Dream of self-improvement, fixed on the idea of Hollywood as the Holy Grail, Jackson had lived and breathed the main-stream showbusiness ethic since he had been old enough to think. The result is that for him, the value of a record seems measurable primarily in terms of the size of audience it attracts. The outlandish crossover popularity of *Thriller* left him hoist by his own petard. After that, where could he go but down? The result was four years of nothing.

But Prince claims for himself a saner balance of priorities. 'Record sales and things like that, it really doesn't matter, you know,' he declared to the Electrifying Mojo. 'It keeps the roof over your head, and it keeps money in all these folks' pockets that I got hanging around here, but it basically stems from the music and I'm just hoping that people understand that. You know, money's one thing, but soul is another and that's all we're really trying to do. I wouldn't mind if I just went broke you know, 'cause as long as I could play this type of thing and come here, you know . . . I just have fun and I'm thankful to be alive.' Easy words to say, and easy to dismiss as platitudes. And yet the singularity of his artistry gives them a certain credence. While Michael Jackson seemed paralysed with worry, Prince responded to his mighty crossover by putting out eight LP sides of new music in three years, none of them designed to be cost-effective in terms of the expectations of those who discovered him simply as the new sensation when *Purple Rain* fever took hold. There is a celebrated tale, told by Jackson's manager Frank Dileo in *The Face* magazine, that Prince had been invited to share lead vocals on the *Bad* album's title track. Dileo added that Prince declined, and asserts that this was Prince's loss. Another version of this story, though, says that Jackson's producer, Quincy Jones, asked Prince along hoping a meeting would help jerk MJ out of his creative inhibitions.

Prince had none of those. *Sign 'O' The Times'* title track might be seen as a nod to a changing rock climate, but the rest of it simply brought to fruition the artistic growth and emotional maturity fitfully promised by *Parade*. Most strikingly, the album's sensuality continued Prince's transition from the pornographic towards the truly erotic. There is as much frenzied sexual longing as ever, but even at his most gropingly sexist, or politically naïve, the lusting is always human where once it was robotic or just plain crude. Part of the difference is that Prince seemed to have really picked up on the idea of *soul*. 'Slow Love', slipped into the middle of side two, is a divine bedroom ballad, with horns as full and fat as prime Stax, and Clare Fischer's orchestration measured with the usual precision. There is a playfulness about the way his voice skews off between octaves, but the lyrics – co-written by one Carol Davis – are of a devotional simplicity that permits no corruption of his sincerity. It is a song about love *and* about sex, with no ulterior motive within earshot. It is also a song which celebrates the physicality of black musical culture, without abusing it to fit the myths created to denounce it.

Sex gets everywhere on *Sign 'O' The Times*, sometimes nasty, sometimes silly, sometimes just sublime, but never in a way that sells the complexities of sexuality short. It is simply more profound. The coasting pop-rock 'Strange Relationship', for instance, details a complicated set of feelings with eloquent economy. Prince's protagonist cannot stand to see his lover happy, but her sadness hurts him more – a no-win, love-hate situation of confused roles, for which he wishes to apologize. The lead vocal is attributed to someone called 'Camille'. As with 'Jamie Starr', no one from Prince's inner circle, or its intermediaries with the outside world, has ever enlightened us as to whom this Camille person is. Nor, however, have they ever troubled themselves to contradict the universal assumption that 'Camille' is Prince, his voice minutely tampered with to sound like a female *alter ego*.

As a device to elaborate more deeply the infinite confusions of gender and desire, 'Camille' is a very handy 'girl' to have around. In total, she makes four appearances on *Sign 'O' The Times*. It is she who jabbers away on 'Housequake', and her other steps into the vocal spotlight are the first three tracks on the album's third side: 'Strange Relationship' is the last of them, preceded by 'If I Was Your Girlfriend' and the opening 'U Got The Look'.

Each of these songs deals in contradictory romantic fascinations, though each is very different from the others. On first listening, 'U Got The Look' is simply a particularly grabby piece of hard American guitar rock, with the vocals shared out to create a turned-on duet. The singers are 'Camille' and Sheena Easton, at that time enjoying gossip column prominence as Prince's latest flame (and making a total of no less than *four* women appearing on the album with whom Prince had been romantically linked: there was media speculation that he and Jill Jones were once a bit more than friends, and he was also supposedly at one time engaged to Susannah Melvoin). Together, the pair of them 'rock out' in the regular girl-meets-axe-riff fashion. But closer inspection suggests the possibility of a more complex undercurrent of meaning which touches the volatile nerve-ends of sexual and racial rivalries. If Prince had struggled to escape from a 'black' racial identity before, then in 'U Got The Look' he positively embraced it, at least in his use of language. All the linguistic idiom he employees is of a semantic and grammatical character that – like 'bad' meaning 'good' – alters and inverts 'standard' (white) rules for governing the use of words. It is black-American English of a concentrated type he had not used before.

Sheena Easton reflects many of the same words and phrases back at him. And yet we know – and if we didn't, we can see from the video – that she is white, a white woman, slicked up and made up like a strutting, stiletto punkette. What does Prince *mean* when he talks about the colours peach and black? Is she the peach and he the black, or is there some obtuse anatomical metaphor at work here? Whatever precisely it was that had fermented in Prince's mind, some black girls definitely took the song to express a preference for Caucasian women which went right against the grain. There is still a school of thought that considers a black man taking a white woman to be a mark of status, of symbolic entry into what is perceived as a superior white world. (It also inflames the deep-seated fears of white racists, although that is strictly their problem.) By logical extension, such values imply an insult to the black world left behind, and in particular to black womanhood.

It was not the first time Prince's work had inflamed these sensitive spots in socio-sexual mores. In *Under The Cherry Moon*, where he otherwise plays fast, loose and frivolous with racial codes and images, dodging from one identity to the next, all the leading women characters are positive and white, whereas the only black female to utter a sound appears as a three-second nightmare visitation representing everything Christopher Tracy yearns to escape. Where the racial and sexual composition of his bands, after Stone and Clinton, was obviously inspired by a combination of hippie idealism and a desire to shock, that scene from *Cherry Moon* seems more than a little insensitive. As for 'U Got The Look', well, only Prince himself could provide the definitive explanation – and he's keeping quiet. Sometimes, music is best *not* left to speak for itself.

In 'U Got The Look', the complications provided by the 'Camille' persona are ultimately whimsical. We all know that 'Camille' is Prince, and in any case, every minor nuance in this song is subservient to the grind of guitars, the chorus and the beat. On 'If I Was Your Girlfriend', though, 'Camille' is right there at the palpitating heart of the matter. If the whole thrust of Prince's art can be understood in terms of a desire to escape the social identities thrust upon him by simple virtue of his being small, black and male, then 'If I Was Your Girlfriend' is a landmark in his quest to wriggle out of the gender straitjacket.

This extraordinary song aches for the emotional intimacy that so often exists between women, and which men look upon with such defensive enmity. Here, 'Camille' is really just a phantom for the 'femininity' that Prince's lyric wistfully tells us – and the woman to whom the song is addressed – he aspires to. 'She' is simply delivering Prince's aching sense of frustration that for women the possibility of sex with a man can be more of a threat than a promise. If only there was a chance for him to enter the world of girls' talk, girls' comfort with each other, the ever so tender prospect of stress-free mutual nakedness. Why, he wails, exquisitely, can't we just be like best girlfriends?

The parabolic pulse of the rhythm imitates the thump of an anxiously beating heart, while being just off-centre enough to anticipate the hilarious irritability of the spoken passages into which the song finally transforms. As the music throttles back to fit the skip and timbre of dialogue, Prince's agony mounts as he glimpses the scale of the seemingly insurmountable disadvantage he finds himself at. And then, as his sensitivity turns to impatience, and his beautifully pained persuasion slumps into despair, he first becomes prickly, then sinks into surreal sarcasm before careering headlong into a feverish fantasy of cunnilingus and perfect post-coital silence. Phew. So *that's* what it means when Prince becomes your girlfriend. With 'If I Was Your Girlfriend', a peerless examination of the point where heterosexual true love and gender jealousy collide, it was as if Prince had finally acknowledged – or maybe just owned up to – all the power games that were involved in 'I Wanna Be Your Lover', 'Private Joy', 'Lady Cab Driver', and his other wide-eyed insinuations into the hearts of womankind. Whatever, it stands as one of the great love songs of modern times.

The enigmatic 'Camille' seems at one time to have been a contender for taking on an entire life of her own. All four of the numbers 'she' sings on *Sign 'O' The Times* also appear on a Prince bootleg simply entitled *Camille*, which seeped from the underground around the same time as *Sign 'O' The Times*. Of the other five tracks, one was an instrumental version of 'Housequake', another, 'Shockadelica' (whose title seems likely to have been a dig at Jesse Johnson's album of the same name), appeared on the B-side of 'If I Was Your Girlfriend' when it was released as a single, and 'Good Love' surfaced on the soundtrack of the film based on Jay McInerney's novel *Bright Lights, Big City*. Of the remaining three, 'Fill You Up' and 'Rebirth Of The Flesh' have not been heard of again (at least, not at the time of writing), while the third, the sumptuous 'Rock Hard In A Funky Place', was all lined up for inclusion on the infamous, aborted *Black Album*.

Taken together, the *Camille* material has no overall conceptual unity constructed around the 'Camille' persona. Unless possessed of polymorphous reproductive organs – which is, in fact, a possibility – 'she' isn't even a woman some of the time, certainly not on 'Rock Hard In A Funky Place'. Maybe she *is* a girl who – as 'she' declares during the song's fade – hates to see an erection go to waste: but not one attached, in full rigid splendour, to 'herself'. However, the three appearances 'she' makes on the third side of *Sign 'O' The Times* add up to a splendidly disruptive spanner in the sex-role works.

Elsewhere on *Sign 'O' The Times*, the libidinal urge is communicated more animalistically: 'It', for example, is a trip into sheer lusting delirium, all throbbing dementia and half-psychotic synthetic strings; 'Hot Thing' is a silicon Rolling Stones' parody from subject-matter to lecherous enunciation. It is the nearest to the 'old' Prince he gets here, but even then he wants to read poetry when he has wooed his quarry home. Both tracks are effective in their own terms, and leavened by the sheer variety of sound and vision spread through the double album's sixteen tracks. It is as though Prince is simply asserting his right to have more than one side to his personality. He can be Lord Byron *and* he can be a 'Sex Machine'. Side two, which contains 'Hot Thing', 'It' and 'Slow Love', also accommodates a piece of utter hippy-dippyness, 'Starfish And Coffee' (lyric co-written by Susannah Melvoin), and a rare declaration of undying fidelity, 'Forever In My Life', where a rolling, groaning rhythm and Prince's own flattened back-ups provide the framework for a lead vocal that brims with exhausted ardour.

Sign 'O' The Times is really a compendium of Prince's favourite musical and thematic things, executed with even more irrepressible invention than before. Every cut provides some surprise dislocation of the standard way of composing, singing a melody, playing a solo, or fitting voices and instruments together. It is impressive to consider that something as dense and frantic as 'Play In The Sunshine', a nostalgic return to the environment of 'Paisley Park' (and containing a secreted anti-drug message), would have been put together so carefully, one sonic stitch at a time. Here as everywhere else, each element is executed with a profound sense of control over the studio environment and the possibilities for adventure within the framework of a pop song.

In the summer of 1987, Prince and his new band undertook a major European tour. Compared to the almost ascetic, soul revue approach of *Parade*, the *Sign 'O' The Times* show was very much a *spectacle*, devised as if with the rock extravaganza tastes of a mass European audience in mind, and well suited to its subsequent adaptation as a full length in-concert film. It also showed that Prince's popularity still reached a long way into 'crossover' land. In Stockholm, for instance, close to 40,000 showed up for three nights at the city's main ice hockey stadium, advised by hoardings in advance to 'wear something peach . . . or black' – and you don't get too many black people in Scandinavia. For the *Parade* production, the props and personnel were basically there as foils for Prince's performance as a dancer and leader of an ensemble. For *Sign 'O' The Times* he was, obviously, the central figure again, but far more integrated into the metabolism of a grand-scale production piece, where all the imagery carried the equal possibility of being interpreted as seductive or corrupt.

The show opened up with a version of 'Sign 'O' The Times', with Prince raising hell on his guitar, and the song building up to a climax with the remainder of the ensemble marching down gantries at the sides of the set, beating a military tattoo on marching drums. Then 'Play In The Sunshine' sent the whole lot off to grab their regular instruments and participate in the ensuing blur of theatre and choreography. Looming up behind the shelved stage stood a huge, neon-lit mock-up of an urban downtown zone, whose signs flashed on and off throughout the show in combinations which at one point yielded the sequence 'Eat – Girls, Girls, Girls – All Night'. With the lower levels strewn with flowers, and the front end of a dead Cadillac glaring out from under Sheila E's drum riser, you could pick your own implication. For the Swedish shows, Prince took the stage in a storm of dry ice, modelling a kind of revised Jesus-freak look that combined the denim, furs, braids and adornments of the Hendrix–Stones era with spectacles which – though in the shape of flattened hexagons rather than circles – smacked of John Lennon's peacenik phase. For this tour, the band comprised Sheila E on drums, 'Doctor' Matt Fink – the only surviving old-hand from The Revolution – Boni Boyer on keyboards, and Mico Weaver on guitar, with Leeds and Bliss providing horns. Gregory Brooks and Wally Safford continued in their role as dancers and humorous interest, but Jerome Benton had gone. It transpired that Benton, no doubt assisted by the connections of his buddies at Flyte Tyme Productions, had negotiated a record deal with A & M. Consorting with the competition was not allowed, and local wisdom has it that Benton – one of Prince's best friends and most favoured protégés – had been fired.

There was, though, a dramatic newcomer to the entourage, Cathy 'Cat' Glover. The way Cat told it to Black Entertainment Television's *Video Soul* show, she and Prince met for the first time on the dancefloor. 'I've always wanted to dance with him, but it was never the right time. I finally got to meet him at a club in LA and he asked me to dance and I said, "Sure!" I was real excited.' Cat claimed to have been a Prince fan since 'Soft And Wet'. She had appeared on a TV talent show, *Star Search*, winning several times, hoping that Prince would spot her. Her recruitment to the team opened up still more possibilities for Prince to play identity games. In the first place, Glover looks very much like him. The 'Sign 'O' The Times' single picture-sleeve features a skinny, dark-haired figure with light-brown skin wearing a peach-coloured cut-away mini-dress and holding up a huge black heart-shape which obscures the body and face. More than one reviewer assumed that the figure was Prince himself, when in fact it was 'Cat'.

With all this visual apparatus in tow, Cat was an integral element in the chemistry of the *Sign 'O' The Times* show. Twisting and writhing anarchically in the back- and foreground, her perpetual motion provided a continual foil for Prince, who featured with her in a number of little set-piece interpretations of songs. One of these, for 'If I Was Your Girlfriend', concluded with Prince pressing her tight up against a giant silver heart. As the beat faded away, the heart tipped backwards and the pair of them disappeared behind the set. It was this scene which led to the *Daily Mirror*'s notorious 'Prince Of Darkness' splash, insisting that on stage Prince 'turns into an evil, wicked, all-powerful monster', and even describing the wrong woman, mistaking Ms Glover for Ms E. In truth, devil-worship was the last thing the *Sign 'O' The Times* presentation was all about. Far more divine than demonic, its grand finale tunes are those which make up the fourth and final side of the album. 'It's Gonna Be A Beautiful Night' (music co-written with Dr Fink and Eric Leeds; vocal chorus chant lifted direct from *The Wizard Of Oz*; fast rap from Sheila E by *telephone*?) is an obvious concert party-piece. But the more overtly spiritual 'Adore' and 'The Cross' define the glow with which Prince's live audience went home.

On record, 'The Cross' is a slow, thundering, ravaged rock piece with an anthemic feel and a mordant, distorted guitar motif that sounds like the Doors' 'The End' played from the pulpit. Some call Prince a Devil, but 'The Cross' is a howling assertion that the pain of living on earth will be assuaged by the beauty of the afterlife. On stage, Prince performed it, guitar blazing, in the ecclesiastical spectacles and clerical two-piece he sports on one of the album's inside picture-bags. And where 'The Cross' describes salvation in words, 'Adore' does the same with music, a sweetly fashioned secular love song which closes the album in a cool, easy, black gospel style.

Sign 'O' The Times has a flavour of just about everything. While making the implicit assertion that a black musician is perfectly entitled to draw upon white styles, it also provides a kind of mystery tour through popular black music history, viewed from the unchartable insides of Prince's head: body and soul, harmony and dissonance, minimalism and the ornate, he paints in every shade of sensuous catharsis, so much at one with his driving inner forces that he is able to parade them in full colour, and under near-perfect control.

'Anybody's music is made up of a lot of things that are not musical,' said the scholarly jazz pianist Cecil Taylor. 'Music is an attitude, a group of symbols of a way of life whether you're conscious of it or not. Any music is an expression of those who created it . . . simply the feeling of the American Negro with that tradition.'

Prince is an 'American Negro' in a time when the tradition Taylor described has been infused with a vast range of new inputs and influences. Twenty years of cultural evolution and uneven social mobility, of mass media explosion and the institutionalization of pop music into the daily pattern of consumption has seen to that. The atypical circumstances of Prince's whole life-experience – first in the Twin Cities, then as a Star – have created the potential for him to express those changes subliminally in a fashion exaggerated still more by his ecstatic imagination, and made vivid by his experitise. What was special about *Sign 'O' The Times* was the way he resurrected the bridge between the new creative territory he had contrived to inhabit and the rich musical inheritance he had built on to get there. Whether Prince was conscious of it or not, he was revisiting his roots, and finding a tremendous breadth of inspiration.

For example, running through the whole of *Sign 'O' The Times* there is a concealed but distinct influence of jazz. It is not there by simple virtue of the horns, or the fleeting moments when the music touches what we think of as a specifically jazz form, but because of the way the vibrations from the album feel so spontaneous, so improvised. Closing the first side, a total curio, 'The Ballad Of Dorothy Parker', just seems to have floated straight out of Prince's head, a muse made audible on the spot. The rhythm is elliptical and complex, and as if in some hallucinogenic daydream, he murmurs to us of bubble baths and zany cocktail-waitresses with a penchant for Joni Mitchell's 'Help Me', from which he lifts and impersonates an entire line. It is a song that appears on Mitchell's 1974 album *Court And Spark*, the one that marked her transition from acoustic singer-songwriter to melancholy beat-poet – a journey that went on to take in a full-length tribute to avant-garde jazz master Charlie Mingus.

But Prince's connections with the jazz world – the black classical music genre – now ran deeper than Mitchell's experiments. He had also made contact with one of the great innovators in the field, Miles Davis, a man who had never been afraid to ruffle a few feathers when it came to the question of race. In *Under The Cherry Moon*, Davis's album *You're Under Arrest* makes a cameo appearance as a prop in Tracy and Tricky's rented room. The godfather of The Cool and His Royal Badness had been sending each other tapes. Davis has been attributed with calling Prince 'the [Duke] Ellington of the '80s'. And in the *New Musical Express* of 20 September 1986, he described him as 'a thoroughbred. He's like an Arabian breed . . . possesses that extra something. When I listen to Prince, I hear James Brown, but it's updated . . . modified. I also hear Marvin Gaye, Sly Stone . . . a whole bunch of other good people. *That's* the part I like.'

According to the *NME* story, Prince had sent to Davis a vocal and an instrumental version of a song called 'Can I Play With U?' with a note attached: 'We think alike, I know how you feel. I know what you're doing . . .' Davis edited the tape down, added some blows of his own and returned it. But Prince himself vetoed the song for inclusion on Davis's *Tutu* album (1986), apparently not considering his own input to be up to scratch. The talk was then of a possible studio match between the two, and apart from anything else, Davis spent a few minutes on the Paisley Park studio stage with Prince and his band during a New Year's Eve charity show in aid of local under-privileged children, at the close of 1987.

If the Davis connection was one indication of Prince's interest in invoking the black improvisational mode, the recruitment of Madhouse was another. Originally a part-time band, Eric Leeds, drummer John Lewis, bassman Bill Lewis and keyboardist Austra Chanel were signed up to do an album as part of the planned expansion of the Paisley Park label. The resultant *8* contained an octet of varied instrumentals which ranged across jazz/fusion territory using just the basic instruments, and is one of the more successful records among Paisley Park's generally rather indifferent output. A different Madhouse line-up supported Prince on the *Sign 'O' The Times* tour, with Leeds joined by his friend Matt 'Atlanta Bliss' Blistan, Minneapolis multi-instrumentalist Dale Alexander (the former member of 94 East) on drums, plus Matt Fink and Prince's new bass player Levi Seacar (like Mico Weaver, from Sheila E's old band) filling the vacant posts. A second Madhouse album, *16*, emerged in 1988, featuring the live line-up with the exception of John Lewis, who returned to fill the drummer's berth.

The signing of Madhouse was an important pointer to the evolution of the Paisley Park label, and hence the kinds of artists Prince was surrounding himself with. By the end of 1987, the roster was eclectic, but orienting itself towards more sophisticated musics rooted in the black tradition. At the poppier end of the scale was Taja Sevelle, a sweet-voiced local singer who had been a DJ, was an extra in *Purple Rain*, provided back-ups on a track from *Around The World In A Day* under the pseudonym 'Taj', and was a protégée of Morris Wilson. Her eponymous 1987 album was a true product of the changed status of Minneapolis as a centre for music. Though Prince contributed a song, 'Wouldn't You Love To Love Me', her main collaborator, a writer-producer named Bennett, had moved out to the Twin Cities from LA – something which would have been unthinkable even five years before.

But the most dramatic recruits to Paisley Park were a long way from being the unknowns Prince had made it his habit to single out for greater things in the past. One was Mavis Staples, whose smouldering soul voice had put the gospel fire into a string of hits for the Staple Singers in the late sixties and early seventies. The other, as if in poetic completion of an entire funk cycle, was none other than George Clinton himself, one of whose concerts is said to have been the direct inspiration for Prince's 'Erotic City'. A DJ at First Avenue remembers him showing up with an acetate the *day after* Clinton had played a local show.

What had always separated Clinton – and, for that matter, Sly Stone – from Prince was their attitude towards the politics of being black in America. Stone's Family was a prototype for The Revolution, but no way did Stone ever seek to dissociate himself from the black world that made him. On the contrary, his entire act was a celebration of it and its right to equal, unadulterated recognition by the powers that be. It is a failure to appreciate this which makes many comparisons between Stone and Prince so shallow and glib. Similarly, Clinton's entire creative output is bursting with the 'blackness' of its maker – even his maggot-brained rock 'n' roll. Every space-age caricature, every piece of mind-expanding language, all those rhythms, every detail of a P-Funk sleeve was an affirmative metaphor for some aspect or other of black America's condition. Notwithstanding rumours of his involvement in the project, it is appropriate that Clinton's arrival at Paisley Park coincided with the period when Prince and his latest band would have been putting together the fizziest exercise in pure funk he had yet conceived.

The saga of *The Black Album* is a vintage example of the erratic fashion in which Prince habitually conducts his affairs. With Christmas 1987 on the horizon, an LP, attributed to 'Somebody', appeared on the Warner Brothers release schedule. The original plan was for *The Black Album* to be slipped into the shops with no artist details and no promotion, and aimed directly at the dance clubs. Then suddenly, amid a flurry of rumour, it became clear that the project had been shelved, if not permanently dumped. One story was that Prince had taken umbrage at the main Warner Brothers pressing plant being fully occupied with Madonna's remix album *You Can Dance* – and no way was he taking second place to that. Another theory was that Warners had been so shocked by the Prince album's X-rated material, they refused to put it out, though history suggests this to be unlikely. *Dirty Mind* was every bit as naughty, and back then, in corporate terms, Prince was more of a liability than a budding superstar. In the end, the project seems to have bitten the dust through a more mundane combination of business pragmatism and sheer caprice. With 'I Could Never Take The Place Of Your Man' – a song of unlikely temperance from *Sign 'O' The Times* – doing well in the singles chart, it would have been financially counter-productive to put more new product on the market in the same year as a double album. The idea is to milk what you have bone-dry first. So, as Prince's press officer at the Bloom Organization put it, 'he changed his mind'. Something which, by several persons' accounts, happens all the time.

It is certainly a pity the decision was made. *The Black Album* draws again on the fine-tuned loose jam ambience that is a feature of *Sign 'O' The Times*, but this time with an ensemble feel, and the emphasis on knife-edge funk. Whether the use of the word 'Black' as the album title was intended to denote an affirmation of racial identity, of anonymity, or both, its content would have showcased Prince's mastery of contemporary dance music at its most feverish and kinky. The opening cut, 'Le Grind', sets the standard as both a rhythm track and an introduction to the overall spoofing sensibility at work – a send-up of party manners that might persuade the most devoted wallflower to party all night. Female voices (almost certainly Cat, Boni Boyer and Sheila E) pant perkily, as horns, piano, and one almighty rhythm section threaten to blow the roof right off. You just can't argue with the heat whipped up by otherwise impossibly silly grooves about getting model girls into their birthday suits ('Cindy C'), the wired-up fun poked at the rap fraternity on 'Dead On It', or the tensile loony-tune fizz of 'Supercalifragafunkasexy' – a Clintonesque title if ever there was one. 'Rock Hard In a Funky Place' reappears, big, rude and bawdy, from the *Camille* bootleg (its juicy hornlines also pop up in a segue section in the later *Sign 'O' The Times* concert film), and there is a ballad, 'When 2 R In Love', splendid in the delicacy of its melody and lewdly graphic images. There is also a long, rather too long, splurge of storming free jazz with the impossibly oblique – and, again, racially encoded – '2 Nigs United 4 West Compton', and, in yet another radical departure, a mordant comedy number called 'Bob George'. To a bare, dull thud of electronic rhythm (another rap put-down?), a deep, flaccid black man's voice (can this *really* be Prince slowed down, the 'Camille' process in reverse, or is it Gregory Allen Brooks in disguise?) mutters threats at his unfaithful wife and eventually shoots her in a fit of wounded Neanderthal pride. She's been off seeing some Flash Harry paramour who manages rock stars for a living. No medals for guessing which one of his clients gets a name-check.

The Black Album celebrates the black party animal satirically but with affection. It also indicates a dislike for the musical crudity, blunt materialism and indiscriminate aggression that Hip Hop – the new force in black music in the eighties – often seemed uncritically to embody now it had become established in the pop mainstream. These are precisely the opposite tendencies to those that characterize Prince's own output from Paisley Park studios since *Sign 'O' The Times*.

Paisley Park is an institution whose reputation reflects the precise combination of characteristics in the make-up of Prince Roger(s) Nelson himself. Its massive resources are chaotically organized, and the business structure within it – PRN – is authoritarian and uncommunicative. At the same time, there is an important aspect to it which prizes artistry above profit, and it is that which has continued to find expression in Prince's own work. By the end of 1987, there were rumours running around the Twin Cities that the finances of Paisley Park were not working out quite as handsomely as planned. There had been a rationalization of the payroll, and word had it that the complex's elaborate facilities were draining the coffers rather than topping them up.

Certainly the Prince empire had suffered some cash reverses. *Under The Cherry Moon* had been a major flop, while Prince's own record sales, though far from disastrous, had plunged from the *Purple Rain* apex, and levelled off at a rather less rarefied height. Other projects once in the pipeline had also failed to reach fruition. Encouraged by the legend at the close of *Under The Cherry Moon*'s credits - 'May U Live To See The Dawn' – there had been speculation that a third Prince feature-film was on the way, to be entitled *The Dawn*. But of this there was no sign.

209

Albums by a couple of other Paisley Park artists – Dale Bozzio and Tony LeMans – had also, apparently, been shelved, and none of the Paisley Park albums that *did* make the shops had sold outstandingly. And soon after the release of *Sign 'O' The Times*, Prince had found himself on the wrong end of a family feud, when Lorna Nelson, his elder half-sister on his father's side, took out a lawsuit against him for alleged plagiarism. Her contention was that the lyrics of 'U Got The Look' had been based on that of a song called 'What's Cooking In This Book' which she had written and had found its way into Prince's possession through another member of the Nelson family. As of writing, the case was still unresolved.

But if the possible shortcomings of his business organization put Prince under any pressure to produce pragmatic hit material, he did not appear to take any notice. His tenth album, *Lovesexy*, was an Event simply on the strength of its unbelievable cover. Vogueish fashion-photographer Jean Baptiste Mondino (who also directed Jill Jones's video for her 'Mia Bocca' single) is responsible for capturing Prince stark naked and beatific, perched, nymph-like in the petals of a vast, blowsy white flower. His left leg is coyly cocked to conceal his private parts, but a strategically located stamen – the pollen-bearing male organ of a flower – provides a compensatory phallic implication. Concealing what is presumably a crucifix, Prince's right hand rests just below his left nipple, giving succour to the pain in his heart. *Lovesexy* is an album about love and sex, peace and war, and most of all heaven and hell. Bible study was never like this.

On *Lovesexy* the potential of the *Sign 'O' The Times* band as a studio entity is thoroughly explored. All the instrumentalists – Boyer (also a great, churchy singer), Leeds, Bliss, Weaver, Seacer, Sheila E and Fink – are credited equally with Prince, as is Cat Glover, who proves that she can handle vocals as well as dance. Musically, it is probably the most complex and unconventional body of work he has ever produced. The dense undergrowth of twists and disjunctures to which even the most structured songs are subjected brings to mind once again the extended jam rehearsal technique Prince has always favoured. People keep giving each other cues: 'We need some bottom in there.' It adds to the *group* chemistry about the whole proceedings, and on the very last track – the peroration, 'Positivity' – Prince actually invites his collected courtiers all to sing to save our souls.

Lovesexy is constructed with certain symphonic aspirations. The tracks are segued together with great ingenuity, linking songs of quite different shape and texture into an overall mood of garish religious fervour. In an escalation of his personal theology to a crusading intensity, refined lust and a love of the Lord are lavishly celebrated as synonymous. It emerges as the guiding tenet of an entire alternative cosmos. The album's very first words are uttered with cool, nursery-rhyme innuendo by a female person called Ingrid, described in the sleeve notes as The Spirit Child: 'Rain is wet, and sugar is sweet . . . clap your hands, and stomp your feet . . . everybody . . . everybody knows . . . when love calls . . . you gotta go.' Speaking against a background of undulating ambient music, she sounds like the first-born of some new and nubile Earth species. Prince's voice breaks in with news of 'a new power generation' and delivers an off-the-cuff anti-heroin remark. There is the sound of crackling, like the fires of Hades . . . and suddenly we're breezed away into a clatter of carnival funk, in which Prince celebrates his knowledge of God and the devil with a certainty so joyous, even the Peters brothers might envy him.

This opening song is called 'Eye No' (trans.: 'I Know'), with the first word fashioned on the sleeve in the actual shape of an eye, just to make life hell for everyone who works in the print media. The predominant sounds are the ones which distinctively characterize parts of the entire album: lots of rattling percussion, the guitar mixed up high, and a squealing female chorus that bobs and weaves intricate extra-terrestrial patterns around Prince's voice, itself flipping in and out of falsetto mode – 'Camille' one minute, dark-brown the next. The horn section blasts and swerves, and the whole thing feels on the brink of a delirious collapse. Finally it *does* collapse . . . into a rhubarb of liggers' voices jostling for free food and drinks, and a preacher intoning sombrely in the background. Suddenly, the Bo Diddley-ish beat of the second track leaps from the back of the mix to the front, and we're into the happy hysteria of 'Alphabet St', which, in an edited version, had preceded the album as a single. 'Eye No' is a *paarty* song. 'Alphabet St' is a kind of hand-clapping, skiffle R & B, the rhythm built into a stiff mesh by the way the guitar, and scattered fragments of voices, fit into it. The mere quality of the sound gives the song a simple but distinctive *presence*. 'Alphabet St' also contains a reference to the white Thunderbird car John Nelson gave to his son, and a long, frisky rap by Cat, who is ushered to the mike (as it were) by her cohorts.

In both these opening tracks, the idea emerges that the title *Lovesexy* actually describes a particular, euphoric state of consciousness which, once attained, enables contact to be made with His Omnipotence upstairs. There is even an inscription on the inner sleeve to explain it, just above the lyric to the title track: 'the feeling U get when U fall in love not with a girl or boy but with the heavens above'. One song, all repeated chorus line, is simply called 'I Wish U Heaven'. But *Lovesexy* was hardly an album designed to mend Prince's reputation in the eyes of the Godly Establishment. While there is moralizing, there is very little of what anyone calling himself or herself a Christian would recognize as morality. Nor could *Lovesexy* be in any sense considered a ploy to woo the masses. It has its accessible side, veering between the brightest, prettiest pop melodies and brittle, playful funk, with 'When 2 R In Love' – the ballad from *The Black Album* – finally enjoying legitimate exposure halfway through side two. But it is all just too volatile, too *abstract* to fit easily into Top 40 radio. Just when a tune has settled down it capsizes into free-form, or somebody starts talking about burning rubber in their pants. The Spirit Child keeps dropping in to offer mellifluous asides. Prince sings in about five different voices, sometimes switching from one to another in the space of a single line, and there are all these women carrying on in the background.

'Glam Slam' is one of the most effective pop efforts, almost bubblegum with its instant, ingratiating chorus. Prince gasps that the love he shares in goes beyond the merely physical. And yet within a couple of lines he is declaring himself as horny as hell. What, pray, does this horniness signify? The thing about *Lovesexy* is that it is well and truly *sanctified*. It is an album of true Prince gospel music, and no two ways about it, unabashedly *worshipful* in its non-conformist faith. Every touch and kiss takes him nearer to Heaven. Every act of fornication lifts him closer to the angels. For Prince, the libido is the great gift from above, and the finest way to praise Him is to use it.

In terms of production, arrangement and song construction, *Lovesexy* is impossibly clever and eclectic, turning familiar melodies into full-scale adventures in weird words and sound. 'Glam Slam' resolves itself as a virtual concerto of spiralling guitar and synthetic strings. 'Anna Stesia', which follows, has the loveliest tune, a low, swaying paean to the painless state that its punning title alludes to, decorated with zig-zagging guitar, and totally devoted to edging closer to Him. The polarities which were once spelled out with such rhetorical spite are now just meshed together as self-evident truths, articulated in a great clamour of treated voices, with 'real' and artificial instruments in unexpected combinations, jockeying for space.

'Lovesexy' itself opens with Prince testifying over the intro, before delivering one of several bizarre lyrics on the album to a four-square beat, Boni Boyer's Hammond organ, great shafts of horns and a repeated synthesizer fanfare redolent of '1999'. He then melts the whole thing down into a crazy seduction scene with *all those girls*, where no touching is allowed – only sweet and dirty words. Cat, the girl, goes first. Her voice is speeded up to a jabbering climax and by the time it has wound back down, has turned into the voice of Prince. At one moment a short, high-pitched buzz intrudes on the music, like a moment of accidental feedback. Who knows why it is there?

Former members of his band had predicted that Prince was due to go through another religious phase, but it still comes as a shocking implication that his idea of the ultimate offering is to dedicate all his orgasms to God. That is what he does on *Lovesexy*, although this spirituality is

212

spiked with social comment. It is not something Prince has always pulled off well, although 'Dance On' – driven by Sheila E's helter-skelter drumming – is impressively brutal. The song employs a bludgeoning bass guitar as a gun symbol, as Prince, name-checking Detroit *en route*, bemoans the violence of the modern world. But Prince is not an artist cut out to address reality as most of us know it. And for the most part his eyes are tilted adoringly upwards. 'Positivity', the final track, sees him right up there on the mountain side, exhorting, extracting responses from his wailing chorus, urging us to seek out the Lovesexy spirit and deny the temptations of a character called Spooky Electric – presumably his metaphor for Satan.

On one level, *Lovesexy* may be just the loopiest thing Prince has ever done. On another, with its ecstatically disordered music and celebration of wildly transcendental sex, it could be considered to sum up His Royal Badness absolutely, blending the astral cravings of *Around The World In A Day* with the manifesto of *Controversy* into something altogether more strange and fluid. Religious unorthodoxy is not new among rock superstars, and nor is sexual abandon. The craving for some idyllic, spiritual sanctuary is hardly unheard of either, though it is rather less fashionable than it was. But to pull them all together in one place, a little Eden summoned up from inside your own head, in quite the way Prince has, makes him pretty much unique. *Lovesexy* may lack definition, but it tells us most of what we need to know about him.

As for the man himself, he continues to view the world as if from inside some great big playpen, where he and a divine creative force at his command get things done for all the Purple People out there – the multitudes whose adoration and approval all stars need. Asked by the Electrifying Mojo why he thinks it is that he's so driven and industrious, and so far ahead, Prince said: 'The thing is that when you're called, you're called, you know, and I hear things in my sleep. I walk around, I go in the bathroom and try to brush my teeth, and all of a sudden the toothbrush'll start vibrating. That's a groove, you know, and you gotta go with that. And that means drop the toothbrush and get down to the studio or get to a bass guitar quick. I dunno, my best things just come out like that. To me, making a song is like a new girl walking in the room, you know. You never know what's gonna happen till all the things come together . . . and there she stands! And she says, "Hi. You wanna take a bite of this orange?" You bite it and it's cool . . . and I send it to you.'

Bibliography

Books

Baldwin, James, *The Price of the Ticket: Collected Non-Fiction 1948–1985*, Michael Joseph, 1985

Bream, Jon, *Prince: Inside the Purple Reign*, Collier Books/Macmillan Publishing Company, 1984

Brown, James (with Bruce Tucker), *The Godfather of Soul*, Sidgwick & Jackson, 1987

Chambers, Iain, *Urban Rhythms: Pop Music and Popular Culture*, Macmillan, 1985

Christgau, Robert, *Rock Albums of the '70s (Christgau's Guide)*, Vermillion, 1981

Cripps, Thomas, *Black Film as Genre*, Indiana University Press, 1978

Cullis, Ann, *Close to Perfection: Girls, Boys, Discos and Capitalism*, unpublished paper, 1986

Feldman, Jim, *Prince*, Ballantine, 1984

Frith, Simon, *Sound Effects: Youth, Leisure, and the Politics of Rock 'n' Roll*, Constable, 1978

George, Nelson, *Where Did Our Love Go?: The Rise & Fall of the Motown Sound*, Omnibus, 1985

Gilroy, Paul, *There Ain't No Black in the Union Jack*, Hutchinson, 1987

Guralnik, Peter, *Sweet Soul Music: Rhythm and Blues and the Southern Dream of Freedom*, Virgin, 1986

Hill, Dave, *Designer Boys and Material Girls: Manufacturing the '80s Pop Dream*, Blandford, 1986

Hirshey, Gerri, *Nowhere To Run*, Pan/Macmillan, 1984

Hoare, Ian (ed.), *The Soul Book*, Methuen, 1975

Ivory, Steven, *Prince*, Bantam, 1985

Lahr, John, *Automatic Vaudeville: Essays on Star Turns*, Heinemann, 1984

Malcolm X, *By Any Means Necessary*, Pathfinder, 1970

Marable, Manning, *Black American Politics: From the Washington Marches to Jesse Jackson*, Verso, 1985

Marcus, Greil, *Mystery Train: Images of America in Rock 'n' Roll Music*, Omnibus, 1977

Marsh, Dave, *Trapped: Michael Jackson and the Crossover Dream*,

Peters, Dan and Steve, *Hit Rock's Bottom – Expsong To The Light The Real World Behind The False Image Of Rock*, Truth About Rock, 1984

Ritz, David, *Divided Soul: The Life of Marvin Gaye*, Grafton, 1986

Tosches, Nick, *Hellfire: The Jerry Lee Lewis Story*, Plexus, 1982

Spangler, Earl, *The Negro in Minnesota*, T. S. Denison, 1961

Staples, Robert, *Black Masculinity: The Black Male's Role in American Society*, Black Scholar Press, 1982

White, Charles, *The Life and Times of Little Richard, The Quasar Of Rock*, Pan, 1984

Wilmer, Valerie, *Jazz People*, Allison & Busby, 1970

Articles

Adler, Bill, 'Will the Little Girls Understand?', *Rolling Stone*, 19 February 1981

Ansen, David, 'The New Prince of Hollywood', *Newsweek*, 23 July 1984

Barol, Bill, 'His Royal Badness Inc', *Newsweek*, 4 May 1987

Berkoff, Steven, 'Berkoff Bites the Cherry', *Time Out*, August 1986

Bernard, Edwin J., 'Prince is Better as a Friend' – interview with Jill Jones, *Record Mirror*, 25 July 1987

Bloom, Steve, 'Paint it Black', *Soho Weekly News*, 20 February 1980

Bream, Jon, 'Prince Gives City Claim to a Star', *Minneapolis Star*, 10 March 1981

Carr, Roy, 'Man of Many Colours', *New Musical Express*, 20 September 1986

Cocks, Jay, 'His Highness of Haze', *Time*, 6 August 1984

Cooper, Carol, 'Some Day Your Prince Will Come', *The Face*, June 1983

Cuba, Dave, 'A Look into the Dirty Mind of Prince', *Calumet City Night Rock News*, February 1981

Davis, Sharon, 'Rick v Prince', *Blues and Soul*, 4 December 1984

Fricke, David, 'Crowning Folly', *Melody Maker*, 19 December 1987

Goldberg, Michael, '*Purple Rain* Star Morris Day Goes it Alone', *Rolling Stone*, 13 September 1984

Graustark, Barbara, 'Prince's Purple Reign', *People Weekly*, 19 November 1984

Guzman, Pablo, 'Rock's New Prince', *Village Voice*, 1981

Hilburn, Robert, 'The Renegade Prince', *Los Angeles Times*, 21 November 1982

Hilburn, Robert, 'A Sexual Outlaw of the Eighties', *Los Angeles Times*, 2 April 1981

Hill, Michael, 'Prince: Born to Come', *New York Rocker*, June 1981

Hunt, Dennis, 'A Strange Man Who's Too Hot for Radio', *San Francisco Examiner-Chronicle*, 25 January 1981

Kael, Pauline, 'The Charismatic Half-And-Halfs', *New Yorker*, 20 September 1984

Kalbacher, Gene, 'Prince in the Afternoon', *Aquarian 'Night Owl' Supplement*, 25 February–4 March 1981

Karlen, Neal, 'Ladies in Waiting', *Rolling Stone*, 24 April 1986

Karlen, Neal, 'Prince Talks', *Rolling Stone*, Spring 1985

Katz, Larry, 'Prince – Vice is Nice', *Boston Real Paper*, 2 April 1981

Kordosh, J., 'Prince's Purple Rain', *Creem*, September 1984

Lamont, Paul, 'Is Prince Getting Too Big for his Lace Britches?', *Right On!*, June 1985

Loder, Kurt, 'Prince Reigns', *Rolling Stone*, 30 August 1984

Marsh, Dave, 'Why Prince and Bruce Springsteen Now Seem Hotter than Michael Jackson', *TV Guide*, 23 February 1985

Miller, Jim, with Huck, Janet, 'Rock's Mystery Prince', *Newsweek*, 29 April 1985

Miller, Debby, 'Prince's Hot Rock', *Rolling Stone*, 28 April 1983

Mitchell, Tony, 'Posin' Till Closin'', *Sounds*, 6 June 1981

Norment, Lynn, 'Prince – The Story Behind his Passion for Purple and Privacy', *Ebony*, November 1984

Palmer, Robert, 'Is Prince Leading Music to a True Biracism?' *New York Times*, 2 December 1981

Russell, Lisa, 'Prince Got the Girl in *Purple Rain* but Movie Rival Morris Day is Stealing Some of his Thunder', *People*, Summer 1984

Salholz, Eloise and Tibbett, Linda, 'Getting the Princely Look', *Newsweek*, 1 October 1985

Sigerson, Davitt, 'Prince Strips Down', *Rolling Stone*, 24 April 1986

Sutherland, Steve, 'Some Day your Prince will Come', *Melody Maker*, 6 June 1981

Tate, Greg, 'Painted Black', *Village Voice*, 14 April 1987

Tucker, Ken, 'Someday my Prince will Come' – *Dirty Mind* LP review, *Rolling Stone*, 19 February 1981

Wilen, Dennis, 'Prince Explains his Royal Secrets', *LA Herald-Examiner*, 27 March 1981

Witter, Simon, 'Prince is an Asshole', interview with Jesse Johnson, *New Musical Express*, 29 November 1986

The following articles appeared without being credited to any author, and in some cases came to me only as xeroxes with no precise details as to date of publication. They are listed here with as much information as I have been able to gather. Each was an important source of information or ideas:

'Prince – *Purple Rain* is Everywhere', *Right On!*, 1984

'Prince Breaks his Long Silence', *Right On!*, 1986 – published in two parts

'Punk Funk – Gettin' Down and Dirty', *Soul Teen*, March 1981

'The Day that Prince Unveiled his New Album', *Tiger Beat*, August 1985

Finally, issues 1–10 of *Controversy*, the unofficial Prince magazine, provided a wealth of anecdotal and factual information with regard to Prince and associated artists. All correspondence to: P. O. Box 310, Croydon CR9 6AP.

Discography

━━━━━━━

The discography is divided into five sections; Prince's US releases; Prince's UK releases; miscellaneous Prince recordings; bootlegs; and releases by associated artists.

Prince's releases are listed with the following information (where available): date of release; title; catalogue number (in brackets); track-listing (for albums); highest chart position reached; and number of weeks in chart (in brackets after chart position). In the case of US releases, Billboard Pop and Black chart listings are given (in that order); if the record reached No. 1, the first bracketed number after the chart position is the number of weeks it stayed there. For UK releases, positions given are from the Gallup chart. Chart placings for 7″ singles include sales of other formats (12″, picture discs, etc.).

The Associated Artists discography lists: (i) cover versions of Prince songs; (ii) songs written or co-written by Prince for other artists; and (iii) singles or albums by other artists for which Prince is credited with production or co-production, either by name or by a regularly assumed pseudonym (such as The Starr Company). In each case, artist, title, co-writer/co-producer (if any) and year of release are given.

1. Prince: US Releases
1978

Album/Cassette

7 Apr.	*For You* (BSK 3150) 'For You', 'In Love', 'Soft and Wet', 'Crazy You', 'Just As Long As We're Together', 'Baby', 'My Love Is Forever', 'So Blue', 'I'm Yours'	163 (5)	21 (23)

Singles

June '78	'Soft and Wet'/'So Blue' (WBS-8619)	92 (4)	12 (20)
Nov. '78	'Just As Long As We're Together'/'In Love' (WBS-8713)		91 (7)

1979

Album/Cassette

19 Oct.   *Prince* (BSK 3366)   22 (28)   3 (23)
              'I Wanna Be Your Lover', 'Why You Wanna
              Treat Me So Bad?', 'Sexy Dancer', 'When We're
              Dancing Close And Slow', 'With You', 'Bambi',
              'Still Waiting', 'I Feel For You', 'It's Gonna Be
              Lonely'

Single

24 Aug.   'I Wanna Be Your Lover'/'My Love Is Forever'   11 (16)   1 (2)(23)
              (WBS-49050)

1980

Album/Cassette

8 Oct.   *Dirty Mind* (BSK 3478)   45 (52)   7 (26)
              'Dirty Mind', 'When You Were Mine', 'Do It All
              Night', 'Gotta Broken Heart Again', 'Uptown',
              'Head', 'Sister', 'Partyup'

Singles

23 Jan.   'Why You Wanna Treat Me So Bad?'/'Baby' (WBS-   13 (15)
              49178)
25 Mar.   'Still Waiting'/'Bambi'   (WBS-49226) 65 (8)
10 Sept.   'Uptown'/'Crazy You' (WBS-49559)   101 (6)   5 (18)
26 Nov.   'Dirty Mind'/'When We're Dancing Close & Slow'   65 (6)
              (WBS-49638)

1981

Album/Cassette

14 Oct.   *Controversy* (BSK 3601)   21 (63)   3 (30)
              'Controversy', 'Sexuality', 'Do Me, Baby',
              'Private Joy', 'Ronnie, Talk to Russia', 'Let's
              Work', 'Annie Christian', 'Jack U Off'

Single

2 Sept.   'Controversy'/'When You Were Mine' (WBS-49808)

1982

Album/Cassette

27 Oct.   *1999* (1–23720) [double LP]   9 (125)   4 (39)
              '1999', 'Little Red Corvette', 'Delirious', 'Let's

Pretend We're Married', 'DMSR', 'Automatic',
'Something In The Water (Does Not Compute)',
'Free', 'Lady Cab Driver', 'All The Critics Love
U In New York', 'International Lover'

Singles

6 Jan.	'Let's Work'/'Ronnie Talk To Russia' (WBS-50002)		9 (16)
16 July.	'Do Me Baby'/'Private Joy' (7–29942)		
24 Sept.	'1999'/'How Come U Don't Call Me Anymore?' (7-298883)	44 (12)	4 (19)

12″ Maxi-Single

17 Feb.	'Let's Work'/'Gotta Stop (Messin' About)' (WBS-50028)

1983

Two-on-One Cassette

17 Aug.	*Dirty Mind*/*Controversy* (4–23953)

CD

14 Dec.	*Controversy* (2–3601)

Singles

9 Feb.	'Little Red Corvette'/'All the Critics Love U in New York' (7–29746)	6 (22)	15 (17)
17 Aug.	'Delirious'/'Horny Toad' (7–29503)	8 (18)	18 (15)
23 Nov.	'Let's Pretend We're Married'/'Irresistible Bitch' (7–29548)	52 (10)	55 (8)

12″ Maxi-Singles

7 Sept.	'1999'/'Little Red Corvette' (0–20120)
16 Nov.	'Let's Pretend We're Married'/'Irresistible Bitch' (0-20170)

7″ Picture-Disc

'Little Red Corvette'/'1999' [Limited Edition]
(9–20129)

1984

Album/Cassette

25 Jun.	*Purple Rain* [R]** (1–25110) 'Let's Go Crazy', 'Take Me With U', 'The	1 (24) (39)	1 (19) (48)

Beautiful Ones', 'Computer Blue', 'Darling
Nikki', 'When Doves Cry', 'I Would Die 4 U',
'Baby I'm A Star', 'Purple Rain'

CDs

6 Aug.	*Purple Rain* [R] (2–25110)	27 (3)	
17 Dec.	*1999* (2–23720)		
17 Dec.	*Dirty Mind* (2–3478)		

Singles

16 May	'When Doves Cry'/'17 Days' [R]** (0–29286)	1 (5) (21)	1 (8) (20)
18 Jul.	'Let's Go Crazy'/'Erotic City' [R]* (0–29216)	1 (2) (19)	1 (1) (17)
26 Sept.	'Purple Rain'/'God' [R]* (0–29174)	2 (16)	4 (14)
28 Nov.	'I Would Die 4 U'/'Another Lonely Christmas' (0–29121)	8 (15)	11 (11)

Back-to-Back Single

22 Feb.	'1999'/'Little Red Corvette' (GWB-468)

12″ Maxi-Singles

13 Jun.	'When Doves Cry'/'17 Days' [R] (7–20228)
29 Aug.	'Let's Go Crazy'/'Erotic City' [R] (7–20246)
26 Sept.	'Purple Rain'/'God' [R] (7–20267)
19 Dec.	'I Would Die 4 U'/'Another Lonely Christmas' [R] (7–20291)

Video

Nov. 84	*Purple Rain* [R] (3–11398)

1985

Album/Cassette

22 Apr.	*Around The World In A Day*** (1–25286) 'Around The World In A Day', 'Paisley Park', 'Condition Of The Heart', 'Raspberry Beret', 'Tamborine', 'America', 'Pop Life', 'The Ladder', 'Temptation'	1 (3) (40)	4 (43)

CD

22 Apr.	*Around The World In A Day* (2–25206)	3 (24)	

Singles

25 Jan.	'Take Me With U'/'Baby I'm a Star' [R] (7–29079)	25 (12)	40 (9)
15 May	'Raspberry Beret'/'She's Always In My Hair' (7–28972)	2 (17)	3 (14)

10 Jul.	'Pop Life'/'Hello' (7–28998)	7 (14)	8 (13)
2 Oct.	'America'/'Girl' (7–28999)	46 (7)	35 (8)

Back-to-Back Singles

26 Aug.	'When Doves Cry'/'Let's Go Crazy' [R] (GWB-0516)
26 Aug.	'I Would Die 4 U'/'Take Me With U' [R] (GWB-0517)

12" Maxi-Singles

19 Jun.	'Raspberry Beret'/'She's Always In My Hair' (7–20355)
31 Jul.	'Pop Life'/'Hello' (7–20357)
2 Oct.	'America'/'Girl' (7–20389)

Video

29 Jul.	*Prince & The Revolution LIVE* [R] (3–38102)

1986

Album/Cassette

31 Mar.	*Parade*** (1–25395) 'Christopher Tracy's Parade', 'New Position', 'I Wonder U', 'Under The Cherry Moon', 'Girls And Boys', 'Life Can Be So Nice', 'Venus De Milo', 'Mountains', 'Do U Lie?', 'Kiss', 'Anotherloverholenyohead', 'Sometimes It Snows In April'	3 (28)	2 (26)

CD

19 May	*Parade* (2–25395)

Singles

5 Feb.	'Kiss'/'Love Or Money'* (7–28751)	1 (2) (18)	1 (4) (17)
7 May	'Mountains'/'Alexa de Paris' (7–28711)	23 (11)	15 (12)
2 Jul.	'Anotherloverholenyohead'/'Girls And Boys' (7–28620)	63 (10)	18 (12)

Back-to-Back Singles

17 Mar.	'Purple Rain'/'Raspberry Beret' (GWB-0528)
17 Mar.	'Pop Life'/'America' (GWB–0529)

12" Maxi-Singles

5 Mar.	'Kiss'/'Love Or Money' (0–20442)
21 May.	'Mountains'/'Alexa de Paris' (0–20465)

30 Jul.   'Anotherloverholenyohead'/'Girls And Boys'
           (0–20466)

1987

Album/Cassette

30 Mar.   *Sign 'O' The Times*★★ (1–25577) [double LP]   6 (45)   4 (45)
           'Sign 'O' The Times', 'Play In The Sunshine',
           'Housequake', 'The Ballad Of Dorothy Parker',
           'It', 'Starfish And Coffee', 'Slow Love', 'Hot
           Thing', 'Forever In My Life', 'U Got The Look',
           'If I Was Your Girlfriend', 'Strange
           Relationship', 'I Could Never Take The Place Of
           Your Man', 'The Cross', 'It's Gonna Be A
           Beautiful Night', 'Adore'

CDs

30 Mar.   *Sign 'O' The Times* (2–25577)
20 Apr.   *For You* (2–3150)
20 Apr.   *Prince* (2–3366)

Singles

18 Feb.   'Sign 'O' The Times'/'La La La He He Hee'   3 (14)   1 (3) (16)
           (7–28399)
6 May   'If I Was Your Girlfriend'/'Shockadelica' (7–28334) 67 (6)   12 (14)
14 Jul.   'U Got The Look'/'Housequake' (7–28289)   2 (24)   11 (15)
3 Nov.   'I Could Never Take the Place of Your Man'/'Hot   10 (15+)   14 (14+)
           Thing' (7–28288)

Back-to-Back Singles

4 Mar.   'Kiss'/'Soft and Wet' (7–21982)
4 Mar.   'Anotherloverholenyohead'/'Mountains' (7–21980)
3 Apr.   'Uptown'/'Controversy' (7–21981)

Cassette-Singles

3 Jan.   'I Could Never Take the Place Of Your Man'/'Hot
           Thing' (4–28288)
14 Jul.   'U Got the Look'/'Housequake' (4–28289)

12″ Maxi-Singles

18 Feb.   'Sign 'O' The Times'/'La La La He He Hee'
           (0–20648)
13 May   'If I Was Your Girlfriend'/'Shockadelica' (0–20697)
21 Jul.   'U Got the Look'/'Housequake' (0–20727)
3 Nov.   'I Could Never Take the Place Of Your Man'/'Hot
           Thing' (0–20728)

Maxi-Cassettes

18 Feb.	'Sign 'O' The Times'/'La La La He He Hee' (4–20648)
13 May	'If I Was Your Girlfriend'/'Shockadelica' (4–20697)
21.7.87	'U Got the Look'/'Housequake' (4–20727)
3 Nov.	'I Could Never Take the Place Of Your Man'/'Hot Thing' (4–20728)

1988

Album/Cassette

| 9 May | *Lovesexy* (1–25720) |
| | 'Eye No', 'Alphabet St', 'Glam Slam', 'Anna Stesia', 'Dance On', 'Lovesexy', 'When 2 R In Love', 'I Wish U Heaven', 'Positivity' |

CD

| 9 May | *Lovesexy* (2–25720) |

Singles

| 23 Apr. | 'Alphabet St'/'Alphabet St' (edit) |
| 11 Jul. | 'Glam Slam'/'Escape' (edit) |

12" Maxi-Singles

| 23 Apr. | 'Alphabet St'/'Alphabet St' (edit) |
| 11 Jul. | 'Glam Slam' (Remix)/'Escape (Free yo mind from this rat race)' |

* Certified Gold: 500,000 copies
** Certified Platinum: 1 million copies
[R] Prince and The Revolution

2. Prince: UK Releases
1979

Single

| Dec. | 'I Wanna Be Your Lover'/'Just As Long As We're Together' (KI75378) | 41 (1) |

12" Single

| Dec. | 'I Wanna Be Your Lover'/'Just As Long As We're Together' (KI75378T) |

1980

Albums/Cassettes

Jan.   *Prince* (K56772)
'I Wanna Be Your Lover', 'Why You Wanna Treat Me So Bad?', 'Sexy Dancer', 'When We're Dancing Close And Slow', 'With You', 'Bambi', 'Still Waiting', 'I Feel For You', 'It's Gonna Be Lonely'

Oct.   *Dirty Mind* (K56862)
'Dirty Mind', 'When You Were Mine', 'Do It All Night', 'Gotta Broken Heart Again', 'Uptown', 'Head', 'Sister', 'Partyup'

Single

Apr.   'Sexy Dancer'/'Bambi' (K17590)

1981

Album-Cassette

Nov.   *Controversy* (K56950)
'Controversy', 'Sexuality', 'Do Me, Baby', 'Private Joy', 'Ronnie, Talk To Russia', 'Let's Work', 'Annie Christian', 'Jack U Off'

Singles

Mar.   'Do It All Night'/'Head' (K17768)
Jun.   'Gotta Stop (Messin' About)'/'Uptown' (K17819)
Jul.   'Gotta Stop (Messin' About)'/'I Wanna Be Your Lover' (K17819)
Oct.   'Controversy'/'When You Were Mine' (K17866)

12″ Single

Mar.   'Do It All Night'/'Head' (K17768T)

1982

Single

Apr.   'Let's Work'/'Ronnie Talk To Russia' (K17922)

12″ Single

Apr.   'Let's Work'/'Ronnie Talk To Russia' (K17922T)

1983

Albums/Cassettes

Feb.   *1999* (92–3809–1) [single LP]
          '1999', 'Little Red Corvette', 'Delirious', 'Free',
          'Let's Pretend We're Married', 'Something In The
          Water (Does Not Compute)', 'Lady Cab Driver'
Nov.   *1999* (92–3720–1) [double LP]
          '1999', 'Little Red Corvette', 'Delirious', 'Let's
          Pretend We're Married', 'DMSR', 'Automatic',
          'Something In The Water (Does Not Compute)',
          'Free', 'Lady Cab Driver', 'All The Critics Love
          U In New York', 'International Lover'

Singles

Jan.   '1999'/'How Come U Don't Call Me Anymore'?
          (W9896)   25
Apr.   'Little Red Corvette'/'Lady Cab Driver' (W9688) 54
Sept.   'Let's Pretend We're Married'/'All The Critics Love
          U In New York' (W9613)
Nov.   'Little Red Corvette'/'Horny Toad' (W9436)

12″ Singles

Jan.   '1999'/'How Come U Don't Call Me Anymore?'
          (w9896T)
Apr.   'Little Red Corvette'/'Lady Cab Driver'/
          'Automatic'/'International Lover' (W9688T)
Nov.   'Little Red Corvette'/'Horny Toad'/'DMSR'
          (W9436T)

1984

Album/Cassette

Jul.   *Purple Rain*★★ (925 1101–1)   7
          'Let's Go Crazy', 'Take Me With U', 'The
          Beautiful Ones', 'Computer Blue', 'Darling
          Nikki', 'When Doves Cry', 'I Would Die 4 U',
          'Baby I'm A Star', 'Purple Rain'

Singles

Jun.   'When Doves Cry'/'17 Days' (w9286)   4
Sept.   'Purple Rain'/'God' (W9174)   8
Nov.   'I Would Die 4 U'/'Another Loney Christmas' 58
          (W9121)
Dec.   '1999'/'Little Red Corvette' (W1999)   2

12″ Singles

'When Doves Cry'/'17 Days'/'1999' (W9286T)
'When Doves Cry'/'17 Days'/'1999'/'DMSR'
(W9286T) [double 12″]
'I Would Die 4 U'/'Another Lonely Christmas'
(W9121T)

Cassette-Singles

'When Doves Cry'/'17 Days'/'1999'/'DMSR'
(W9286)
'1999'/'Uptown'/'Controversy'/'Sexy Dancer'/
'DMSR' (W1999C)

1985

Album/Cassette

Apr.   *Around The World In A Day*** (925 286–1)   5
            'Around The World In A Day'/'Paisley Park'/
            'Condition Of The Heart'/'Raspberry Beret'/
            'Tamborine'/'America'/'Pop Life'/'The Ladder'/
            'Temptation'

Singles

Feb.   'Let's Go Crazy'/'Take Me With U' (W2000)   7
May   'Paisley Park'/'She's Always In My Hair' (W9052)   18
Jul.   'Raspberry Beret'/'Hello' (W8929)   25
Oct.   'Pop Life'/'Girl' (W8858)   60

12″ Singles

'Let's Go Crazy'/'Take Me With U'/'Erotic City'
(W2000T)
'Paisley Park'/'She's Always In My Hair'/'Paisley
Park' [instrumental] (W9052T)

1986

Album/Cassette

Apr.   *Parade*** (WX39)   4
            'Christopher Tracy's Parade', 'New Position', 'I
            Wonder U', 'Under The Cherry Moon', 'Girls
            And Boys', 'Life Can Be So Nice', 'Venus De
            Milo', 'Mountains', 'Do U Lie?', 'Kiss',
            'Anotherloverholenyohead', 'Sometimes It Snows
            In April'

Singles

Mar.   'Kiss'/'Love Or Money' (W8751)   6

226

Jun.	'Mountains'/'Alexa De Paris' (w8711)	-	45
Aug.	'Girls And Boys'/'Under The Cherry Moon' (w8586)	11	
Oct.	'Anotherloverholenyohead'/'I Wanna Be Your		36
	Lover' (w8521)		

'Girls And Boys'/'Under The Cherry Moon'/'She's
Always In My Hair'/'17 Days' (w8488F) [double
pack]

12" Singles

'Kiss'/'Love Or Money' (w8751T)
'Mountains'/'Alexa De Paris' (w8711T)
'Girls And Boys'/'Under The Cherry Moon'/'Erotic
City' (w8586T)

10" Single

'Mountains'/'Alexa De Paris' (w8711W) [white
vinyl]

Picture-Discs

'Kiss'/'Love Or Money' (w8751P) [shaped]
'Girls And Boys'/'Under The Cherry Moon',
(w8586P)

1987

Album/Cassette

Mar.   *Sign 'O' The Times* (wx88) [double LP]
'Sign 'O' The Times', 'Play In The Sunshine',
'Housequake', 'The Ballad Of Dorothy Parker',
'It', 'Starfish And Coffee', 'Slow Love', 'Hot
Thing', 'Forever In My Life', 'U Got The
Look', 'If I Was Your Girlfriend', 'Strange
Relationship', 'I Could Never Take The Place
Of Your Man', 'The Cross', 'It's Gonna Be A
Beautiful Night', 'Adore'

Singles

Mar.	'Sign 'O' The Times', 'La La La La He He Hee'	8
	(w8399)	
Jun.	'If I Was Your Girlfriend'/'Shockadelica' (w8334)	13
Aug.	'U Got The Look'/'Housequake' (w8289)	11
Nov.	'I Could Never Take The Place Of Your Man'/'Hot	29
	Thing' (w8288)	

12" Singles

'Sign 'O' The Times'/'La La La La He He Hee'
(W8399T)

'If I Was Your Girlfriend'/'Shockadelica' (w8334T)
'U Got The Look'/'Housequake' (w8289T)
'I Could Never Take The Place Of Your Man'/'Hot
Thing' (w8288T)

12″ Picture-Discs

'If I Was Your Girlfriend'/'Shockadelica' (w8334TP)
'U Got The Look'/'Housequake' (w8289TP)
'I Could Never Take The Place Of Your Man'/'Hot
Thing' (w8288TP)

Cassette-Singles

'If I Was Your Girlfriend'/'Shockadelica' (w8334C)
'U Got The Look'/'Housequake' (w8289C)
'I Could Never Take The Place Of Your Man'/'Hot
Thing' (w8288C)

1988

Album/Cassette

May   *Lovesexy* (WX 164)   1
             'Eye No', 'Alphabet St', 'Glam Slam', 'Anna Stesia',
             'Dance On', 'Lovesexy', 'When 2 R In Love', 'I
             Wish U Heaven', 'Positivity'

Singles

Apr.   'Alphabet St'/'Alphabet St' (edit) (w7900)   9
Jul.   'Glam Slam'/'Escape' (w7806)   29

12″ Singles

             'Alphabet St'/'Alphabet St' (This Is Not Music,
             This Is A Trip) (w7900T)
             'Glam Slam' (Remix)/'Escape (Free yo mind from
             this rat race)' (w7806T)

3. Miscellaneous Prince Recordings

'4 The Tears In Your Eyes'
Prince's contribution to the *USA For Africa* album (USA IDF1) (various artists, US release
only)

'Good Love'
Opening track of the album *Bright Light, Big City (Original Soundtrack)* (various artists). Also
on the *Camille* bootleg.

Minneapolis Genius – The Historic 1977 Recordings (Hot Pink 11 LP 3223)
The earliest recordings of Prince, multi-instrumentalist, with Minneapolis band 94 East

4. Bootlegs

There are many Prince bootlegs floating around if you care to look, but these are the ones most worth the expense. There are also several live-in-concert recordings in circulation, as well as collections of out-takes from official albums.

The Black Album
The brilliant collection of funny funk that never made it to the shops. Available on cassette and black-market vinyl.

Camille
The 'girl' herself, playing in a variety of parts. Several tracks turned up on *Sign 'O' The Times*, and others on B-sides and soundtracks. Cassette only.

5. Associated Artists

(i) Cover Versions of Prince Songs

Age Of Chance	'Kiss' 7″ and 12″ singles, 1986
Bette Bright & The Illuminations	'When U Were Mine' 7″ single, 1982
Blood Uncles	'Let's Go Crazy' 7″ and 12″ singles, also track on album *Libertine*, 1987
Hurd, Debra	'Gotta Broken Heart Again' 7″ single, 1983
Jackson, LaToya	'Private Joy' Track on album *Heart Don't Lie*, 1984
Jackson, Millie	'[I] Wanna Be Your Lover' 7″ and 12″ singles, 1987
Jones, Jill	'With You' Track on album *Jill Jones*, 1987
Khan, Chaka	'I Feel For You' 7″ and 12″ singles, also title track of album *I Feel For You*, 1984
Lauper, Cyndi	'When U Were Mine' Track on album, *She's So Unusual*, 1983
Mills, Stephanie	'How Come You Don't Call Me Anymore?' Track on album *Merciless*, 1983
Morgan, Meli'sa	'Do Me, Baby' 7″ and 12″ singles, also title track of album *Do Me, Baby*, 1986

229

Nieve, Steve	'Condition Of The Heart' Track on album *Playboy*, 1987
Pointer Sisters	'I Feel For You' Track on album *So Excited*, 1982
Ryder, Mitch	'When You Were Mine' Track on album *Never Kick A Sleeping Dog*, 1983
Turner, Tina	'Let's Pretend We're Married' B-side of 'I Can't Stand The Rain', 7″ and 12″ singles, 1983

(ii) Prince Compositions For Other Artists

Apollonia 6	'Sex Shooter' 7″ and 12″ singles, also track on album *Apollonia 6*, 1984
Bangles, The	'Manic Monday' [credit: Christopher Tracy] 7″ and 12″ singles, also track on album *Different Light*, 1986
Cymone, André	'The Dance Electric' 7″ and 12″ singles, also track on album *A.C.*, 1985
E, Sheila	'A Love Bizarre' [with Sheila E] 7″ and 12″ singles, also track on album *Romance 1600*, 1985
Easton, Sheena	'Eternity' 7″ and 12″ singles, also track on album *No Sound But A Heart*, 1987 (US only) 'Sugar Walls' [credit: Alexander Nevermind] 7″ and 12″ singles, also track on album *A Private Heaven*, 1984
Family, The	'Nothing Compares 2 U' Track on album *The Family*, 1985

'St Paul' Peterson and others close to Prince at the time assert that Prince actually wrote all the material on *The Family*, save for 'River Run Dry', by Bobby Z. Despite this, writing credits are distributed randomly among the members of this short-lived quasi-group on the album's label.

Hendryx, Nona	'Baby Go-Go' [credit: Joey Coco] 7″ and 12″ singles, also track on album *Female Trouble*, 1987
Jones, Jill	'All Day, All Night' [with Jill Jones]

'For Love' [with Jill Jones]
7″ and 12″ singles, 1987

'G-Spot [with Jill Jones]
7″ and 12″ singles, 1987

'Mia Bocca' [with Jill Jones]
7″ and 12″ singles, 1987.

All above tracks on album *Jill Jones*, 1987.

Mazarati
'100 MPH'
Track on album *Mazarati*, 1985

Rogers, Kenny
'You're My Love' [credit: Joey Coco]
Track on album *They Don't Make Them Like
They Used To*, 1986

Sevelle, Taja
'Wouldn't You Love To Love Me?'
7″ and 12″ singles, also track on album *Taja
Sevelle*, 1987

Time, The
'Cool' [with Dez Dickerson]
7″ and 12″ singles, 1981

'Get It Up' [with Morris Day]
7″ and 12″ singles, 1981

'Girl' [with Morris Day]
7″ and 12″ singles, 1982

'Oh, Baby' [with Morris Day]
'The Stick' [with Morris Day]

All above are tracks from album *The Time*, 1981. The album is unusual in that neither label nor sleeve contains any songwriting credits, but the evidence strongly supports those attributed here.

'I Don't Wanna Leave You'

'Onedayi'mgonnabesomebody' [with Morris Day]

'The Walk' [with Morris Day]
7″ and 12″ singles, 1982

'Wild And Loose' (with Dez Dickerson)

All above are tracks from album *What Time Is It?*, 1982. On the album, they are credited collectively to The Time, and it seems various group members probably contributed to some or all of these songs. However, the consensus is that Prince and Morris Day continued to be the dominant creative forces.

Prince's compositional input into The Time's third album, *Ice Cream Castle* (1984), is less easily defined. It seems probable that he was as much executive producer as songwriter for this final release from Morris Day and his revised line-up.

231

Vanity 6

In John Bream's biography, *Prince: Inside The Purple Reign*, Prince is credited with writing the Vanity 6 songs 'Nasty Girl', 'Wet Dreams', 'Drive Me Wild', $3 \times 2 = 6$', 'Bite The Beat' [with Jesse Johnson], and 'If A Girl Answers (Don't Hang Up)' [with Terry Lewis]. All of these appear on the album *Vanity 6*, with 'Nasty Girl', 'Bite The Beat' and 'Drive Me Wild' each being released as singles. I was unable to authenticate this claim in my own researches, but that is not to doubt the veracity of Bream's assertion.

(iii) Other Artists Produced by Prince

Apollonia 6

Apollonia 6 [credit: Another Starr Production)
Album, 1984

'Sex Shooter'
7″ and 12″ singles, 1984
Also track on album *Apollonia 6*

E, Sheila

The Glamorous Life [with Sheila E] [credit: The Starr Company]
Album, 1984

'The Belle Of St Mark'
7″ and 12″ singles, 1984

'The Glamourous Life'
7″ and 12″ singles, 1984
Both the above also tracks on album *The Glamorous Life*

'A Love Bizarre' [with Sheila E]
7″ and 12″ singles, 1985
Also track on album *Romance 1600*, 1985

Jones, Jill

'All Day, All Night' [with Jill Jones and David Z]
7″ and 12″ singles, 1987

'For Love' [with Jill Jones and David Z]

'Mia Bocca' [with Jill Jones and David Z]
7″ and 12″ singles, 1987

All above tracks on album *Jill Jones*, 1987

Time, The

The Time [with Morris Day] [credit: Jamie Starr]
Album, 1981

'Cool'
7″ and 12″ singles, 1981

232

'Get It Up'
7″ and 12″ singles, 1982

'Girl'
7″ and 12″ singles, 1982

All above also tracks on album *The Time*

What Time Is It? [with Morris Day] [credit: The Starr Company]
Album, 1982

'Gigolos Get Lonely Too'
7″ and 12″ singles, 1983

'777–9311'
7″ and 12″ singles, 1982

'The Walk'
7″ and 12″ singles, 1982
All above also tracks on album *What Time Is It?*

Ice Cream Castle [with Morris Day] [credit: The Starr Company]
Album, 1984

'Ice Cream Castles'
7″ and 12″ singles, 1984

'Jungle Love'
7″ and 12″ singles, 1984

Both the above also tracks on album *Ice Cream Castle*

Vanity 6

Vanity 6 [credit: Another Starr Production]
Album, 1982

'Bite The Beat'
7″ and 12″ singles, 1983

'Drive Me Wild'
7″ and 12″ singles, 1983

'He's So Dull'
7″ and 12″ singles, 1982

'Nasty Girl'
7″ and 12″ singles, 1982

All above also tracks on album *Vanity 6*

Index

237